HB

Sunnyside Down

Sunnyside Down

GROWING UP IN '50S BRITAIN

KEN BLAKEMORE

LARGE PRINT
Oxford

First published in Great Britain 2005
by
Sutton Publishing Ltd.

Published in Large Print 2006 by ISIS Publishing Ltd.,
7 Centremead, Osney Mead, Oxford OX2 0ES
by arrangement with
Sutton Publishing Ltd.

British Library Cataloguing in Publication Data
Blakemore, Ken
    Sunnyside down: growing up in '50s Britain. –
Large print ed. – (Isis reminiscence series)
1. Blakemore, Ken – Childhood and youth
2. Nineteen fifties
3. Large type books
4. Cheshire (England) – Social life and customs –
20th century
5. Cheshire (England) – Biography
I. Title
942.7'10855'092

ISBN 0–7531–9360–4 (hb)
ISBN 0–7531–9361–2 (pb)

Printed and bound in Great Britain by
T. J. International, Padstow, Cornwall

Contents

Foreword by Blake Morrison

Few decades are as remote as the 1950s. Looked back on half a century later, they seem magically cosy and placid — like a becalmed liner, adrift from the dramas on the mainland. Historians tend to treat the period with patronising affection, as a time when nothing much happened. These were the years of the Conservative slogan "You've never had it so good", when Britain slowly rebuilt after the war — and when ordinary families began to acquire unimaginably luxurious consumer items, such as a fridge, a television and a car. It was also the era of Suez, when our leaders, refusing to accept that Britain's role on the world stage had become a bit-part, tried to flex our imperial muscle one last time. Few could feel nostalgic for the jingoism, class division, snobbery, racism, insularity, complacency, bureaucratic meddling and all-pervasive political incorrectness of the period. But in the provinces at least, Britain seemed a safer place then, freer, friendlier, more trusting. And despite the narrow-mindedness, it could also be strangely tolerant. These were the years of the newly created Welfare State, and notions of social justice — of caring for others less fortunate than ourselves — were more active than they are today.

Ken Blakemore is truly a child of the period. He was born on 5 July 1948, the day the National Health Service came into being — in terms of British social history, the equivalent of one of Salman Rushdie's "midnight's children" (the babies born in the hours after India's independence in 1947). Too young to recollect much before Coronation Day in 1953, he more than compensates with his powers of recall for the rest of the decade. It's all here — the sweets he ate, the books he read, the radio he listened to, the first television programmes he watched, the trips he took, the punishments he endured, the illnesses he contracted, the fears, the pleasures, the upsets, the hobbies, the horrible stink of the primary school toilets — so horrible that boys and girls would wet themselves rather than go there. For anyone who knows the period, the names and brand-names are enough in themselves to bring it back: *Sing Something Simple*, *Lassie*, Nuttall's Mintoes, *Wagon Train*, Sugar Puffs, Uncle Mac, *Champion the Wonder Horse*, Heinz Sandwich Spread, *Two-Way Family Favourites*, *Davy Crockett*, polio, *Dr Finlay's Casebook*, Energen rolls, *Music While You Work*, acid drops, Austin 8s, Smiths' crisps (and the little blue salt twist secreted in the bag). Even the name of the village in which Ken Blakemore grew up, Bunbury, seems perfectly in keeping with the period, a place that might have been made for a Hovis ad.

I should declare an interest. My own birth-date was just a couple of years after the author's, and I grew up, as he did, in a village in the north of England (in my case Yorkshire rather than Cheshire). More intimately, though I have never met Ken Blakemore, I know we come from the same family: the Blakemores were nuts-and-bolts makers based in Bolton (when the Mersey Tunnel was built, the firm supplied the nuts and bolts), and it's because of my father's mother, born Kathleen Blakemore, that I was given the name Blake. All that makes Ken's story particularly interesting to me. But the good news for other readers is that he wastes little time on the matter of lineage. Where relations cross his path, they're described, in all their eccentricity. But he recalls them as he perceived them at the time, not as a researcher into family history. And although his infant impressions are sometimes supplemented by the hindsight of an adult (one who makes his living as an academic, and who has thought long and hard about social change), it's the sharpness and freshness of the child's eye, his unclouded vision, that gives *Sunnyside Down* its distinction. Even for those born later, to whom names like Uncle Mac or Harold Macmillan mean nothing, he brings the era alive.

One other quality of the book, implicit in its title, deserves mention: however sunny and upbeat, it is not so nostalgic as to omit the downside. Pessimism, or rather realism, is a quality which Ken Blakemore associates with the Pennines, as typified for him by the image of a granite headstone in a bleak cemetery with the inscription "Well — What Did you Expect?" Being honest about the 1950s means acknowledging its vices as well as its virtues: he doesn't pretend all was once right with the world until the sixties, or some other imagined villain (Beeching or Mrs Thatcher or Tony Blair), came along and ruined everything. We glimpse his mother Beryl's frustrations in her role as mother and housewife, for instance; are reminded how sadistic teachers could be to their charges (the village school Ken went to was a forced agricultural labour camp for children); observe the cruel divisiveness of the 11-plus system (one of Ken's twin brothers passed the exam, the other failed); are made to realise that, however secure the fifties seemed, they were a much rougher and tougher era than our own.

Ken Blakemore subtitles his book "a family and social history". It's a difficult combination to get right; too personal and you alienate readers whose stories don't connect with yours; too social and there is no story, merely a dry academic text. Here, unusually, the balance is perfect. *Sunnyside Down* is Ken Blakemore's story, but the story of countless other people, too.

Acknowledgements

Many people have helped me with the preparation and writing of this book, but two stand out immediately because, without their kind support and positive reactions to the project, it wouldn't have made it into print at all. The first is my old mate Steve Taylor, who encouraged me to develop the idea of *Sunnyside Down* in the first place (and to put some other, pretty bad, ideas on the backburner), and who then read several chapters and made useful comments. The second is Simon Fletcher, who listened patiently to my rather garbled summary of the book when I first contacted Sutton Publishing. Thankfully he made the time to read the manuscript, despite a very pressured workload, and to follow it up with the offer of publication.

Next, I must acknowledge the help of various members of my family. I'm particularly grateful to my daughter Elin, who read much of the manuscript with enthusiasm (partly to discover her paternal grandparents, whom she never knew). Also, as a young student of English, Elin gave me a critical perspective on what it's like for a 20-year-old to read about the 1950s. In a different but equally valuable way, my partner Helen Thomas — who shares a strong interest in social history — was prepared not only to put up with my preoccupation with northern village life in the 1950s but went beyond this to offer her own reflections, ideas and much else besides.

My twin brothers, Henry and Fred, have both been extremely supportive in reading the manuscript, putting me right about various details of our family life and, above all, being very understanding about having their photographs reproduced and personal aspects of their own earlier lives written about by their kid brother! My cousin Thelma Potter and my second cousin Maggie Ainley have also been very helpful indeed, both in supplying family photos and in helping me, through shared reminiscences about the quirky behaviour of our parents, aunts and uncles, to retrieve some of the colour and spirit of that generation.

Sadly, my sister Jay MacArthur, who died early in 2005, will never see this book in print. However, I am glad that at least she was able to read some of the manuscript before she died, and that I am able to acknowledge her help in making some corrections and to record here her reactions of laughter and tears when she read it.

Another vital set of contributions to the preparation of this book must be acknowledged, and they were from a stalwart and very supportive group of Bunburians. In particular, I would like to thank Blanche and George Wilgose, our kindly neighbours at Sunnyside from the early 1960s onwards, who at the time of writing are still living "next door", forty and more years on. They unfailingly provided me with reminders and details of who lived where and did what in the village in the 1950s and 1960s, gave me a copy of a splendid collection of old photographs produced by the Bunbury Society, *Bunbury 1898–1998*, and were hospitable and welcoming in every sense. Similarly, I am extremely grateful to Jean Healey and to the Bunbury Society for their help in tracing sources of old photographs, and to John Elsworth, Gordon Jones, Hester Wade and Bob Welch for giving me permission to reproduce copies of their old photos and postcards in this book. Alan Jervis, of the *Nantwich Chronicle*, kindly allowed me to reproduce the photograph of the street at the level crossing in Nantwich. I am also grateful to Richard and Gill Mayers, the current residents of Sunnyside, for their permission to photograph the house and to reproduce it in this book, and to Richard Casserley for his kind permission to reproduce a photograph of Bunbury Castle station.

Friends in Swansea read through various chapters of the manuscript and provided some very helpful and supportive comments — in particular, Gillian and Bob Drake, and Sarah Harris. Ian Moore also read some of the manuscript, and helped with many ideas for writing about childhood and suggestions for the design of the book.

It should go without saying, but is probably worth re-stating, that while I acknowledge the kind support of everyone mentioned above, I must accept full responsibility for the contents of *Sunnyside Down*. This is an impressionistic, personal view of the 1950s — a view through the lens of my own childhood and how the world appeared to me then. No doubt there will be some who read this and think "No, it wasn't quite like that", or, among younger readers who never experienced the 1950s or 1960s themselves, "Could it *really* have been like that?" When this happens, I apologise in advance for any errors or inaccuracies. I have tried to be as accurate as possible with regard to the historical details of the 1950s and the biographical details of my family. However, this book is primarily a personal account, and a view of social history anchored in biography. It is a narrative of a period, and of a world, that was changing fast but, in some ways, didn't want to change. I hope that you enjoy reading about it as much as I enjoyed writing about it.

Ken Blakemore
Swansea, March 2005

Prologue

Before we're born we circle the earth, waiting for our special time and place.

Do you remember the photo of the swimming baby? Eyes wide open, a hint of a smile, limbs outstretched? I like to imagine millions of us doing just that, circling in the pure blue-green light around the earth. The planet is streaked with cloud here and there, the oceans a deeper blue. It is curving away from us, and it will be our home. We're all waiting patiently, smilingly, timelessly but with some excitement, for the mysterious inner voice that will tell us where our next life will be.

Here come the assignments: a gritty, smoky town in central China, a farm in New Zealand, a house of mud bricks in Zaire. The wise, knowing babies silently nod and slip away over the curve to their destinations. The next is a drought-stricken village in Afghanistan, recently ruined by earthquakes. "Ah," murmurs a shoal of babies nearby, sympathetically. "Tough assignment." But the chosen one still nods her head, smiles, stretches out her plump golden arms and dips over the horizon to meet her mother.

Now come a string of assignments to dull green, cloudy islands moored untidily off the north-west coast of Europe. Those not going down here look quizzically at the ones who are, little thumbs moving uncertainly up, then down. Could be good, could be bad. No one's sure. But those of us chosen here, now, know that this is our place.

Soon, it will matter very much exactly where we go and who our family will be — assuming we get one. But just for this moment, we're all special and yet equal. I've been at this moment and you've been here too, poised above the Earth. It doesn't matter if it's the year 1205, 1856, 1948, 1976, 1985 or 2020. It doesn't matter, just at this moment, whether it's going to be America, Asia or Africa. And it doesn't matter, just now, that one baby is going to 15 Chemical Road in Port Talbot and another to Rose Cottage in Bourton-on-the-Water. Or that one is gliding effortlessly through a pink dawn over motorways to Birmingham and another through mists to Orkney. Here we go-o-o-o-oh . . .

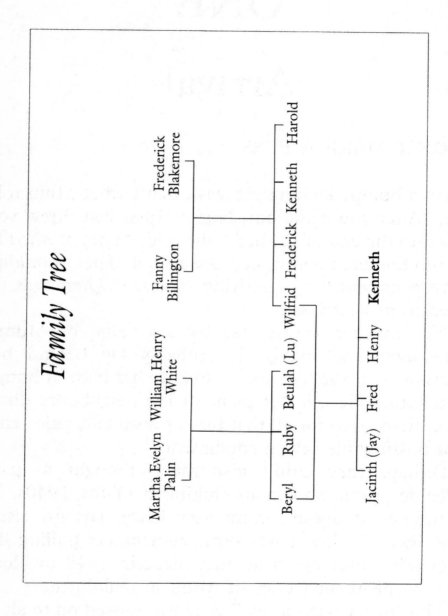

Family Tree

Martha Evelyn William Henry   Fanny   Frederick
Palin   White   Billington   Blakemore

Beryl   Ruby   Beulah (Lu)   Wilfrid   Frederick   Kenneth   Harold

Jacinth (Jay)   Fred   Henry   **Kenneth**

CHAPTER
ONE

Arrival

Don't make a fuss

I had a bumpy landing. At least, that's what Mum told me. "After you came out, Nurse Hurst just threw you down to the end of the bed," she said. "They seemed to be too bothered about me," she added. *They shouldn't have been* was the underlying message. *There was no need to make a fuss.*

Not making a fuss was a core value of Mum's generation and family. It probably lay behind her decision — if she had one — to have her baby at home. Better to stifle cries of pain, so the neighbours don't hear, than go in for all that fuss of hospitals, pain relief and possibly life-saving equipment.

Perhaps they didn't give much thought to pain relief for rural women in childbirth in the 1940s. In retrospect, it doesn't seem very likely. Jay, my sister who was 15 when I was born, remembers pulling the bedclothes over her head that night in 1948 to block out the distressing cries of Mum in childbirth.

The "not making a fuss" gene was passed on to all of us in that house, I suspect. It was certainly in my sister Jay, a no-nonsense, stoical person who grew up to be a nurse, and in my twin brothers, Henry and Fred, who were aged 9 in 1948.

When I lay, a few minutes old, at the foot of my parents' double bed, tossed aside by Nurse Hurst as she attended urgently to my mother, I was beginning to learn this first lesson — we don't make a fuss. How wonderful to have been born after 1970, when the idea that newborn babies needed to touch their mother's milky, salty skin as soon as they can, and be pressed gently to their mother's breast, became widely acceptable again.

Maybe I didn't miss out on any of that, though — I just don't know. And probably it was much better to have been born at home than in a cold, starched hospital of that day and age. They wrapped you tightly in bandages then, and waited to see if you could struggle free before the rigidly scheduled feeding time.

Probably the small front bedroom was stuffy and full of the smells of human birth, with a yellowish light coming from the single shade dangling in the centre of the ceiling (I think I was born in the small hours). There might have been one or two summer moths banging against it, as they usually did if you left a light on and a window open.

Outside it would have been dark, inky black — there were no streetlights — until dawn at four. The sweet leather smell of cow manure and Cheshire grass would have been drifting through the little top windows. Perhaps there would have been the bleating of a calf and the corresponding mooing of its anxious separated mother. At least once there would have been the

2

swishing of train wheels on tracks a mile or so north, as the London–Holyhead express stitched its way through dark folds of night.

Looming next to the bed was my parents' wardrobe. It had double doors with mirrors, and was stained dark brown. When I was a child, much later on, I was going to discover items loaded with deep, secret knowledge in that wardrobe.

The place that I'd been assigned to was a village called Bunbury, on a breezy plain where the north of England starts and the Midlands ends. If I had swooped low towards Bunbury to join my mother from a northerly direction, I would have passed between two lines of red sandstone hills, each decorated with a castle. One, Beeston Castle, sits on a huge craggy rock. It's a twelfth-century castle, now mostly in ruins, but its keep still frowns at the surrounding lush plain. A mile or so to the west of Beeston is Peckforton, a nineteenth-century replica of a medieval castle, complete with drawbridge, battlements and a large tower at its eastern end.

Beyond both castles lies Bunbury itself, a loosely scattered collection of red brick and black-and-white houses and farms. The Shropshire Union canal and London Midland railway mark its eastern side, and at the southern end of the village is a large, impressive red sandstone church, recently damaged in the Second World War by incendiary bombs and a land-mine.

The whole nation, not only our mothers and fathers, had been expecting us. This was because we were to be the first babies of a brand-new National Health

3

Service. The day before the NHS and I were born, 5 July 1948, my mother cut a cartoon out of the newspaper (and it's one I still haven't found). It showed an anxious-looking father holding a shotgun, looking up at their moonlit house, wanting to keep away a circling stork with its little bundle of baby. The caption read "4 July". The message was clear. Keep your baby away until 5 July, when all medical and nursing services would be free, as well as prescriptions and medicines.

As it happened, the house at which I arrived — Sunnyside, my home for the next eighteen years — was just a few doors along from the local district nurse, Nurse Hurst. And as Mum was so near there was no need for Nurse Hurst, a diminutive figure with a kindly, stoical face, to clamber on to her motorbike. A large bike it was, and she wore appropriately huge leather gauntlets to protect her thin, wiry arms. A mini-Valkyrie in goggles, the thundering bike beneath her and the gauntlets lending an air of combat, Nurse Hurst was a formidable sight in the lanes around Bunbury. As she scorched dangerously around tight bends, looking for the next woman in labour to assist, she and her thrumming machine became as one, an angel of birth.

An uncertain future

Nurse Hurst must have been busy in the three years before I was born, weaving her way through the country lanes from one woman to another, because after the Second World War it started raining babies. From 1945 to 1947 the flow of babies poured incessantly. All that yearning, so much postponed holding and wanting, the prospect of life after so much death, or news of it, burst the banks and out came millions of children — the baby boom, the baby bulge.

By 1948 the surge was beginning to ease. The level of new babies began to sink, so people could take the sandbags away from their doorsteps, start to mop up and safely open their windows again without fear of yet more babies gliding through. So I was one of the afterthoughts, both of the baby boom and of the family. My mother might have been expecting me, but was anyone else? Dad perhaps, though it's doubtful he gave much thought to it until a week or so before the birth. Jay, possibly — as she was 15. My twin brothers, Henry and Fred, probably not.

Henry had been expecting *something*. He'd detected the air of anticipation in the house and became convinced it was about something he particularly wanted. He remembers being told by Dad, out of the blue one day, that there was some good news. Mum had something to show him, but it was asleep at the moment. "A kitten!" he exclaimed. He'd been right all along. He'd been so much looking forward to having and looking after his very own kitten.

"No, a baby," was the reply.

So I was a disappointment from the start to Henry, and not only for this reason.

Equal to the shocks of not having a kitten and of Mum producing a baby unexpectedly that day, there

5

was another shock — the use of all the eggs in the house to make a single omelette. Post-war rationing might have resulted in the healthiest diet the British have ever had, but it also meant that many people, especially 9-year-old boys like my brothers, were preoccupied with food and on the edge of hunger the whole time. Everyone in the house knew that there were precious eggs in the pantry, and everyone expected each egg's fate to be pondered carefully.

But on the evening of the day I was born a midwife swept into the kitchen to look for some sustaining food for Mum. To Henry's amazement and horror, she broke *all* the eggs (there were perhaps as many as five) into a bowl, and made a super-omelette for her. "Your mother needs the strength," was the explanation. There was no question about it, no debate, and the effect on Henry was profoundly unsettling. From then on he expected the worst as far as the new baby was concerned, and perhaps the worst of the world in general. It was like a military coup for him, that day. All eggs commandeered. All hopes of kittens or pet rabbits dashed.

So Henry and Fred weren't expecting me, Dad and Jay only a bit, and Mum had thought she was having a girl. So, roughly speaking, that meant there was about half a family vote for expecting what I was — a baby, and a boy — and about four and a half votes expecting either a girl or no baby, or a kitten, or possibly a rabbit. All this confusion and uncertainty soon showed itself in a lack of decisive thought about what I would be called.

Mum had convinced herself the baby needed a name that would do for either sex, if the worst came to the worst and another boy came along. These names (the first had been my maternal grandmother's name) were to be "Evelyn Frances".

I doubt very much whether I could have stood tall when I was older and thought, I'm extra lucky because I'm called Evelyn Francis. With a name like that I might have gone far, but in what direction? What on earth could she have been thinking of? Perhaps she had chosen the names hoping to avoid a fuss — a sort of compromise — but I think it showed the ambivalence she felt about having delivered another boy. She had almost certainly shuddered at the prospect, given the social havoc, worry and sheer damage, physical and human, that had been wrought by my twin brothers since the day they had first toddled into action.

At the christening service the indecision about my name manifested itself font-side. There had been muted family disagreement about my names on the way to the church. Mum told me that she had tried to maintain her Evelyn Francis line, but was weakening in the face of silent, subtle opposition (nothing too definite could be said for fear of making a fuss). So I was handed to a vicar who was still in some doubt about what names to call me when he came to sprinkle me with the special icy Anglican water.

At the crucial moment, when he could go no further without having a definite ruling, he paused and looked expectantly around the small gathering. Apparently there was an awkward silence. No one wanted to tread on anyone else's toes by suggesting names that others might not like. The seconds ticked by. The dreaded words "Evelyn Francis" hung in the air, unheard but ready to be trundled out, like old, awkward-looking reserve fire engines, if no one said anything else. Eventually someone called out "Kenneth!" — not a bad choice for that era. My uncle, one of Dad's younger brothers, was a Kenneth. Several heads nodded discreetly, as at auction when a bid has been accepted. The vicar picked up his order of service and was beginning to resume when someone else called out "Peter!" — so I inadvertently got that name too.

Later, when she became a nurse and then moved to Canada, my sister Jay worked for a short period with Inuit people in the far north. She wrote home about how Inuit women at the point of birth, or at least in labour, spot something and call out its name, which then becomes the baby's. I remember my mother reading out the letter and hearing how one baby my sister helped to deliver had been called "Jimmy Frying Pan". I felt both a strong affinity with the Inuit people and some envy of their system. How much simpler and less demoralising it would be, I thought, if everyone got named by accident, and were called things like "Net Curtain" or "Lampshade". Mind you, I concluded, even that system could go wrong. What if you ended up with names such as "HP Sauce", "Wardrobe" or "Bra"?

So I started life on an uncertain note. I was just one little millionth of uncertainty in the general sea of uncertainty of post-war, late 1940s Britain. I must have picked up on this. It came out in the way I cried and squalled and fretted constantly. Mum told me later that

8

I was a nagging, unhappy baby who was beginning to wear everyone down in the first few months.

The only day of perfect peace and tranquillity she got was the day I was circumcised. "You just slept the whole day through", she said. "The general anaesthetic was wonderful. I was able to get on top of the ironing at last." When I heard this I thought that arranging for your son to be circumcised and to be heavily drugged, just for one day's peace, seemed a little harsh. But having gone through the parenting ordeal myself, I now understand completely and approvingly.

However, I still sometimes wonder whether they couldn't have said to the doctor, "One junior general anaesthetic to go, please. Could you make that two days? But hold the side order of circumcision, that's OK." But that's a very recent way of thinking, isn't it? Under the new NHS everything was free, so they thought they might as well throw in the circumcision with the anaesthetic anyway.

To offset these momentous changes it's reassuring to know that the summer of 1948 had been mildly disappointing, in a familiar British way, with lots of cloudy weather and occasional weeks of sun and showers. As all local papers do, the *Chester Chronicle* gave a good impression of not very much happening in the week after I was born.

There were little things like the launch of the National Health Service ("Doctors, Dentists and Opticians Line Up for 5 July") and a claim by the Labour government (on 3 July) to have "Abolished Poverty". But these were given equal space in the news pages to items such as "Visitor Left Train That Did Not Stop". Apparently the alien "visitor" — a man from the Planet Warrington — did not believe fellow passengers when told that the train was not scheduled to stop at Chester, and got off anyway. "He entered the station at 15 miles per hour," the article continued, "and had discussions with station staff later on."

Other dramatic events worth reporting in the week of 5 July included the exciting story "Motorcycle Ran Up a Bank". Interviewed by a *Chronicle* reporter in Chester Royal Infirmary, the injured motorcyclist was asked about the cause of the accident. "I was proceeding on the lane towards Waverton," the man explained, "and my bike just . . . ran up a bank."

Meanwhile, Chester Zoo was getting "Bigger, Better", with new enclosures and "tropical islands" being planted with appropriate vegetation. Visitors could look forward to the construction of a new transparent Perspex roof for the Reptile House, and startling additions to the Aquarium.

Appropriately, at the Odeon cinema in Chester, you could follow up with a viewing of *Miranda* ("It's all about a mermaid who's caught by a human"), a British comedy starring Googie Withers, Glynis Johns and Griffith Johns. Or, if you preferred, there were other British films on offer — for instance, *Three Weird Sisters* and Rex Harrison in John Galsworthy's *Escape* at the Gaumont. And there were yet more films to watch that week, showing just how important "going to the flicks" was in those days. There was Marlene Dietrich in *Golden Earrings* (Majestic), Alan Ladd in

Saigon (Music Hall) and, if you wanted to gallop across the rolling Cheshire prairie to the small town of Frodsham, it was possible to see Roy Rogers and his horse Trigger in *Under Nevada Skies* at the Grand.

But best of all, and because I wouldn't have been able to make any more sense of it now than I would the day I was born, I would love to have been on a trip to the Royal Variety Theatre in Chester. Here, commencing twice nightly at 6.15 and 8.20 in the week beginning 5 July, there was a fabulous show featuring "Gorgeous Girls, Spectacular Scenes, Lovely Gowns, Laughs Galore." This must have been a leftover from Second World War army entertainment days — it was the official fourteenth Army Review, *Hello From S.E.A.C.* The cast included a string of ex-officers with charismatic names such as Ex-Flight Officer "Dick" Richards. But what on earth would "Torpedoman" Johnny Rainsey's act have consisted of — let alone "The Glorious Memsahibs"?

In the next few years I was going to discover a village and a world around me that became even stranger. When I was born the dark shadows of war still hung over Bunbury and the whole of England. Later on, in the 1950s, the country started to move uncertainly towards newer, bolder ways of doing things.

THE BOOKS OF KNOWLEDGE

One way that I was going to learn about this strange world was by secretly reading the Books of Knowledge.

One was blue and one was red. I can't now remember whether the blue one was the Book of Illnesses and the red one the Book of Life, but that was how I saw their contents when I was a child. You couldn't go and look at them any time. You had to wait until everyone was out and Mum had gone to the village shops or somewhere. They were extremely heavy books — hardbacks, of course — about a foot high and several inches thick. The page ends were flecked with colour (red or blue), making the books look freckled when you looked at them side on. And when you opened them, straining to prise the weighty pages apart, they smelled of mothballs from the wardrobe, and of secret, privileged knowledge.

I think Mum must have discovered in the end that I had been reading them. Nothing was said, but they disappeared without trace when I was 13 or so. I never got many chances to look at them before that, though, and sometimes months would go by because I'd forgotten them. But occasionally, when an unusual stillness fell upon the house and there was nothing to do, the books would float back into my mind.

With one eye and one ear open to catch signs of anyone coming, I would stand next to the dark wardrobe and, taking one of the books out, place it on Mum and Dad's bed. Which one would be first — blue or red? Each was mystifying yet revealing, fascinating yet puzzling.

The Book of Illnesses had an excellent description of what happens when someone dies, how they feel colder and colder, and how relatives stand around asking the

12

nurse to put more blankets or warm things around them, but the nurse gently and firmly doesn't do that.

It contained vivid explanations of measles, mumps, diphtheria and all sorts of child-killing diseases. It also had a really eloquent section on bed baths, and how people with raging temperatures could have blissful release from their burning skin by being wrapped in cool, wet sheets. And there were encouraging diagrams of broken bones in cross-section, and how they could be mended. I learned that blood flowed around the body in arteries and veins, that people were bodies and had mysterious things called spleens, and that thoughts happen in your brain, which is a grey, spongy material. It was terrific.

But the Book of Life was even better. It was less factual and more philosophical than the Book of Illnesses. Occasionally my hands would tremble as I took in the awe-inspiring secrets of life and the dazzling insights it could give to a 10-year-old. Yet some of the passages were intriguing precisely because their purpose and meaning were not yet clear, although you just knew the knowledge was going to be important.

One particularly puzzling section was about mothers and sons. It seemed to be about boys much older then me — in their late teens, perhaps. It described, in a roundabout way, how a mother might be flattered by a son who preferred to take her out to the pictures, buy her flowers or little presents, or go out to the shops or a café with her rather than with a girl. What girl, I wondered, but read on.

I pictured the mother in this passage as a woman who was not like my mother. She was younger, more affluent somehow, with a fur stole and an elegant hat, smiling indulgently at her son over a cream tea. The book said firmly that the mother in these circumstances must gently rebuff her son's attentions. The son was probably going through a passing phase and should be steered girlwards. On no account should the mother encourage or enjoy the son's unusual affection or attention. Quietly nodding my agreement and thanking the book yet again for providing another gem of insight, I resolved never to buy Mum any flowers, gifts (including birthday and Christmas presents) or cinema tickets when I was older, just to be on the safe side.

The best section in the Book of Life, though — you've guessed it — was the section dealing with sex. Its only disappointment was that it contained no diagrams — no equivalents of the cross-sections of broken limbs, as in the Book of Illnesses. But when I say it "dealt with" sex, that was its attraction. It didn't refer to feelings or desires I didn't yet have, or celebrate the physical sensations or emotional joy of sex, in the way the Book of Illnesses celebrated bed baths. Nor was there any hint of "nod, nod, wink, wink, know what I mean?" No allusions to information the reader should have known about already, or to shameful or embarrassing things — and that was its chief attraction to a boy who knew nothing.

All was laid out in detached, scientific prose. The man "placed" his penis inside the woman's vagina. That was perfectly clear. With simultaneous access to the

14

Book of Illnesses, I could cross-check what these bodily items were. So that was it, that was how it all began. The man placed his penis. I didn't ponder long over the mechanics of this — it was enough just to have read about the basic idea. I had a fleeting but recurrent image of groups of men standing about in a casino, dressed in dinner jackets and bowties. A white-haired, black-suited croupier comes over to one, a father-to-be, and whispers discreetly, "Time to place your penis, sir," gesturing towards the door in much the same way as he might say, "Place your bets, gentlemen," before spinning a roulette wheel.

This image was one way that I could imagine my own father placing his penis. But this mental leap didn't happen instantly. It was a slowly dawning realisation that crept over me and said, yes, he too must once have done this — actually, four times!

When I was 9, and before that, Dad was in the habit of going to the Club, a small wooden building just a few houses along the road from where we lived. It was a British Legion hut (and later became the village Scout hut) containing a billiard table. Some nights after work Dad would put on his stained cream linen jacket and go to play a game of snooker. On summer nights, if you were passing, you could see the men in there, wreathed in pipe and cigarette smoke, lit like suspended fish in a green aquarium by the big light over the baize. I saw him once when I was 8, as he was nonchalantly chalking the end of a cue.

As boys do (or did then), I glanced at my dad and he became a hero in that moment — an expert, an

15

impressive person of many skills. So two or three years later, digesting the news of conception from the Book of Life, I was able to apply the basic idea to my dad perfectly well. He had nonchalantly and expertly placed his penis, just as he had placed one of the coloured balls into the little net sacs on the billiard table. He had placed it, discreetly and with no fuss (we don't make a fuss about anything, remember?), like a limp leather glove on a sort of table in my mother's living room, or womb, or something.

Funnily enough, I didn't detain myself with any thoughts about what all this had meant for Mum. As a male, I had identified with the onerous task facing dads. I didn't really connect any of the physical information to what my mum had done. But then I hardly thought about any of the physical details at that stage. Once the basic principle had been absorbed, what fascinated me about all this was the *philosophy*. It was not *how* mums and dads do these things, or *what* they did, that really interested me. It was *why* they did it and, in particular, *why did I exist?*

Once I realised that we were not just here because we were and that was that, and once I knew some sort of decision was involved — the Placing of the Penis — I began to reflect on whether I *should* be here. Wasn't I getting in the way?

There seemed to be ample evidence for this. Brothers — Henry, in particular — would often scowl at me. Dad would shake his newspaper irritably and refuse to get out of his chair to entertain me. Mum could be impatient with me at times. The dog snarled at me and bared his teeth. Also — more evidence — my twin brothers were nine years older than me. After such a long gap, did my parents really mean to have another child? Wasn't I a mistake?

These questions would become fundamental when I was a young teenager. Should I be here, on this planet, in this village, in this family? Maybe the first seeds of doubt were sown when I was thrown down to the end of the bed, a few minutes old. But they developed after I had read the Book of Life. Perhaps this riddle of existence is shared by a lot of people, and especially only children.

The problem was, in a family like mine, you couldn't talk about it. It was not that I *did* want to talk about it and was frustrated by lack of opportunity. It was more that I had a vague, continuing sense of unease about whether I should be here. I couldn't mention anything because I didn't actually have the language to do it. Our family didn't really "do" anger, so it was pretty impossible to lash out and shout, "Why was I ever born?" and storm out of the room. No one stormed out of rooms. For one thing, there weren't enough *other* rooms to storm into. Also, that behaviour didn't exist as a concept, just as the distinction between red and green doesn't exist in colour-blind people.

Nor did the family really "do" talking about how you felt, or what your worries were. So the only way I could have asked would have been to adopt the normally polite rules of family conversation in a staid, lower-middle-class northern family of the time. It might have gone something like this: "Don't worry if

17

you can't be bothered to answer at the moment, or if you're too busy, but — er — are you sure I'm supposed to *be* here?"

In any case, this kind of question had an implied subtext, an unsaid additional clause "*Because if not, I'll go away if you like.*" As I couldn't in all honesty say I was willing to offer this, I had to settle for staying on, and feeling rather guilty and embarrassed, from time to time, about being here.

Smouldering stubble

But this wasn't going to be the whole story. True, I was going to be a boy who felt insecure at times, not quite sure I was supposed to be where I was. But I was also the opposite. Sometimes I felt lucky — really, really lucky — to be here. Even if it was a lucky chance, something random, I was here, and no one could take that away from me.

Have you ever had that feeling? Sometimes, for no reason at all, the world stops. If there is noise it becomes pleasant background sound. No matter what you're up against, or how troublesome life is, suddenly — and just for a few moments — you see it all differently. You might be looking at someone you love pouring coffee into a cup, or ironing a shirt, or stroking a cat. You might be in a car on a hot day. You put the window down and look through the rushing wind at a tree in full leaf. If you're in a room, you're blissfully aware of the dust motes in the air and the rays of sunlight passing through them. If it's a person you're looking at, you see the flecks of colour in their eyes. It's all over as soon as it's happened, but it leaves behind a feeling of discovery, awe and connection. *Ah, so that's what it's all about*, the soul inside us says, remembering the time we circled the Earth together, waiting to be born.

The moment that told me I was lucky to be here came when I was 6. Mr Ewing, a near neighbour, owned a field that lay behind our houses. He was a gentle, muscular man who did a bit of this and that — some painting and decorating, for instance — and drove a small van. He was often sawing or chiselling or whittling bits of wood in his dark, long shed, though why and for what purpose was never clear. He did a lot of musing and standing, smoking aromatic tobacco in a pipe that emitted clean blue smoke, like a mature bonfire.

One particular year he hit on the idea of growing a crop in his field. Normally it was mostly left to grass, and a neighbouring farmer was allowed to put heifers in it. But this one year a cereal crop was sown. It duly sprouted, grew, and was rained on heavily. It was called "corn", but I found out much later that the adults in my bit of the planet didn't really know what corn was. They probably thought it meant wheat, but might not have been sure. Cereal-growing wasn't a strong agricultural skill around Bunbury. Cows were more important. Anyway, once the "corn" in Mr Ewing's field got wet it refused to stand up again, and then it rotted and became worthless. Back to the whittling, sawing and musing.

Mr Ewing decided to go back to grass. But it also grew too long (perhaps the cows forgot to eat it, or he forgot to arrange for the cows to be there) and rotted. Eventually — in high summer — Mr Ewing decided to burn all the by now dry, horizontal, rotted grass in one great glorious field fire. It's just occurred to me that this is what he had been secretly planning all along — not for the sake of some wily insurance claim, but for the drama of it. There was a Hollywood, Errol Flynn-ish air about Mr Ewing. He could have starred as a rugged pioneer or frontiersman in a film version of *The Call of the Wild.* When he was younger he could have played Rhett Butler in *Gone With The Wind.* The idea of bringing the plot to a conclusion with a blaze certainly appealed. Atlanta had to burn.

That day — hot and brilliantly sunny — was the best day of my life so far. Mr Ewing ran back and forth with sacks to hit the increasingly delinquent fire. It went out of control. Henry came to help. There were muffled shouts from shadowy figures inside blue clouds of smoke, but no obscene swearwords because, after all, this was the 1950s.

They tried to thrash out new fires that were beginning to burn the tall hedges all around the field. White, dense smoke curled upwards in liquid spouts a full five feet in front of the main blaze, preparing the ground for the next wall of flame. A whole section of dry raspberry canes in one corner of the field went up with a satisfying *whoosh* and much crackling. My

20

brother Henry appeared from the smoke, red-eyed and shirtless like Mr Ewing, to drink Corona pop. Mr Ewing, pipe in mouth, tensely smoked in the smoke. Later, when the blaze had subsided and all naked flames had been extinguished, Mr Ewing wanted to re-light his pipe, but found that he couldn't because he had no matches. The irony of it: no way to light his pipe, after all that blazing.

In the evening, after tea, I stood in the smouldering stubble. The heat from the ground was intense. It pulsed through the soles of my sandals. The sky was clear, green-blue and seemed to speak to me of where I had come from. I looked at my home. It was one of a row of small, semi-detached 1920s red brick houses. I saw it for the first time, in a conscious way, as a place on this planet. I had arrived. I stood, a 6-year-old boy, in a burnt-out field with an intense aroma of smoke around me, watching the sun go down. The first few points of stars appeared in the twilight above me, and they told me that I was so, so lucky.

CHAPTER
TWO

School

THE ELEVEN-PLUS

It's the eleven-plus exam results day, a bright early summer morning in 1959. Thousands of flimsy brown envelopes flutter down from letterboxes in family homes all over the Cheshire Education Authority's green and pleasant turf, as they do every year. In the 1950s everyone aged 10 or 11 sat the eleven-plus — it wasn't an option. It was a strange government exercise in mass pessimism, informing about two-thirds of all children that they were failures.

So each envelope contained a slip of paper quivering with important news. Will your life turn out to be a fairly low-key event in the history of the universe? Or do they think you're going to be a sparkling star? If you're in the first group you'll have to attend the local secondary school. The instant successes are in for the grammar school and probably a life of anxiety, homework and later on — in the seventies and eighties perhaps — their very own executive dream homes.

In some families there's going to be elation, in others burning resentment, while in yet others there'll be children saying, "Stuff it, never wanted to go to that stuck-up grammar school anyway", and parents who'll just shrug their shoulders.

Was I going to fail or pass? I really wasn't sure. The portents and signs that I'd received as a 10-year-old boy hadn't been very clear. Dad, in a rare moment of solicitude, had told me weeks before the eleven-plus exam that it really didn't matter at the end of the day what the result was going to be.

"Just do your best and don't try too hard or worry about it," he said. These words felt comforting and calming.

Warming to his theme, Dad explained that this was why he and Mum hadn't even thought of trying to "bribe" me to do well with promises of a bike, or some such lavish present if I passed. He implied that this kind of thing was just plain wrong. It was going to put far too much strain on children. It would lead to life-blighting, crippling disappointment if I failed the exam *and* lost out on the present.

He was right, though looking back it does now seem a convenient ideology for a man who might not have had the ready cash, just at that moment, for a new bike.

Other portents existed in the shape of Henry not passing the eleven-plus, though Fred — his twin brother — had.

Henry *not* getting the eleven-plus seemed to me, as a 10-year-old, a much stronger and more telling example than Fred passing it. The soft mist of pessimism and self-doubt that permeated our household had already got under my skin. I'd already begun to look at life "Sunnyside down".

Also, there was something more generally pessimistic in the air of northern England that the brash optimism of the rock 'n' roll times after 1955 couldn't dispel. That strangely comforting gloom is detectable in the theme tune of *Coronation Street*. I believe northern doubt leaks out of the canyons of Yorkshire. Dark clouds of it roll over the moors, east, north, and west over the Pennines, and I reckon its southern edges seep across to Cheshire. To me, the image of a grey granite headstone in a bleak cemetery, with the inscription "Well — What Did You Expect?" just about sums up this northern cheerfulness.

However, Henry's "failure" also had a big impact on me because it seemed so unfair. If the eleven-plus was a razor-sharp but random axe that could easily whack apart the branch between twin brothers, then how was I to know whether I'd pass? But despite what must have been fairly narrow differences between them at that age, the twins weren't identical. I was a little bit like Fred, perhaps, but also a little bit like Henry, and, then again, I was not like either of them.

Later, Mum told me regretfully how she wished that she and Dad had questioned Henry's eleven-plus result. They found out too late that if they had "made a fuss" the Education Authority would probably have applied a recommendation that if one of a pair of twins passes, both pass.

Raising the matter would have been difficult if not impossible for Mum and Dad, however, because it ran counter to the "don't make a fuss" gene embedded in their physical makeup. Also, in their defence, the eleven-plus was still relatively new when the twins took the exam (1950), and perhaps no one knew what to do, or was readily on hand to advise, when this kind of thing happened. In 1950 it was like one of those mad scientific experiments pictured in the black-and-white films of those days. You can picture a boffin with a white coat and heavy, black-framed glasses saying, "Twins, eh? Ai nevaire thought of thet. Demn!"

But not everything can be blamed on the machine. As Mum said, Henry apparently stomped off on the morning of his eleven-plus exam in a dark mood, determined on principle to do the opposite of what Fred was trying to do — pass. Thus fraternal rivalry probably played its part, and I've always been suspicious of educational and psychological tests for that reason. Can they ever measure people's abilities and IQs objectively, when some of us *want* to score low? And even if the outcome for Henry had been altered after the results had come out, so that he could go to the grammar school after all — on the strengths of his brother's result rather than his own — how would he and Fred have felt about that?

SNOT SURPRISE

The end of the fifties and the eleven-plus exam represent, for me, the end of childhood. And if 1959 was the end of that chapter, starting school in 1953 was the beginning.

At that time Bunbury had two separate schools. One, near the church, was the so-called Girls' School, though boys aged 5 to 7 attended it as well as girls from 5 to 15. It was a single-storey, nineteenth-century building with bricks arranged in a cheerful blue-and-red checkerboard pattern along the front. After two years boys left here and went to the Boys' School, which was situated about a mile away on Bunbury Heath at the other side of the village, just a few doors from my house.

Children in the 1950s were somehow younger than they are now. Now, most of them get some forewarning of the busyness of the life that is to come later, by being plonked in a playgroup or nursery, or being whizzed back and forth in cars to childminders', or to friends' and relatives' houses by working parents. And most now start school earlier than we did, as "rising fives".

For me and for the little motley collection of rural 5-year-olds starting in September 1953, though, it was all a bit of a shock. Most if not all of us emerged from a chrysalis stage in little houses in a placid countryside with no television and few distractions except the odd moving cow. In almost every family there was a mother who stayed at home ironing, cooking, talking to the children and probably, in some cases, to the trees and the wall as well. But even if our mums were hallucinating or hearing voices from time to time, we didn't know it. We got used to all the attention.

So from today's perspective it wouldn't look like much of an upheaval to walk a mile or so with your mother from these homes every morning, down quiet lanes to a little village school surrounded by the sounds of birdsong and the occasional tractor. But for us it was a devastating blow.

For me, three things in particular summed up the shattering of everyday reality. The first thing that I noticed, and was fascinated by, was that the snot underneath girls' nostrils would vanish when they were surprised or afraid. Was it just the girls? Or is my memory a result of early sex discrimination on my part? I honestly don't remember the boys having fingers of snot, though my perceptions were probably a bit distorted by never having seen so many girls in one place before. In my class there must have been at least *eight* of them! The only one I had ever seen or talked to much was Susan Walker, a girl who was about my age and who lived in the wooden bungalow across the road from my house.

Susan Walker had never done the disappearing snot trick, but all these girls were doing it frequently. One moment they would be standing around, looking forlorn or bored, faces empty of emotion, with one or two trails of green or opaque gluey snot lying at ease above their lips. Then, a sudden noise or a teacher's shout might alarm them. Their faces would register surprise and their eyes darken with fear, and the two snot fingers would vanish *in a split second*, like two mice into their holes, only to be cautiously winched down again once the cause for alarm had receded.

The second thing that seemed to symbolise the abrupt change of going to school was the sudden sight of dozens of recently torn-off cows' horns lying on the ground. They lay in the farmer's yard and on the lane leading up to the Girls' School. Grey-white and with matted tufts of hair and blood on the bottom ends, they lay silently in the morning autumn sun. They spoke of wrenching agony and of the shock of the new and the strange. Each morning for a week or so we picked our way through the crop of horns, not saying anything. It was a scene worthy of a surreal Spanish art film.

Thirdly, going to school spelled a new regime for our bowels and bladders, and this too was a shock to the system. One glance into the toilets was enough for me. I took a policy decision that it just wasn't going to be an option during the school day. I can still remember the voice in my head telling me this, and it was an adult voice, like that of a solicitor or surveyor I had called in to give professional advice.

A swift recollection of the state of the toilets always saw me through. Those toilets really reeked. They were as bad as the giraffe house at Chester Zoo, crossed with the excrement of pigs that have been partying on Guinness and filled croissants. The problem was not that they were flushing toilets that had failed to work or had been blocked, but because they were based on a primitive collection bin technology. Except that one vital element in the technology seemed to have broken down — the collection part.

For boys, urinating is an easier prospect than it is for girls, as long as a suitable wall or target is provided. For the girls, though, it was much, much harder, because they had been trained to sit down. And this, of course, meant a trip to the giraffe house and the stench of medieval excrement. Any other strategy such as disappearing into the bushes at the edge of the playing fields to crouch down must have been unthinkable. Well, I sincerely hope so, anyway, because that's where I used to lie low in games of hide-and-seek.

So, for a lot of the girls, opportunities to pee were a problem and, as they never used the toilets, some of the little ones didn't manage to hold on.

"Look, the girl in the pink cardigan's bought it," John Vickers, the boy I used to sit next to most of the time, would whisper to me. We would look sympathetically, never sniggering, at the girl a few tables away, and at the dark pool widening beneath her chair, soaking into the wooden floor. Half an hour later it would happen again, to another girl, and we would look across again, sad-faced and wondering, as the teacher — the aptly named Miss Bratt — came up, sighing and stern of face, to lead her away from the embarrassing scene.

JUST ADD "NING"

The shock of separation from our mothers at the start of the school day soon wore off. I was disconcerted, in the first few days of school, by red-faced weeping mums, including John Vickers's mother. Why were they so upset? My mum wasn't like this. I had wanted to cry, and had felt my throat tightening. I did continue to lament and grizzle a lot at home, especially on Sunday evenings when I realised it was school yet again on Monday morning. But after the first few days at school it didn't happen much. I had more of a disembodied feeling, as if I were watching an accident happening in slow motion in front of me.

John Vickers and I discussed the theory that his mother would stop crying after the third day and, sure enough, this is what happened. We took heart from our new-found ability to predict human behaviour, and cemented a friendship. We were put to sit together at one of the little tables and eventually we began to learn to read.

The sense of disorientation I experienced in school and the general weirdness of the place was maintained by the strangeness of the reading books we had to work with. They seemed to have been written by someone with Asperger's Syndrome who was obsessed with the minute details of the physical movements of Janet, John and a large frisky collie called Rover. Or perhaps they were the work of a retired secret policeman whose specialism had been breaking down suspects by repeating the same words over and over again.

John sits. Rover runs. Janet runs. Rover sits. Sit, Rover. Janet sits. John runs. Sit, John. John sits, reluctantly. Rover runs. Janet runs. John runs. Sit, John. John sticks two fingers in the air and runs to . . . Paris, where, after a personal struggle with alcoholism, he joins an alternative circus and later becomes a successful cross-dressing juggler.

The only bit of excitement in these junior textbooks was the crocodile at the bottom of each page of the arithmetic book. John Vickers and I would try to rush through the sums on the page we'd been asked to work on, in case the crocodile got us. Pathetic, but it helped.

But we'd then have to wait, before we could turn the page, until the slowest table in the classroom had completed it. It was agonisingly boring, a bit like the progress, later in the decade, of *Wagon Train* through the TV schedules. Just when you had at last begun to roll forward in a slow, creaking way, the convoy would grind to a halt as, metaphorically, another wheel fell off someone's wagon. This meant that someone on another table couldn't do a sum, or had wee'd on the floor or something, so we had to twiddle our thumbs while Miss Bratt sorted it out.

These methods of learning how to count and add up, and how to read, had a sort of hypnotic effect and began to make us all as obsessive as the author of the reading book. Once, when I missed a few days of school because of a heavy cold, I got quite worried about which permutations of Janet, John and Rover in various physical positions or activities I might have missed in my absence. It was especially worrying because I'd heard on the grapevine that a quantum leap in literacy had taken place. In an unexpectedly daring push Miss Bratt had introduced to the class the breathtakingly long word "running". Now John, Janet and Rover were running everywhere.

"Don't worry," John Vickers called to me from across the road, when I saw him with his mum in the village later that week, "it's just 'run' and you put 'ning' on the end." Phew. That wasn't so bad then.

Not everything in the first years of junior school was a step-by-step training in Asperger's Syndrome, however. There was Music and Movement to brighten the day. Most mornings Miss Bratt would tune the wireless to the Schools Broadcasting Service and the children from the other room would troop in to join us. On wet days we always had to remove our footwear, so the running and marching that we did in a big circle around the room was relatively quiet, apart from the blaring radio itself. A large chunk of Verdi's operatic marching music would fill the room as we skipped around, giggling self-consciously.

But when it was dry outside we were allowed to retain our footwear. Most of us wore wellingtons, except in the summer, when it was sandals made of a cardboard-like material. The wellies weren't the shiny, trendy kind that you can buy for kids today. They were just ordinary matt black rubber, often a bit too big and evil-smelling inside because they had belonged to an older child first. So when we had Music and Movement in wellies, Verdi was combined with the plonking, hollow, rubbery sound of scores of wellington boots drumming around the room. It was like a little rubber fetishists' barn dance.

Another less boring part of school routine was lunchtime or "school dinner". Some benighted souls, including the two schoolmistresses, were forced to participate in the undercover biological warfare experiments being conducted by Cheshire's School Meals Service. Luckily I was not one of them. My parents, among others, seemed to have reached a consensus that meals prepared at some unspecified date and delivered by unmarked van from a location unknown were not only going to be disgusting to eat but also a health hazard.

John Vickers and I looked very sceptically at the school meals van chugging up to the school every day. We sniffed the battered aluminium containers of Irish stew and custard resting in the back. Horrifically, the containers had a similar design and battered appearance to those in the small brick giraffe house at the back of the school.

If you didn't have school dinners then you either went home for lunch or stayed to eat something that you'd brought with you. Most of us were in the latter category, though a few did go home every lunchtime, especially the kids who lived in the new white-painted council houses nearby. One day Miss Bratt asked a wispy, thin girl with red raw cheeks what she'd had to eat at home.

"Taters," she whispered, two lines of green snot vanishing quickly up her veined snub nose.

"Oh. And how do you have them? With anything?"

"Just taters."

"Oh. And who gets them ready?"

"Mum leaves them in a saucepan on the fire."

I sensed there was something wrong. I continued to stand and listen to this, but Miss Bratt didn't say anything. I now realise that she was probably weighing up whether she should tell anyone about the frail six-year-old heaving a heavy blackened saucepan full of boiling water up to a kitchen sink every day. I pondered on the fact that there was no mum around at home for that girl, and wondered what it would be like.

My school lunch consisted of Heinz Sandwich Spread sandwiches, washed down with a very weak solution of pink liquid from a jug that the school gave us. Heinz Sandwich Spread, if you're not familiar with it, is still with us, and consists of a sharp-tasting mayonnaise shot through with tiny pieces of chopped-up preserved vegetables. As a child I loved the stuff, and refused to eat anything else in sandwiches for a year or two. However, it can't be denied that to some children's eyes its appearance, when applied, resembles vomit.

"We've come to tell you," said one of a posse of three wise girls standing in front of me one lunchtime, "that you shouldn't eat that. It'll make you sick." All three had serious, responsible expressions and stood with their arms akimbo, waiting for me to agree with them and put the offending sandwiches away.

"It's Sandwich Spread," I explained, swallowing. "I can't eat banana sandwiches any more. The banana goes brown when you leave the sandwiches by the pipes."

"You can't eat it!" shouted the girls, adding noises such as "Urgh!" and repeating "It'll make you sick, oooh, look!"

I realised that the girls had never come across Sandwich Spread before, so I could turn it into whatever I wanted.

"It can't make me sick," I explained again patiently, "because it *is* sick."

The three girls gasped as their lines of snot vanished up their noses with the shock.

I pressed the point home, opening up another sandwich for them to see. "Look, it's *my* sick. You can't be sick on your own sick."

The girls screamed hysterically and ran away, chanting, "He eats sick! He eats his *own* sick! Uurrrgh!" I chased after them, chuckling and brandishing an open sandwich or two of Sandwich Spread, until Miss Bratt sharply told me to sit down.

WALKING HOME THROUGH BETHLEHEM

I did learn things in the first two years of school — how to read, write, spell, recognise numbers, plant seeds, sit still — but the main thing I learned was that somehow I'd been trapped. Not only was there that awful sinking feeling at home on Sunday nights, of remembering that the most boring experience on earth was about to be inflicted yet again, but also I had flashes of insight into this entrapment while I was sitting in class.

One very sunny afternoon — it must have been the first summer in school — I looked up from my desk, which was positioned near an open door. I could see, through the doorway, the intensely blue sky, feel the warm wind and smell the playing field with its fresh grass and buttercups. All those things combined into a heady rushing spirit of freedom. I wanted to run, right then, out of the dark classroom and into the field, shouting and whooping with other children, singing with the wind until I lost myself in it and vanished. It was then that I realised, quite consciously, that I'd been trapped and that life couldn't be the same again. School meant having to sit there, and you couldn't just get up and run.

There were other times, too, when I felt that school had got it all wrong. One of these was just before Christmas, when we were told to make nativity scenes with plasticine. Each of us had a wooden board, and a large ball of mixed-up plasticine with which to make figures of Mary, Joseph, innkeeper, shepherds, wise men, donkeys, sheep, tax inspectors, palm trees, ice cream vendors, ticket touts, star in the sky and, of course, a crib with baby.

As the plasticine was public property and had been much used already, most of it had lost its original distinctive colours. So our tableaux were composed of grey-greenish figures, some with streaks of red or yellow. I can honestly say that our efforts — ashen, stooping, malformed figures in a desolate landscape — looked more like figures in a depressing Bertolt Brecht play, or commemorations of the after-effects of a terrible nuclear accident, than the Nativity.

Except one. The thin, wispy potato-eating girl with the blotchy red face and scared expression had quietly made what I thought was a masterpiece — very detailed, carefully moulded figures of the Holy Family and assorted hangers-on, in a spacious stable. The only thing that was different about her scene was that it was *two*-dimensional. It was a flat, elegant drawing in plasticine. I thought that her effort was original, whereas our horrible little statues and grotesque farm animals stood up, but looked like the playthings of a brilliant, but deeply troubled, geneticist and cloning expert.

The telling-off that the poor girl got from Miss Bratt made a deep impression on me. Strong acid of teacher's ridicule and sarcasm was poured all over her neat little plasticine drawing.

"Didn't you *realise* what you were supposed to do, you *stupid* little girl?" The teacher's hot, scalding voice made the girl's face blanch. It lost all its redness. But she didn't cry. I could see her withdrawing into herself for safety, a panicky, uncomprehending look in her eye as in a child running from an invading army. Slowly, the tears now dripping as the teacher walked away, she began to unpeel her two-dimensional figures from the board.

This was very unfair, I thought. School, it dawned on me, was not a place that tasted bad but did you good, like medicine was supposed to do. It tasted bad and *was* bad.

The good bit, though, was going home. That Christmas our class had to do a Nativity Play and, after this mysterious event, I remember walking home through the already-dark lanes with Mum, and the other children and their mums.

The meaning of the Nativity Play itself had been lost on me. No one seemed to know what was going on, in fact. Janet, John and Rover had vanished from the scene. They'd either been picked up by the secret police for further questioning, or had gone into hiding and were on the run to a neutral country. Miss Bratt appeared with armfuls of musty-smelling robes — Biblical, Nativity Play clothes — and distributed them fairly randomly around the class.

Most of us boys were supposed to be shepherds, but we were never told what shepherds were, or what we were supposed to do except to hang around, existentially, with the angels. As we lived in Cow Country, the shepherd concept was too foreign for us to get our heads around. So we stood in small knots wondering about the meaning of life, awkward smirks on our faces, making sheep-like noises until we were told off angrily — *being* sheep was someone else's job, though no sheep or sheep's clothing were ever supplied. We wore drab, ankle-length shepherds' robes, blue-and-white striped, which in retrospect I think must have been old men's shirts. On our thin little bodies they looked like the shirts that concentration camp victims wore in the Second World War.

The other odd thing about the preparations for the Nativity Play was the sudden urgent demand from top management for paper chains. The demands were insatiable. Hour after hour we dabbed porridge-like glue on to the ends of strips of stiff, coloured paper, bent them over and made link after link after link. I couldn't connect this to the imminent arrival of Baby Jesus at all. Just when we thought we'd surely done enough, though, shrieking demands for yet more would be passed down and production would have to be stepped up. It was exhausting, but at least it was a role and perhaps preferable to the meaninglessness of shepherding.

It was on that walk home, though, that everything fell into place. You have to remember that a village like Bunbury had no street lighting in those days and so, on clear frosty nights like this one just before Christmas, the sky was swathed with bright stars. They seemed to buzz and crackle with electricity, so that if you paused and listened you could almost hear the galaxies fizzing. A silver new moon stood over the farm next to the school, suspended just over the barn as it would be in a child's drawing.

We spilled into the narrow lane, so glad to be out of school. The Christmas holidays were actually going to happen! They weren't going to be cancelled as part of some sick joke by the capricious school, and we weren't going back until after Christmas — which to us meant possibly never.

As we walked through the village and up the hill towards home I suddenly saw Bethlehem. We were in it. In the darkness the houses in the village shuffled their outlines to become the square, flat-roofed houses with zig-zag external stairs we'd all drawn in our Bethlehem pictures at school. Under the same scimitar-sharp moon there was an equally big sky with stars, and under them were dark purple mountains, palm trees and tents. The tents stood around in desert sand, and when I looked inside I saw rich red and gold carpets. There was a laughing girl inside one of the tents, smiling and holding a large copper bowl. I looked up at the moon, much higher in the sky now, and felt the existence of that place and of another country, elsewhere. There really was another world, with goats nibbling thorns, dusty streets and tents with brass bowls in them, and I wanted to be there.

BACK TO THE NINETEENTH CENTURY

No one had told us, when we were starting school, what it was all in aid of. I'm sure that we would have appreciated an explanation, suitably adapted to be understandable to young minds, rather than being left in the dark. Why the heck were we doing this?

Still less, though, did anyone think to explain to us, when we changed sex from the Girls' to the Boys' School at the age of 7, that the school we were going into was actually a time machine. It was, in effect, a living museum of an elementary school with a live connection to the Victorian period. It's a pity we weren't told this, as I think we would have enjoyed the time travel part of it a lot more than we actually did.

It could have been like one of those "living history" museum theme parks that you can go to now, where you can smell real Vikings or listen to actors' voices shouting long-forgotten street vendors' cries: "Visit Bunbury School, where you can dip your own scratchy nib in a real inkwell! Watch children being whipped across their palms with a real willow stick — it could be you next! And perform tedious arithmetic exercises involving medieval units of measurement such as pecks, chains and gills!"

40

There were two main reasons why we had to go back in time. The first was that Cheshire Education Authority still hadn't got round to building a secondary school for our area. This was 1955, eleven years after the wartime Act of Parliament that told local authorities to divide schooling into primary and secondary stages, but Cheshire somehow seemed to have put this message in a filing cabinet somewhere and forgotten about it.

This meant that when I went to the Boys' School there were still boys up to the age of 15 there — in fact, my brother Henry, nine years older than me, had only just left, a year or two after I started. So in 1955 the old pre-*First* World War elementary school system was still ticking along — just — in Bunbury.

But it was beginning to wind down. A new secondary modern school was being built in Tarporley, the small town-village that was 4 miles away, and, two or three years after I started at the Boys' School, all the boys aged over 11 vanished. The large echoing hall inside the school, which was the main teaching area, was suddenly deserted. We were left — a small band of bewildered 7- to 11-year-olds — like the children left behind in a Cornish coastal village after a sudden Moorish pirate slave raid for young men and women. Where on earth had all the older ones gone, we asked ourselves.

The second reason for time travel back to pre-war days was that the school was run by a silver-haired husband and wife team, Mr and Mrs Steventon. Mr Steventon was a tall, red-faced man with white curly hair and angry, blue-grey eyes that would tolerate no nonsense. He limped around, wincing from the pain of a faulty hip, and he often had to walk with the aid of a stick. Mrs Steventon had yellowish-white hair and a kinder, smiling expression, though her china-blue eyes could also frost over with anger or sarcasm very quickly. Her skin had a waxy appearance and little white whiskers shot out of her cheeks.

They were both coasting down to retirement. Understandably, perhaps, after a long working life of shouting and being sarcastic, they'd had enough. They certainly didn't want to have much to do with the 1950s. Most things smacking of the modern age were rejected with scowling sarcasm by the Steventons — especially coffee bars, Teddy boys and hanging around in small aimless groups.

There were two exceptions to this anti-modernism. For some reason Mr Steventon identified washable Terylene trousers as a marvellous invention, and he went on about them quite a bit. He also accepted that the huge new electricity pylons that were being erected in the 1950s could be strangely beautiful in natural landscapes — preferably those of Wales. This opinion might have been more to do with Mr Steventon's view of Wales than pylons. "They give a bit of perspective, don't they?" I heard him say to another grown-up. "Where it's needed."

So we were told, more or less directly, that — pylons and Terylene trousers excepted — most of what was on offer in the present-day world around us was to be treated with deep suspicion. A key element in this

42

training, or the Steventon Historical Experience as I like to look back on it now, was gardening.

Mr and Mrs Steventon were very proud of the school garden. It lay around two sides of the spacious redbrick school building and continued into the grounds of the Steventons' home, a large, elegant early-Victorian detached house. They were very big gardens indeed, with rosebeds and vegetable plots, a pond, gravelled paths, and different sections artfully screened by trellises with climbing, flowering plants and neatly clipped yew hedges.

Not that we were ever told much about the names of these flowers, shrubs and different plants. I can't ever remember being personally enticed or coached into an interest in growing things, or watching the miracle of germination or experiencing the satisfaction of tending my own things. This was not to be, because our role as little gardeners was to be the underlings, like automated garden robots. Weeding, flaying, digging, more weeding, clipping, raking paths, weeding again, cleaning spades and forks with dirty oily rags — these were our mechanical tasks, hour after hour after hour.

We had a taste of what it must have been like for young children in China during the Cultural Revolution: endless backbreaking toil in the paddy fields, weeding, planting and weeding, under the pitiless gaze of party officials and the Red Guards; working in the blinding sun to try to meet the crazy demands of an authoritarian government for food production.

The parallels with Red China, and the insane element in the Steventons' demands for forced labour, became really noticeable when the big boys left. Suddenly, when I was 9 or so, the school was denuded of its main source of muscle and experience. All that was left was a small, raggle-taggle peasant brigade of little boys aged under 11. There were only six or seven of us in each year, so that meant a tiny labour force compared with the collective farm-sized unit that the Steventons had previously had at their disposal.

The key problem was that Mr and Mrs Steventon were reluctant to let go of the pre-war style of garden to which they had become accustomed. For one thing, the lavish and well-cultivated vegetable plots and zones of soft fruit cultivation had kept them well provided with free food. Secondly, there were appearances to keep up, and Mr Steventon loved nothing more than showing parents around their gardens every summer on Prize Day.

"I really must apologise for the state of the garden these days," I once heard him saying to a knot of parents, in the quiet summer evening light. "We can't do it justice now, you know."

So perhaps, in their minds, they had already made big compromises. But be that as it may, the demands of gardening on our school timetable were extraordinary and reached fever-pitch during the peak growing and planting-out season. Day after day in the spring and early summer we were hauled away from our books into the bright sunshine to hack away at the huge garden. We ran panting from plot to plot, pushing squeaking wheelbarrows like emergency vehicles full of weeds or compost or loam, as Mr and Mrs Steventon barked incomprehensible orders. Our hands got blistered and ingrained with soil, and our backs ached from endless weeding. And when it rained Mr Steventon often hoped that it was just going to be a shower, and kept us on red alert so that we could quickly troop out again if it stopped.

All this was just when you might be thinking of getting ready for a summer exam such as, oh, I don't know, the eleven-plus?

"It's just not *fair*, Mrs Blakemore," I heard Clive, a classmate, say to my mother one day. Clive had been detailed to cut a hedge bordering the road and the Steventons' front lawn. He stood there, angry and frustrated, the shears in his hands, full of worry that he wouldn't pass the eleven-plus — which he didn't.

I wouldn't have blamed the bitterly disappointed Clive if he had returned to the Steventons' garden, years later, with power shears or even a chainsaw. Perhaps he or others full of the desire for revenge could have wreaked havoc upon the garden, slashing the yew hedges and bushes into crude, obscene parodies of root vegetables — but as far as I know, no one ever did.

The thought control of the slave plantation had done its trick. In fact, our early gardening torture seems to have produced two different groups of mental disorder, in adulthood. There are those of us who, like me, sometimes become obsessive about gardening and have to have hypnotherapy or other treatments to make us stop when we're caught weeding at night, under artificial lights. And there are others whose eyelids flutter and twitch and who begin to stammer just at the thought of garden shears or weeding, and who live in houses with no gardens, surrounded by paving and concrete slabs.

A LITTLE BIT OF BREAD AND NO CHEESE

Once upon a time children were regarded as empty vessels or blank slates. Kids could be topped up with knowledge and their blank minds filled in with the teacher's notes. Children were not expected to do anything in this process of being programmed with knowledge, except sit still, learn it and remember it all. All this was supposed to be bad. Later on, from the 1960s on especially, it was replaced by another theory, that children learn a lot better if they actively play a part in their own learning, picking up scraps of knowledge by trial and error, like bewildered shoppers in a large rag market.

Actually, just the first approach would probably have been fine by us. It would have been an educational luxury for us, in our 1950s village school. Unfortunately, though, the Steventons hadn't latched on to the *traditional* approach yet. They seemed to be following some sort of bizarre educational theory of their own. They had hatched it in the relative isolation of the Cheshire countryside and had honed it, over the years, into an unquestionable code.

What Steventon's Law suggested was this:

Firstly, all human beings are born with an encyclopaedic bank of knowledge and a complete set of skills. Thus all children already know what a chaffinch's song sounds like, what leaf mould is, how to double trench, how to spell simple words like "gardening" or "hoe", who Walter de la Mare was, and how to mentally multiply 3 × 6 × 2, add 5 and subtract 10.

The second principle of Steventon's Law was that most, if not all, children, apart from geniuses (who, it went without saying, would never appear in Bunbury), wilfully *forget* or — even worse — deliberately *conceal* their innate knowledge and skills.

Thirdly, then, it follows that the purpose of school and of the understandably weary schoolteacher was to *remind* children of what they knew already. Only a deluge of sarcasm and threats of physical violence could determine whether the child was deliberately concealing what they knew or had irresponsibly forgotten it all. In the latter case, about fifteen minutes' worth of ridicule, sarcasm and vented spleen would probably be enough. Any child still claiming ignorance after such treatment probably fitted the "deliberately concealing" category. This residual group could then be given a further tongue-lashing on the theme of being lazy, irresponsible dreamers who would soon learn that they could never thwart Steventon's Law.

Sometimes, if you seemed to have forgotten something, you might be lucky enough to be given a clue to jog the memory.

"A-little-bit-of-bread-and-no-chee-eese?" Mr Steventon once intoned to me, putting his head on one side like a

47

peculiar great bird, a condor or great bald eagle perhaps. As he sang this his voice, alarmingly, went into a high falsetto. He then glared at me, looking angry and expectant at the same time. I hadn't a clue what he was on about. Gradually, through all the hysterical shouting that then followed, we discerned that Mr Steventon had been imitating the song of yet another kind of local wild bird. To this day I'm still not sure what type it was supposed to be — we were all too transfixed by fear to worry about that — but the main point was that *no one had told us in the first place* which bird goes round singing about odd food specifications. It was simply assumed that, as children growing up in the countryside, we would know which bird was which, without being told. To us, though, birds were just flying objects that stimulated the improvement of spear design.

"And what d'you think will happen now?" asked Mr Rowell the relief teacher one morning, as he held his thumb over the end of a test tube. By this time we'd been promoted from the second year in Mrs Steventon's class to the Big Hall where, in Mr Steventon's absence, we were being taught by Mr Rowell. Mr Rowell was a nice, gentle man who later went on to be a woodwork teacher in the secondary modern. He had served in the RAF in the war, and had been one of those relief teachers who'd been given a brief crash training course before being sent off to work in schools.

So Mr Rowell didn't know much really, but nevertheless he had obviously been instructed in the

Steventon doctrine, because he expected *us* to know what would happen.

We shook our heads, knowing that we could be honest and not get into trouble with Mr Rowell. "Are you sure?" he persisted. Words like "sulphuric acid", "gas" and "iron filings" flew over our heads. We still didn't know. In his disarmingly honest way, Mr Rowell chuckled and admitted he didn't know either really, but it was something to do with acid and gas and reactions, and we really ought to know about it. "It'll pop when I take my thumb off, I thi —."

But he never finished his sentence. As he was talking he'd been shaking the test tube vigorously. Suddenly there was an ear-splitting bang and Mr Rowell's bushy eyebrows disappeared. We then noticed that he was holding just the end fragment of the test tube, and that his face had been grazed by dozens of fine shards of glass. Some of these minor lacerations began to bleed as Mr Rowell looked around uncertainly, smiling and waiting for the sound to come back.

It was a terrific experiment, but one we never learned the point of. That was a pity, as — understandably in Mr Rowell's case — it completed our science education in primary school, at the age of 9.

We only got two other glimpses of science. The first was a large ostrich egg, locked away in a glass-fronted cupboard and never to be examined, and the second, towards the end of primary school, was a wonderful newly arrived set of books with coloured, glossy pages, clear diagrams and exciting pictures. The trouble was, we were rarely allowed to handle or look at these books.

"D'you have any *idea*," shouted Mr Steventon angrily, "how much that set of books *cost*?" as he denied our tentative requests for access yet again, like a sixteenth-century pope forbidding discussion of heretical theories of the universe. And yet we persisted in asking.

We once had a history lesson — it seemed like one of only four in so many years of schooling — and it made me really desperate to know about Greeks, Romans and other ancient empires. I could picture ancient Greece in my head, and saw temples with white pillars and felt the stirring of the wind in the yew trees that stood just outside the school, transformed at that moment into ancient Mediterranean cypresses.

But this pining for knowing more was unrequited. Apart from the endless drudgery of gardening and mental arithmetic, a lot of time in school was just empty, like the "sports" lessons when we were allowed to run round and round unsupervised on the school field like a small mass of hornets.

Or the so-called music lessons, when we were handed old damp wooden recorders and told to go outside and play them. Again, according to Steventon's Law, we should have been pre-equipped with musical talents and abilities to know about scales, tones and notes, and perhaps be able to show adeptness in a small repertoire of English folk tunes. No such luck. We drifted around the field and lay on our backs among the buttercups on the air raid shelters, blowing tunelessly through the recorders like plaintive migrant birds whose navigation systems had been utterly screwed.

FARMERS FOR A NUCLEAR AGE

Gardening, or getting your hands dirty in the soil for various reasons, therefore seemed to be the only point of school with the Steventons. If there wasn't any gardening, time hung heavy. There was one blissful period — I was about 10 — when Mr Steventon had to go into hospital for a hip operation, and was away for about six weeks. A really professional teacher arrived to take his place, and the difference was astounding.

This man — I've forgotten his name, but let's just call him Hero — was enthusiastic. He wore a neat sports jacket and often had a pipe stuck in his mouth, and with his short curly hair he looked a bit like Kenneth More, the actor who played Douglas Bader in *Reach for the Sky*. In fact, Mr Hero talked to us rather like a friendly squadron leader addressing trainee pilots. Above all, he actually began to teach us things. We made models, painted pictures, wrote poems, read books together. In other words, we had a brief glimpse of what it might be like to be educated.

All too soon, though, he had to go. We clubbed together and bought him a present for ten shillings and sixpence, as that seemed to be an appropriately lavish amount to spend on a hero. We bought him the very latest in 1950s smoking technology. It was a pipe from the local newsagent's, and the main attraction of it was that it had a transparent plastic stem so that you could actually *see* how much black gunge and spittle was collecting in there. Handy! We were convinced that the advanced science behind this would particularly appeal to him.

Mr Steventon's return was a real downer. There had been a few heady weeks of liberty and free discussion of ideas, and then he trundled back, like the Russian tanks re-establishing Soviet control over Budapest in 1956. Mr Steventon poured scorn on all the projects we had done with his relief teacher.

"Oh dear, oh dear, oh dear", he thundered in a deeply sarcastic voice. "Look at how *utterly ruined* you've been by your free and easy ways! What a job I've got to do, just to get you back on the straight and narrow!"

But perhaps the return of Mr Steventon was a deeply educational experience for us, after all, because it exposed more clearly than ever what his idea of school was about — gardening, killing ambition, and crowd control. Except the main problem was that he now had an extremely small crowd to control.

This was particularly unfortunate for us because, from Mr Steventon's point of view, a certain minimum frequency of caning still had to take place. We were a pretty blameless lot — just a dozen or so hapless young children — but still the tumbril had to roll occasionally.

When the big boys had still been in school someone seemed to get the stick every couple of days. We always witnessed this because, after we'd left Mrs Steventon's class in the adjoining classroom, we were taught in the same cavernous hall with the older boys. They sat in rows at the far end being harangued by Mr Steventon, while we sat at the other, near the cupboard with the ostrich egg in it, being whispered to by amiable amateurs such as Mr Rowell.

We were always told not to listen or to show any visible signs of attention to Mr Steventon, when he began his build-up of shouting at one of the older boys. If we did happen to glance across at Mr Steventon when he was in harangue take-off mode, we could expect to receive a withering verbal onslaught from him ourselves. We had to keep our heads down. All the same, I'm ashamed to say that, along with everyone else probably, I found it deeply interesting and satisfying to hear someone else being torn to shreds before being sentenced to the cane. I definitely would have been beside the guillotine in the French Revolution.

When it came to the actual caning, though, we were expected to stop work and were *instructed* to watch — it was supposed to be an example. It was such a ponderous performance. All that was missing was a drum roll, possibly, and perhaps the shrouding of the podium in black would have added to the atmosphere. Finally, after repeating the sentence and lingeringly going over the ample justification for it, Mr Steventon would limp slowly over to the cupboard where the supple willow cane was kept. Silently, he'd then lift it to the required height above the offending boy's hand and then: *Whoosh-crack! Whoosh-crack! Whoosh-crack!*

We'd then go back to normal gardening or bird identification — whatever — but at least life had lost its boring edge for a while.

It wasn't so much fun if you got it yourself, though, and, as the number of children in school rapidly diminished, the chances of getting caned increased. To be fair, I only got the stick once — fortunately just three lashes, which seemed to be the going rate for our age group. I can't remember the reason for my punishment now, so it probably did no harm. But what seemed to me to be particularly bad about it was the way the pain crept up on you afterwards. It was a shock and quite painful to feel the crack of the stick on your palm, but it didn't seem so bad. But afterwards the stinging got worse and worse, you felt humiliated and tears began to sting your eyes as well.

I now wonder what effect the caning and shouting had on boys like my brother Henry who had been labelled as educational failures by the eleven-plus but had to trudge through the Steventon Historical Experience right up to the age of 15. But I suppose that, from Mr Steventon's point of view, it was all about Preparing Them For Life.

That was certainly his theme at the end of the school year, when he always gave a long talk to the older boys about What to Expect From Life and How to Avoid Wasting Your Time. I can still remember what was probably the last time he ever had to do this, when the last cohort of older boys was about to leave in 1955.

There was a long preamble about the utter disgust he felt for lads who sat around doing nothing: "Then they ride on motorbikes to Nantwich for a cup of frothy *coffee!*" The last word said with lip-curling disgust, which you need to substitute with any Class A drug to get a sense of the seriousness of the message. And then, an unbelieving note crept into his voice, "they just ride back again!"

"No doubt you'll be wondering what sort of job to get," he said, in more reflective mood. "Well, there're all sorts of jobs on offer, of course. Working in a factory, on the railways, things like that. But y'know, when it comes down to it, you can't beat the one type of work that stands head and shoulders above all the rest — and that's farming."

If Mr Steventon had had a pipe in his mouth, he'd no doubt have sucked on it wisely at this point. "Yes, farming — a varied career. Nothing better."

Perhaps this was only being realistic, though. The village school had produced, year after year, barely educated cohorts of serfs who were sent into the competitive world like a loyal and trusting peasant militia, pitchforks in hand, being pushed into the machine-gun fire of modern warfare. Faced with the demands of the new industrial society, with its car plants and electronics industries and petrochemicals, the school-leavers of Bunbury could only turn to their knowledge of double-digging and various tweeting birds.

"And you'll also find," he added, "that in a few years time they'll let you vote!" *Good God*, he seemed to add, in an undertone. "Now, one thing that needs explaining before you vote is what's the best party to

55

vote for. And that's the Conservative Party. What does it stand for? Well, it's not about keeping everything the same. Oh no. It stands for wisdom. Adapting. Keeping the best from the past, and making it better. Understand me? So if you're in any doubt just remember what I've said. Conservatives — think it over."

At the time, even at the tender age of 7, I remember thinking vaguely that this sort of message couldn't be quite right, or allowed. In fact, looking back, it's amazing what the Steventons got away with: not much actual teaching, loads of free fruit and vegetables grown with slave labour, and a chance to indulge in political indoctrination or to lash out with a stick now and again.

In today's over-cautious atmosphere you can't help wondering what would happen now to any teachers who behaved as they — and probably many other village school teachers of the 1950s — did.

As the Steventons had more or less sketched out a life for most of their students as the farm workers of the nuclear age, the eleven-plus posed a bit of a dilemma for them. It raised the possibility that *too many* children would be selected for an unsuitable life removed from their natural home, the soil. Therefore they played down the eleven-plus as much as possible. For instance, Mr Steventon always refused to entertain the idea of preparing his final-year class for the eleven-plus. In a way he was right, because selective tests have a tendency to begin to dominate the school curriculum, as well as teachers' and parents' every thought.

But as a result of strong pressure from a posse of parents, led by Mrs Cheers, Mr Steventon very reluctantly agreed to let us practise on past test papers. However, it went against the grain. The Steventons preferred to think that the eleven-plus would naturally pick out the right children, and that preparing for the test was somehow unnatural.

They preferred to give their own indications of who they thought was going to pass, through their choices of annual prizes they gave out on Prize Day. If you got a garden spade that was a very bad sign. If you got a book, though, that was a good sign. It wasn't fantastically subtle. I used to make a joke about this, saying that I really didn't know where I was headed, or what they thought of me, because I once got a *gardening book* as a prize.

But it wasn't true. I did get a book, but it wasn't about gardening. As I didn't get a spade or any other kind of horticultural implement, however, they clearly thought I was going to pass. Whether or not this was true I wouldn't know for another two years, until one summer morning in 1959.

CHAPTER
THREE

Life and Death

Angels at eight o'clock

I looked up from my bag of Smith's crisps for a moment, holding the little blue greaseproof paper twist of salt and getting ready to sprinkle its contents inside the crisp packet. I was very young — perhaps 5 or 6. I caught sight of something out of the corner of my eye. Over the pub garden, about thirty feet away, a young woman in a leather jacket was suspended horizontally high in the air. She was close enough for me to see her serious, concentrated expression. She definitely didn't seem to be flying so much as hanging in the corner of the quiet evening sky, like a fixed angel. Or was she a witch? I had time to wonder whether she was in some way connected to the mysterious bottle of Witch-hazel in the bathroom at home. Was this flying person Witch Hazel or, putting it another way, Hazel the Witch?

Of course, she wasn't really fixed in the air, but so extraordinary was the sight, so still the moment, that it seemed as though she was.

The summer evening was fading and in the clear turquoise twilight she was flying properly, her arms stretched in front of her and her long hair streaming out behind. She made no sound. Silently, she now continued her flight, which was tracked by a dozen open-mouthed adults until she coasted over a nearby hedge and landed with a soft thump in a cabbage patch.

There was a murmur of concerned voices as people went to investigate, but I was told to sit still. A few minutes later they said that she had been badly wounded, that was all.

I hadn't noticed the sound of the motorbike crash. As I overheard later from adults talking to each other, the girl's boyfriend had driven the bike far too quickly towards the sharp bend in the road near the pub. He jammed on the brakes but the bike just slid beneath them, colliding with the wall head-on. He was thrown into the bank above the wall; I've no idea what injuries he sustained or whether he survived. Not many people wore crash helmets in the 1950s, as it was considered a bit soft to do that. As the bike's back end reared up the girl was launched miraculously into the sky. That was why she had appeared unto us as an angel in a medieval painting, as she soared above the men with their pints of beer and the women with their lemonade shandies in the pub garden.

But that wasn't the death. That death was after school one still, wintry afternoon. We were walking down the steep stony lane at the side of the school towards the open gateway. Mr Steventon turned round to face us. He was bellowing, with his arms outstretched, angry as he often was but also with a surprisingly different look in his eyes — a panicky, frightened look. His face was red and his watery blue eyes were bulging as he shouted at us, "Get out! You *would* have to walk this way, wouldn't you? Just get out!"

This was a hard instruction to follow without carrying on in the direction we were already heading, downhill towards the exit. We backed off, scared, looking back to the school side entrance, uncertain about what to do and bewildered by Mr Steventon's peculiar state. It was unusual for him to be at the school gate at all, because as soon as school was over he usually lurched slowly back to his house.

"Oh, go *on* then!" he bellowed, his voice almost breaking with emotion. He waved us angrily towards the exit, and added, "You've just come to peer and look, haven't you? Just *go*!"

In fact, we were among the last three or four children to be leaving school. It seemed as though everyone else had been told something that we hadn't heard. No other kids were around.

When I got to the bottom there was a knot of people in the road, including Nurse Hurst in her uniform. She was shaking her head sadly, slowly, in response to someone. I looked to the right. Further down the hill a black coal lorry stood, its blunt bonnet slewed toward the pavement.

Silence was leaking everywhere, blotting out anyone's attempt to speak or even to whisper anything to us. I turned left out of the gate, to walk up to my house and away from the little group. But everything

60

was so hushed, and so peculiar, that I just had to find out what this was all about.

There it was, lying at the edge of the road by the grey kerb. Today you'd think that someone had carelessly left a dark-blue holdall by the roadside. But this was a soft mound covered by a navy raincoat, it was not a bag. A line of blood was stretching out from underneath it, for a foot or so, already drying on the road gravel.

I can't remember the boy's name now. He hadn't been living in Bunbury that long, perhaps a few months at most. He'd been slight, thin, with bright ginger hair and freckles and a lot of smiles. He'd run out of the school gate that afternoon without a care.

Mr Edge

These days I'm sure that more would have been made of that death. At the very least there would be fading bunches of flowers in the hedgerow for months afterwards near the spot where he was run over. The head teacher, or perhaps the vicar, would have talked gravely to all the children in the class about it. And today we'd probably have had a little ceremony of remembrance in the classroom, with each child being encouraged to draw a picture of what we did with him or where we played together. We might have written a poem about him, or a story. Perhaps we'd have been sad and expressed that feeling in tears, even though we were boys.

But none of this happened. Later in the afternoon, as the grey light began to fade, I remembered with a jab of excitement that there was going to be another episode of "Sherlock Holmes" on *Children's Hour*. The shock and excitement of seeing the huddled form under the navy raincoat was beginning to wear off.

"Oh no, we can't put the radio on *yet*," Mum said, "It's only just happened!"

I remember being very disappointed, and unable to counter her argument in any way. Yes, it had been terrible, but I couldn't quite see how me not hearing a "Sherlock Holmes" story on the radio would help very much.

We went to school the next day and nothing was said about the accident. We were told that there was going to be a new rule about walking out through the school gate. We had to stop and look both ways before crossing the road, and an older boy was always going to stand by the gate at hometime to make sure we did this. But that was about it. We didn't see the grieving mum and dad, go to the boy's funeral, draw pictures or write poems.

All that remained of him was a small dark stain on the road, a line of dried blood that gradually darkened into the road surface over the following weeks. I looked at this stain carefully as I passed it nearly every day on my way back home up the hill from the village shops. I wondered how long it would take for the stain to merge into the other black streaks and blemishes on the gravelly surface, and I remember being surprised that it took a year or so, rather than weeks.

Which is better? Today's more openly emotional way of handling sudden tragic death, or the stoical 1950s way? I'm not sure, though I can't say that any of us at the time seemed to have any problems with how it was all smoothed over — no nightmares or fears or worries that I can remember.

But perhaps we were over-protected from human death in those days. None of my friends at school seemed to have been to a funeral, and I don't remember going to any funerals in my childhood or adolescence even though three uncles and other relatives died.

Human deaths occurred mainly on television, and usually in the form of cowboys being shot painlessly in their chests. As children, we acted out these black-and-white deaths in our games, clutching our chests and bending forwards, then wheeling around in several circles before falling into the long grass.

But we did understand that there were real deaths. When I was 8 Mr and Mrs Ewing, our near neighbours, were setting off in their van to Chester.

"Would Kenneth like to come for a ride?" asked the morose Mrs Ewing. "We're going to the cemetery," she added, as if this should be the highlight of anyone's day. She was clutching a bunch of flowers.

The expansive cemetery, with its headstones as far as the eye could see, took me aback. I was only used to the village scale of things. The old graveyard around Bunbury church was a typically sleepy, restful place surrounded by thick, warm red sandstone walls — a place of history, moss on headstones and long grass, rather than a place to remind you of recent deaths. Faced with the *newness* of the seemingly endless headstones in the Chester cemetery, lined up in ranks in what seemed to be a park with neat grass and gaudy flowers, it dawned on me for the first time that dying had caught on in a big way.

That visit to the cemetery with Mr and Mrs Ewing also introduced me to the scent of death. It was a humid, soft, drizzly day. Tears of rain dripped slowly from the bent-over rhododendrons and weeping willows around the edges of the huge graveyard. But above all it was a pervading odour in the damp air, something earthy like the smell of celery wafting up from the gravel around the graves, that left the strongest impression. Was this what death smelt like?

Back in the village there was another sign of the reality of human mortality. This sign — indeed the personification of the gateway to death itself — was the appropriately named Mr Edge. He was the sexton of Bunbury church, but that title didn't mean anything to us. What mattered was that he was nearly always in the graveyard wearing black clothes, or haunting the dark recesses of the church. He was tall and gaunt, and his face was skull-like. It was as if his head was a fine waxy potato, nibbled carefully into a skull shape and with extra large bites taken out for his sunken eye sockets. Deep inside those sockets, if you could bear to look, there was the relief of seeing tiny flecked blue eyes, twinkling with humour. But his face was usually expressionless, his mouth a thin line across yellow stretched skin, and only occasionally was there a ghost of a smile on it.

Mr Edge had the supernatural power of being able to appear suddenly and silently from behind a yew tree in the churchyard or to manifest himself out of a darkened shadow in the nave. But I could never get quite close enough to him to find out whether *he* smelt faintly of celery. To me, if he had, it would have clinched my theory that he not only represented death in the village, but was actually dead himself — one of the walking dead.

THE EXECUTION OF MOLES

But while human death was somewhat shrouded in mystery, the deaths of animals were much less so. In fact, they were commonplace and readily observable, and, for a rural child like me, they were the main way of learning the basic truth that everything that's alive will die.

You could divide the animal endings into the ones that happened naturally or accidentally, and those that were the result of human actions.

Just playing in the fields and walking around the village showed us a lot of the first sort. For instance, there might be a cat lying dead by the side of the busy main road, a carelessly abandoned fur stole in the grit and dust. And once I saw the bloated body of a badger in the canal, feet up, floating in a stately and steady fashion towards the locks. Dead birds were a common sight, too — loose artistic collections of dry feathers that, when you poked them with a stick, revealed writhing colonies of maggots on bony frameworks.

Leading the unnatural category were the lines of dead moles strung up in dozens along barbed-wire fences around the fields. Quite why the mole murderers kept doing this was never explained. But it wasn't something we ever questioned. Looking back now at the memory of the little creatures with their eyes tightly closed, pinioned to the spikes of the fence, I'm more puzzled. Was it perhaps a rustic attempt at black humour? Or was it art? Or was it an echo of medieval justice, when leaving the remains of executed criminals to swing in the wind provided a powerful lesson to potential miscreants? But what had the moles done to deserve such terrible warnings? It seemed unfair that there were no possibilities of probation for moles, or lighter sentences than death by pinioning.

On Cubs' night there were other lessons in sentencing animals to death. The Wolf Cub pack met every Tuesday evening in a large, bare room in outbuildings behind the grocer's and butcher's shops owned by F.W. Burrows & Son. Across the yard was another two-storey building, the bottom floor of which served as a slaughterhouse. So on Cubs' night our dib-dib-dibbing and dob-dob-dobbing, and promising to do our best, was often punctuated by the sound of shrieking animals and small arms fire.

Today animals have to be transported for hundreds of miles this way and that before they're killed. Having a local village slaughterhouse and bringing things to a swift conclusion was more humane than the modern practice of going on a six-day scenic tour of the Highlands and Islands followed by being shot in the head.

But in the village then, even though the time period in which the animals anticipated or feared being killed seemed to be mercifully short, there's no doubt that the pigs seemed to suffer the most. They reached almost human cadences of terror and disbelief when they were pushed into the slaughterhouse and smelt the end. We Cubs would look at each other when a pig was shrieking, and smile grimly when the *thock!* of the humane killer cut the pleading short.

Indecently soon after, within seconds, if you looked out of the window you could see gallons of dark-red blood gushing along the channel under the big door into a nearby grid. Gradually the dark blood turned a lighter red, then pink, before becoming slightly discoloured water. You could hear the slosh of water from the hose inside and Tony Burrows, the butcher's son, whistling cheerfully as he pushed a stiff brush across the floor.

There was one less ordinary form of animal slaughter in the village and I once saw its results. It was the outcome of a collision between a Ford Popular and a cow. It had occurred one foggy night on a narrow lane called Highwayside. The cow, a bulky black-and-white Friesian, had blundered through a badly maintained fence into the lane.

The front end had completely caved in and vital internal fluids, black and green, had spilled all over the road. The dead cow, though, looked mysteriously whole and unharmed, as if peacefully asleep on a spiritual journey back to India, the land where cows are blessed and people are reluctant to kill them.

Milk and smoke

You have to pinch yourself to remember that most people in the 1950s, men especially, could only look forward to three or four years of active life after retiring from work. Death wasn't the lifestyle choice — something you can always postpone — that it's supposed to be now.

The change in attitude from the rather fatalistic 1950s, when people seemed resigned to dropping off their perches, started slowly at first. But in the 1970s immortality was being considered seriously as an option, at least in the circles I was moving in then. The only thing was, you had to do certain things to attain immortality, such as becoming self-reliant by digging up the lawn to grow your own vegetables. The other thing you could do was to go and live in one of those places where you can live for ever. There's the Hunza Valley in the Himalayas, and the remote villages of the Caucasus mountains of Georgia. There's even such an area in England. If you go down to East Anglia you'll find villages there where people have been practising living a long time, for centuries even (you can see the evidence on the gravestones in the local churchyards). Perhaps it's the thin mountainous air in Norfolk that keeps them going for so long.

By contrast, a stroll under the tranquil yew trees and through the lych-gate into the sunny graveyard next to Bunbury church reveals quite a different story. As you crunch along the gravel paths between the headstones the relatively young ages of the people who died — especially the men — are striking. There are lots more in the 40 to 60 age bracket than 70 to 90 — and this seems to be the case among headstones from the 1950s as well as further back in time.

In this respect, though, I don't suppose Bunbury was particularly unusual. It's not as if some peculiar local death wish had been at play. But if Bunbury was a typical place and middle-aged men and women were dying off at a fairly brisk rate when I was a child, we shouldn't blame the 1950s for that. It's more likely that the unhealthy effects of pre-war times, including the malnutrition and poverty of the 1930s, were playing themselves out. Also, two World Wars had had their effects. For instance, when I was in my teens in the 1960s I was press-ganged into the local bell-ringing team where I met Jack Mulloch, a First World War veteran, who was as thin and cheery as a sparrow.

Jack had been gassed in the trenches on the Western Front and was operating on a ghost of one lung, as far as anybody could make out. In fact, he might have given up on lungs altogether and have been trying gills or just breathing through his skin. It was quite nerve-racking to ring the bells with Jack, because his face would turn blue as he raised his arms and looked up at the rope, then red as he looked down. All this was accompanied by apparently terminal wheezing that would sometimes stop for frighteningly long periods. You never knew whether to stop, run down all the steps of the tower to the red phone box half a mile down the road to call an ambulance, or to press on with the intricacies of Bob Major.

All in all, there must have been quite a few people in the village wandering around with serious health problems stemming from the past, though — being a child — I was mostly unaware of them.

On the other hand, living in a village *and* in the 1950s must have included quite a lot of health-giving ingredients. For a start, there were no package holidays in the sun to worry about. Hence there were no holiday marital bust-ups induced by alcohol, long plane journeys and screaming kids. And there weren't many serious injuries caused by falling off Spanish mopeds, sunstroke and heatstroke, or phobias about flying.

In the 1950s there was a lot of healthy, locally produced food: lovely crumbly farmhouse Cheshire cheese that you could buy in the market in Nantwich, fresh local fruit and vegetables, and cooked meats with just a dash of nitrates. And at the butcher's you could buy meat from the animals that had been slaughtered on Cubs' night.

What's more, the gentler pace of life meant that quite a lot of people still had two or three cooked meals a day. If men took sandwiches to eat at work in the middle of the day — "snap" — then they'd probably had a cooked breakfast, and expected a hot meal at a set time in the evening, with the family. Add to this a lot of cycling and fresh air, and it's surprising that the death rate among men in their fifties and sixties *was* so high then.

So unfortunately there must have been a few negative things affecting health in that 1950s village as well as the bad effects of the past. One of the prime suspects, I reckon, was the milk. I've been told that milk is "back in" now as a healthy item, not least because too many girls and women have stopped drinking it and aren't getting enough calcium. But in the days before cholesterol and saturated fats were invented, perhaps the people of Bunbury were glugging a bit too much of the stuff. Milk was everywhere, like alcohol is today. It was available at your local friendly farm, trundling past in churns on milk lorries, or, of course, delivered to your doorstep.

Henry told me that in the school holidays, when Mr Rowell the teacher used to stand in as a driver of a milk lorry for the village firm, Stocktons', he would sometimes go with him for the ride to Liverpool. Early in the morning Mr Rowell would stop the truck on a quiet country lane. He'd dip a large jug into the foaming creamy milk and down it in one, then offer the same to Henry.

You have to remember that the milk then was beautiful stuff, like half-cream is today. Cheshire had thousands of Friesian cows pumping it out, topped up with Jerseys and Guernseys for that extra creamy saturated fat content. No wonder the veins and arteries

71

of everyone in Bunbury were furring up and popping like central heating pipes in a hard water area.

Then there were the cigarettes. The statistics say that not many more men smoked in those days than they do now, and they didn't necessarily smoke a lot. But I can't quite believe it. Men seemed to be smoking everywhere. For instance, they used to smoke in bed, *in hospital*. When I went to have my tonsils out at the local cottage hospital in Tarporley, I clearly remember the men in the ward lighting up after the nurses had finished their last round. I would lie in the warm, enveloping darkness, listening to the rise and fall of the men's gritty, kindly voices, and taking in the sweet cloying smell of untipped Park Drives.

My uncles — Fred, Kenneth and Harold — were all heavy smokers of cigarettes, and all died far too early from illnesses that seemed to be closely related to the habit. Dad smoked a pipe, and seemed to regard this as healthier than cigarettes. It didn't *smell* much healthier, though, especially as he, like the rest of his generation, carried on smoking everywhere — even when he went to the lavatory.

Dad's bowel movements occurred with such precision that you could imagine people today setting those hi-tech astronomical clocks by them. When he disappeared, humming, into the bathroom at 8.27 and 32.09 seconds every morning, in went the pipe as well. It would be fuming gently like a semi-dormant volcano. Perhaps he thought that the smell of tobacco would disguise the noxious sulphurous smell that was emitted when he was in there. This was truly awful — it reached the scale of a small chemical plant. There were various theories knocking about in the household to explain it, but mostly we shrugged our shoulders and gave the toilet a wide berth for an hour or two afterwards. You had to mask up if you wanted to go in a little earlier than that. The effect when combined with pipe smoke was even worse, as if an invading force had capriciously dynamited a sewage works.

THE DOCTOR AND THE NURSE

It wasn't until 1962 that *Dr Finlay's Casebook* started on BBC TV. This was the highly popular "small town doctor" serial, dramatised from the books by A.J. Cronin and starring Bill Simpson as Dr Finlay and Andrew Cruickshank as Dr Cameron.

But while everyone was glued to their TV sets in the early 1960s watching the adventures of the two Scottish doctors in black and white, we didn't realise that in Bunbury in the 1950s we were getting a real-life preview — or at least a preview of *one* of the doctors. We had our own version of Dr Cameron, though we lacked a Dr Finlay.

Dr Campbell — our Dr Cameron — worked from a GP surgery in Tarporley. Rather than register the family with a Bunbury doctor, Mum had insisted on retaining the link with her home town and the highly respected Campbell, who had helped her through all sorts of homemade medical dramas.

Dr Campbell didn't physically resemble the Dr Cameron of the TV series. He was taller than the actor Andrew Cruickshank and he had a fitter, leaner, almost military bearing. Dr Campbell had similar greying hair, but it was slicked back in an elegant fashion with hair oil. He had a small, neatly clipped grey toothbrush moustache and, when he smiled or grimaced, gold fillings and caps gleamed impressively. Whatever the weather, Dr Campbell always wore a long, grey or off-white raincoat. He usually smelled of mints and a faint odour of alcohol, the surgical or clinical sterilising kind, but sometimes with an additional whisky note.

As far as voice and manner of dealing with patients went, though, Dr Campbell was almost an exact replica of Dr Cameron from Tannochbrae. For a start, he preferred noises to words. His tall, imposing figure would stoop down to examine me closely, emitting strange Scottish grunts and drawn-out sounds: "Errh? — Noo thennn" and "Ha! Eh?" or "Waaa! Now, ohpen weede! Urgggh! Ha!"

Soon after these intimidating noises were emitted you knew that some sharp but short-lived pain would come. It might be a fierce poke in the ribs, a gut-wrenching grasp around the tummy, a wrist being grabbed in a vice-like grip, or the shock of a specially chilled stethoscope being clamped to the chest. As the brief examination continued Dr Campbell would be squinting at you, a pipe clenched firmly between his gold-capped teeth.

Then there would be a single word for me, such as "Bed" or "School" or "Drink", followed by a few sentences of noises in a deep rumbling voice for the benefit of any adult bystander, real or imagined. After he had gone no one was quite sure what he had said. We would sit around trying to piece together the jumbled jigsaw of Scottish sounds that he had left behind.

The main clue to the road to recovery would lie in the hastily scrawled prescription that Dr Campbell would have stuffed into Mum's hand. The variety of Arabic script in which he specialised offered at least a permanent, if almost entirely unreadable, record of his visit.

Oddly, from today's perspective, I hardly ever saw Dr Campbell in his surgery. In fact, I didn't know what the surgery looked like until I had to be taken there one evening with a deep cut above my knee when I was 8. The doctor almost always came to us. But this didn't mean that he was a less remote or respected figure than GPs are today — quite the reverse.

Even the faintest notion of the doctor bending to the patient's will, or of being at their beck and call, was dispelled by the *way* in which Dr Campbell visited. First, the black Rover would screech to a halt outside the house, often with the front end slewed untidily across the pavement. The doctor would sprint to the front door, black bag in hand, pipe clenched between gold teeth. There followed a deafening hammering at the front door, a technique apparently modelled on the home-visiting techniques of the Gestapo. But whereas there was a chance that the Gestapo would wait at least thirty seconds for the panicked resident to answer the door or to stuff the British parachutist into a cupboard under the stairs, no such slight concessions to politeness were entertained by Dr Campbell. After the lightning assault on the door he would be in and bounding up the stairs without asking where the patient was precisely located, emitting strange grunts and "Urrggghs!" as he reached the landing. It was simply assumed that, to be counted as genuinely ill, the patient had to be found somewhere in the bedroom area.

Apart from Dr Campbell, I encountered very few medical professionals in my childhood apart from the occasional visits of medical teams to the school to give us injections for immunisation. The only other person in the village to consult about medical matters was Nurse Hurst who, in addition to her district nursing, could be prevailed on to act in a vaguely advisory way from time to time. If I lay in bed with an inexplicably high temperature or a raging headache, for instance, Nurse Hurst would sometimes appear at the end of the bed, wearing her large starched nurse's head-dress and a sympathetic look on her kindly, brown and wrinkled face. "Oh, who's in the wars, then?" she'd say, before departing with the same saddened but helpful expression, blaming everything on constipation.

However, from about the age of 5 onwards I grew increasingly aware of another nurse — my sister Jay. When I was 5 she was 20 and already through her initial training. She'd begun to live away from home, spending time as a resident nurse in hospitals near Manchester and other places around the north-west.

76

Jay was born to be a nurse and, even as a child, I could tell that she loved it, though it was a hard and very demanding form of training in those days. Later, when I was 8 or so, she began working nights in a hospital nearer home, and she'd appear looking drawn and tired from her hot little bedroom on sunny summer afternoons, trying to drag herself into action for the coming evening and night.

Often she'd leave her training books and manuals lying around, and I'd look at them. One in particular grabbed my interest, because it was illustrated with cartoons in a particularly eye-catching way.

There was a section of this little illustrated book on germs and infections, but instead of going for graphic pictures of wounds, the book contained abstract drawings of doors and windows with the germs trotting through. The germs themselves were drawn as female figures in little black dresses and high-heeled shoes. They were chattering cheerfully to each other and holding cocktail glasses as they clip-clopped through doorways left carelessly open. Meanwhile, though, red and white corpuscles in the blood stream were readying themselves to come to the scene — and they wore appropriately red or white high-heeled shoes.

Both Mum and Dad were proud of their daughter. I picked this up from the cheerful banter between Mum and Jay when they were chatting about the funnier side of nursing and words such as "commode" and "bed baths" came into their conversations. I also noticed the admiring look in my mother's eye when she looked at Jay in the mornings after she'd come home, dog-tired, from a night's work at the hospital. Some of Mum's yearning to have had a fuller education and a career undoubtedly found a home in a vicarious experience of Jay's nursing. Jay told us about her struggles with strict matrons and her personal triumphs, and there was plenty of time to listen to these stories over the breakfast table, after her night shifts.

One of these involved a disappearing patient. He'd had a big operation on his stomach. Jay described how he'd been put in a curtained-off area, with tubes and drips leading to and from various parts of his body.

Apparently Jay had been really stretched to look after everyone that night, as she and a colleague had to keep an eye on forty or more patients. When the two nurses eventually got to this particular man's bed they pulled back the curtains to find that he had gone. There were just the tubes dangling there.

When they looked up, Jay and her fellow nurse saw that the window above the patient's bed was open, and that the curtains were fluttering in the breeze. Peering through the window — it was after eleven o'clock by then — they saw their patient stumbling across the grass towards the gates. He was wearing one of those especially short tunics that are used for operations on the area below the navel. Aghast, they realised that he was nearing the main gates, his bum twinkling in the moonlight.

So fierce was the reputation of the matron who controlled the hospital at that time that Jay and her colleague felt the only thing they could do was to climb out of the window to chase after their errant patient.

They raced across the lawn and made it through the front gates without being noticed, only to find that the patient, still woozy from the anaesthetic, had joined the late-night bus queue. The other travellers, it appeared, had merely shifted their feet uncomfortably, in a typically British way, when they had seen a semi-naked man with various tubes dangling around his legs.

The only problem Jay then faced was how to get the patient back into the hospital without getting into trouble with the matron. As she explained, there was only one way to do it and avoid going past the reception desk, and that was to push him back through the window.

BEING SICK

One thing I've noticed about children and young people now is that, compared to my childhood, they are not very good at being sick. It's only when, as teenagers, they start pitching into all kinds of alcoholic drinks that they begin to experience serious throwing-up. And understandably it's quite a shock to them. Some get frightened and think that they are ill. Could more be done to introduce young people to the vomiting experience and how to handle it? Perhaps it could be included in the National Curriculum, at Key Stage *Hwuuuh*!

Quite *why* my friends and I were sick so often is a bit of a mystery. It was definitely more of an occupation or a hobby than a disease. Sometimes I woke up in the night and found myself being sick. I hadn't been particularly ill the day before, and the next day I would be fine. It was inexplicable.

But perhaps some of it — the daytime vomiting, at least — was a reflection of the fact that we didn't travel very much, perhaps once a week in the car, and therefore the unfamiliarity of a vehicle's swaying motion could make us queasy that much more easily.

Lloyd Passey, one of my friends at the village school, would turn green just at the thought of a rare coach trip to the seaside or to the mountains of North Wales. On the latter journey — a long bus trek organised by local schools as a day out for children and parents — Lloyd, like all of us, had eaten his sandwiches by ten o'clock in the morning. By that time we had barely left the relatively easy landscape of the Cheshire plain and were only just beginning to approach the foothills before Snowdonia, with their twisting roads and vertiginous slopes. Lloyd's face turned green, then assumed a deathly chalky-white colour.

He had brought his sandwiches in a rectangular biscuit tin with a tightly fitting lid. Fifteen minutes after the last egg sandwich had gone down, it and its colleagues wanted to come back again for a replay. We were all sitting on the back seat and Lloyd began to try to stand up to walk giddily down to the front end of the careering bus. But before he stood up he looked inquiringly, through waves of nausea, at the biscuit tin.

"Yeah, go on, Lloyd," we urged. He opened the lid quickly and then, very neatly, he threw up into the tin. No mess. No doubt about it, Lloyd was a professional.

With a grave, satisfied face, he snapped down the lid, like an owl that has safely regurgitated a vole into its nest.

Another sign of the way that being sick had somehow got detached from actual illness was the way in which Lloyd, John Cheers and I started to be sick absentmindedly in fields, on the roadside, in school, anywhere. This failing had originated in illness, and it had started as a result of some strange virus that we had all contracted, the main feature of which was to cough and cough and then be sick. In a week or so, however, our racking coughs disappeared and we felt much better. But somehow, although we were basically well, a little cough — or even just clearing our throats or singing "All Things Bright and Beautiful" in school — would make us throw up.

"Oh hello, Kenneth, and how are you today?" Mrs Cheers asked one day, smiling, as I called round at John's house, one of the new council houses near the church. "Oh fine, Mrs Cheers" (pause to clear throat), "I've just come to see . . . HWUUUH!"

This was the occasion when I threw up all over Mrs Cheers's lupins. "Damn, I've been sick again! Sorry, Mrs Cheers."

"So have I, Mum," interrupted John as he came out through the front door. "It's in the hall."

In fairness, though, not all the vomiting we did was a kind of hobby. Some of it must have resulted either from real illness or from the passing effects of the food we ate. In the 1950s food storage and preservation were better, but not that much better, than they had been in late Victorian times.

For instance, no one I knew, except Auntie Ruby, had a fridge. Therefore food and drink that could go off, such as milk, had to be kept in a cool pantry and in a larder where the flies couldn't land on it, bathe in it or generally party around. But these efforts to keep food fresh weren't entirely successful. Even if you got the food every day from one of the village shops, which most families did, it was quite usual in summer months to see large bluebottles practising circuits and bumps on the food that was on display. They were always humming around the darkening lumps of meat in the butcher's window or on the cakes on the grocer's counter.

Sometimes it was the remedies that made you sick, though. The bane of my life when I was feeling nauseous was Milk of Magnesia, a revolting bluish chalky liquid that looked like milk that had gone off. It was streaky and viscous, and somehow managed to taste both insipid and waxy at the same time. My mother insisted on pouring a good dessertspoonful of this so-called medicine into me whenever I had been sick, thus ensuring a repeat performance within fifteen minutes.

There were other medicines and remedies like Milk of Magnesia or Vicks, the eucalyptus rub to relieve nasal congestion, which seemed to go with childhood illnesses — much as decorations go with Christmas — rather than affecting them in any way. Famel, for instance, was a strange, thick, fawn liquid with odd

82

bubbles in it that I had to swallow to relieve a bad cough or sore chest. It tasted strongly of creosote, so that after swallowing a spoonful or two you could single-handedly fill a house with the smell of a dual carriageway being resurfaced.

I remember going to bed one snowy winter's night after being given some Famel, and hearing an odd whistling noise outside. It kept on, that persistent ghostly whistling, as if a man was standing in the quiet field behind the house. It was intriguing rather than frightening, at least to start with, so I got up from my bed and, shivering, scratched away at the frosted flowers of ice on the inside of the window. No one was there, but the whistling continued. I looked across the garden, blanketed in crisp white snow that gleamed with blue moonlight. All was utterly silent, except the rise and fall of the solitary whistler.

I began to get frightened and was about to shout "Mum!" when I realised with a flood of relief where the whistling was coming from. It was my lungs. The Famel was doing its work, and was transforming them, temporarily, into musical instruments. As I lay back in the warmth under the heavy piles of blankets I was able to go to sleep in comfort, listening to a selection of tunes from *Children's Favourites* played by my very own internal bagpipes.

Run-of-the-mill illnesses among children generally seemed to be more common in the 1950s than they are now, except perhaps asthma and allergies, which were rare. For one thing we hadn't been reared on regular doses of antibiotics, as children and livestock animals are today. The first liquid antibiotic medicine I remember taking was *after* the 1950s, when I was 13 or so. It was a thick, pink, sludgy medicine that tasted of artificial strawberry.

But as antibiotics were either rare or unheard of when we were children we had to soldier on through a wide spectrum of illnesses, enjoying fabulously high temperatures and wonderful hallucinations as a result. Chest infections and throat problems were common in the winter, and I could therefore expect to get feverish and delirious at least two or three times between November and March.

Another notable gap in the medical armoury was the absence of immunisation against some serious illnesses, such as polio. As children we were shielded from the concern, even panic, among our parents about the threat of polio. But I can distinctly remember the charged atmosphere in the village one summer — I was 6 or 7 — when polio began to strike in the vicinity. It caught Maurice, a local boy, who eventually came into our class at the village school wearing heavy callipers to support his legs. My mother later told me, after the "sugar lump" vaccine was introduced at the end of the 1950s, how convinced she'd become that I had contracted polio. One day that summer, apparently, I became very listless with a powerful headache and began to run a high temperature. For a few hours she was convinced, and then the panic subsided. But as a result she asked about Maurice from time to time. She also told me about how his mother had watched him, when he was recovering the following summer, determinedly crawling all around the field next to their house, pulling himself along with his arms. "That could so easily have been you," she said to me.

Measles was another illness that we weren't immunised against in those days, and I did catch measles when I was 7. Mum and her friend Mrs Newport watched over me in a concerned way, one evening, when I was delirious with it. It was dark outside so it must have been winter. I felt hot, sweaty and confused. My skin was sore and itched with the measles bumps. The ceiling light, weak though it actually was, dazzled me and pained my eyes. The two women stood at the foot of the bed, looking at me, as I returned to the task of sweeping my hands up and down the wall, trying to catch the little cherubs with diaphanous wings that were hovering there.

Henry, I believe, had had a similar experience when he was younger, and had been discovered by Mum on the landing, in his pyjamas, crouching down with a serious expression on his face, dodging from side to side as dancing squirrels threw nuts at him.

GROWING PAINS

There was quite a bit more pain on offer to a child in the 1950s, compared to the present day. Of course, an unfortunate few children today still have to cope with serious and painful illnesses. But for the majority there's Junior Disprol and Paracetamol, and even little comforts such as a local anaesthetic when the dentist is at work.

Pain for children in the 1950s probably wasn't all that good an idea. Far from making a stronger character, the experiences of pain we experienced might even have made us a bit more squeamish, as adults, than we might otherwise have been. But while the pain itself felt bad, in some ways learning to cope with it did have a positive side. For instance, I developed a sort of meditation technique all by myself for dealing with the pain of having my teeth filled by Mr Parker.

He was an excellent dentist, an expert in his apparently recreational pastime of slowly rebuilding teeth, bit by bit. He was a patient, silver-haired man, very able to conscientiously plod on with his dental stonemasonry, seemingly oblivious to the pain involved in the process.

His surgery was in an impressive Georgian terrace off Abbey Square in Chester, where there was a dark waiting room smelling of floor polish, a very worn Axminster carpet and wrinkled copies of *Country Life* and *Punch* on a low table. Waiting there for ten minutes or so as a child seemed to last a century or two, during which time you could begin to convince yourself that it had all been a mistake. Mr Parker didn't want to see you today after all. You could go outside into the sunshine, have an ice cream and go home.

But no, the large panelled door would swing open and a nurse in a white uniform, wearing a deceptively friendly smile and bright red lipstick, would wave for me to come through. Walking across the lino floor towards the dentist's chair, I gained a sense of what it must have felt like for Charles I on his last bad hair day.

Then the drilling would begin. Dentists' drills in those days were attached to what looked like a small crane. The whole contraption swung into place over your head. Sitting in the chair, you could see the gantries and beams of the drill superstructure over your head, and the cords that ran between pulleys which were situated at various strategic points. When the drill started it hummed and whirred like a small power loom. The pulleys began to pick up speed, but when the drill began to bite home — a sensation rather like having a heavy-duty road drill thudding into your tooth — the pulleys would begin to slow down with the strain, and sometimes they would stall altogether. This was a good sign, though, because it meant that the lancing, jagged pain would stop for a blessed second or two's relief, before the pulleys began to hum into action again.

The interesting thing is that this was all done without any anaesthetic. And it was because of this that I gradually learned that it was much better not to look at the pulleys, but at a cherry tree in the little garden beyond the french windows. In spring I distanced myself from the pain and everything else around me by concentrating on the contrast between the fresh blue sky and the pink flowers on the tree. I really got into studying that tree bit by bit. The worse the pain was, the more I climbed into it, mentally, branch by branch.

In winter I studied intently the patterns of the bare branches, and in summer the fluttering leaves.

In a dentist's chair without any anaesthetic you're on your own. But it's better if you can hold on to someone when you're in pain. This was possible on another occasion, when I cut my knee badly on some glass, playing in the woods near home, and it was the last time I felt really close to my dad.

I didn't think anything of it when I came home for tea that day, as the bleeding had stopped. My mother looked at the cut, said, "Mmm" thoughtfully and put a loose bandage around it. But when both parents looked at the oval-shaped cut and the light-pink flesh underneath, it was decided that I'd need some stitches.

This was the occasion I saw the doctor's surgery for the first time. After tea Dad took me in the car and, when we sat down in the quiet sunny room with Dr Campbell, Dad stuck out his banana-like fingers and told me to hold on tight when it hurt. I was surprised. I couldn't remember ever holding Dad's hand before. But I took it this time, looking enquiringly at the doctor.

Dr Campbell didn't say anything, but smiled in a reassuring way, showing his gold teeth and enveloping me in his smell of tobacco, antiseptic spirit and whisky. Then, after a stinging dab of antiseptic on my cut, he started to sew. As with the dentist, there was no thought of a local anaesthetic.

"Ow-w-w-w!" I cried, holding tight on to Dad's hand. But I didn't move as Dr Campbell very carefully, very patiently, pushed the needle this way and that, drawing the thick black thread through to make three stitches. As he did this the pain branded the image of my dad's hand and the cuff of his old green tweed jacket into my memory.

I didn't know it then, but this was the last time I was to hold my father's hand. I was 8 years old. In the next few years I would start to grow away from him. The hero in the stained cream jacket who could play snooker, nonchalantly put his hands into a running car engine and absorb massive electric shocks, just to test the timing, and who could steer a car with his knees while loading his pipe, was beginning to lose his god-like status. He was going to be replaced by a smaller, much more fallible and sometimes downright irritating, mortal person.

In the next year or so the family in Sunnyside was also going to change — mainly by shrinking from six to four. The following year, 1957, Fred was going to leave home to start his university course. And for Jay, the case of the disappearing patient had proved to be the last straw. This was the time when the NHS was still young, and the expansion and improvement in hospital facilities that was to be carried out in the 1960s hadn't yet begun. It wasn't the hard work that bothered her, but the impossibility of doing a good job with inadequate equipment and nursing cover for the patients.

So one day in 1956, to everyone's surprise, Jay announced that she was leaving her nursing job to go to work on a short-term contract in Alberta. She was going to live in temporary accommodation for a while and "see how it goes", though in fact she never came back, except for three short visits.

"What's a trailer?" I asked Mum, as I read her first airmail letter from Calgary.

"A caravan, but bigger," she said, enthusiastically. She had absorbed some of the excitement from Jay's first letter home but there was also a sad look in her eye.

I don't remember the day Jay actually left. I'm not sure I even had a chance to say goodbye. But one morning soon after she'd gone I went up to her tiny bedroom at the top of the stairs and peeked inside.

I sat on the quilted bedspread and looked at the apple tree in the back garden. Beyond the tree was Mr Ewing's field and, beyond that, the woods where I often played. In the distance, to the right, I could see the Peckforton Hills, lying like the back of a blue whale, and the regular outline of Peckforton Castle.

Inside the room, which could hold little more than the bed and a dressing table, there were a few reminders of Jay: two spindly gold-coloured shoe trees for high-heeled shoes, a hatbox under the bed, a few coppers and a worn-down lipstick on the dressing table, a cookery book.

Suddenly the feeling of being alone, of being an individual, swept over me. I could see myself having this room, so I would no longer have to share the bigger back bedroom with Henry and Fred. *But would Jay come back?* The penny dropped. She might not need this room again, ever.

I slid off the bed and went to the window, glancing down to see Mum pegging out some washing in the back garden. Now I could see her differently, too. Just as the first cracks had begun to appear in Dad's immortality, so I had seen for the first time that Mum wouldn't always be here for ever, either. All those things I'd already absorbed — Mr Edge, the desiccated body of a rabbit or a bird in the field, the big cemetery and its gaudy flowers, came together.

I looked down on one parent and thought about the other. I realised for the first time that, even for parents, they were old. Some day, I thought, they wouldn't be here.

It wasn't a sad thought, but rather a clear, steady voice at the back of my mind. *Before they go*, the voice said, *you will leave. You'll go just as soon as you're grown up, like Jay.*

I let the sunlight coming through the window shine into the back of my closed eyes, so that it burned an orange glow into the back of my eyes and helped me to fix the realisations I'd just had. Then, an 8-year-old boy with grazed knees and a tattered grey-green cardigan, I clattered down the stairs to look for Kim, the red, fox-like puppy Jay had brought home just before she left.

CHAPTER
FOUR

Mum, Dad
and the Family

LIFE'S A BOWL O' BROKEN GLASS

Early one October evening, when I was only 4, I sat at
the table in my pyjamas eating a bowl of Kellogg's
cornflakes. About to take another spoonful, I paused for
a moment. To my surprise, the surface of the milk and
the brown-orange flakes had suddenly been covered
with shards of twinkling glass. Around the scores of
shards was a magic dust that also twinkled delightfully.
I opened my mouth, amazed, and looked in wonder at
the cereal box, trying to work out how this very special
magic had happened.

"Mum, look at *this*!" I cried, lifting a spoonful of
twinkling cornflakes to my mouth. No one seemed to
notice me. But just as I was about to put the spoon in
my mouth someone grabbed it from behind, wrenching
it rudely from my hand.

It was only then that I noticed the hard leather
football lying on the hearth rug. It, too, gleamed with
magic dust. Shortly afterwards I saw the big jagged hole
in the window, noticed the cold breeze with its damp

bonfire smell on my face and heard Dad's exasperated voice. He was asking Henry and Fred, in the back garden, how they thought they were going to pay for the damage.

The more I looked around the room, the more I saw diamonds of broken glass sparkling at me from the carpet, the tablecloth and the sideboard. As a young child in a small, overcrowded house containing twin teenage brothers, I think I must already have begun to learn that all kinds of inexplicable events could happen without a moment's warning. A brother could fall out of a tree and wind himself so badly that he couldn't breathe for a few minutes. Another brother could walk into the front room and crash down through the wooden floor, discovering widespread dry rot. Few if any of these shocks directly affected me very much. So here was another occasion on which it seemed OK to just carry on eating the cereal — except that in this particular case I would have been munching bits of broken glass.

The football smashing through the window sums up a key aspect of living "Sunnyside down". This little house had volatile young people and one child in it, together with two rather exhausted fifty-something parents. To make it work we had to distance ourselves from any sudden explosions, losses of temper or fractious disappointments.

Like Japanese people in rooms with paper walls, we couldn't afford to "do" anger. Outbursts were generally contained, not dissipated by lots of shouting and arguing as might happen in the stereotypical Jewish family. Instead, there were sad parental expressions and shakings of heads. I think Dad occasionally did have to bellow and wave a stick at the twins when they were children and got really out of hand. But by the time I was conscious of what was going on, this way of controlling them had mainly been replaced by him scowling and tut-tutting, and by Mum looking disappointed. Both of these techniques generally worked.

There were occasional insurrections and flashpoints, though. Once, when I was 5 or so, Henry had been teasing me relentlessly about my plump knees. Something snapped in my head. But rather than senselessly lashing out at this large 14-year-old brother, a fiendish psychological scheme suddenly came to me. I stomped determinedly into the back yard to find the flowerpot containing the beloved little oak tree seedling that Henry, like a depressed long-term prisoner of Alcatraz, had been lovingly nurturing for weeks. Angrily, I uprooted the precious little tree and flung the pot and its soil on to the blue bricks of the backyard, smashing it to smithereens. It felt great.

At that stage, and up to the age of 9, I was sharing the larger (but not very big) back bedroom with Henry and Fred. Jay had the tiny bedroom next to ours, at the top of the stairs. Mum and Dad had the front bedroom with its chamber pot under the bed, the dark-brown wardrobe and a view of the small front garden, chestnut tree, road and fields beyond.

To me, as a young child, the house seemed roomy enough, especially as there was an often empty, cool front room to take refuge in. Today, the rooms would probably seem small and a little claustrophobic. In winter, when there was only one fire in the living room, the only hope of keeping warm was to be in there together.

But it would be wrong to describe our family life as a simmering cauldron of emotions that was about to boil over at any time. Most of the time it was a relaxing, placid environment. This was partly because Mum and Dad didn't seem to have been entered for the status race of the post-war 1950s "keeping up with the Joneses" years.

The carpets and the furniture covers were threadbare, the furniture looked worn-out and secondhand, and there were no expensive ornaments, clocks or china — and more strikingly, little sense that acquiring new things was very important. The only object in the house that Dad seemed to treasure was a print of a watercolour by Peter Scott, a picture of geese flying over marshland in yellow-grey wintry light. Just looking at it made you feel a yawn coming on.

The effects of the laid-back atmosphere at home could be seen on any neighbour who called round, such as Mr Shore from next door, the well-meaning but rather ponderous and fussy man who had a whitecollar job with British Railways. People like him might busily visit with some neighbourly concern to discuss. They would leave an hour or so later feeling completely calm and slightly spaced out, shaking their heads in a bemused way as if they were trying to shake a cobweb out.

Perhaps it was something to do with the way that there was never a rush to clear away after meals, and how we would sit around nibbling an extra bit of moist, salty Cheshire cheese, chatting over the crumbs. Or perhaps it was connected to the relaxing weave of blue smoke that drifted out of Dad's pipe. But most of all it was probably because both parents were, firstly, often tired out and, secondly, were generally interested in, and amused by, other people.

This placid atmosphere in Sunnyside could feel deceptive, however, and I began to detect some underlying tension at an early age. Like life in a lot of apparently stable 1950s families, ours might have seemed dependable and routine on the surface. But there were noticeable tremors from time to time, suggesting a fault-line between my parents.

These were like the worrying changes of note or pitch in the deep, reassuring rumbling of a ship's engines. When I was 9 the ship's engine was to stop altogether. Mum left for Canada, the engines fell silent, the family ship began to drift disconcertingly, and I wondered whether she would come back.

The reasons for these underlying flaws and the air of regret that wafted between Mum (Beryl) and Dad (Wilfrid), weren't hard to find. Life hadn't quite turned out for either of them in the way they had expected.

Dad's strategy was to beat a staged retreat from family life. My main memory of him in the family setting is a smell of pipe smoke and an occasional voice coming from behind a copy of the *Daily Telegraph*. He'd be sitting in his chair next to the fire (it was frowned on for any of us to sit in Dad's chair), paper up and legs crossed. His feet, in worn check slippers, would stick out at just the right angle to capture maximum heat and to block warmth from reaching anyone else in the room. Sometimes he'd misjudge this slightly, though. The foot would be angled just a little too close to the fire, and there would be a smell of burning rubber as his slipper sole neared spontaneous combustion point.

He was a man on the short side of medium height, not overweight but with a comfortable rounded belly. When I was a child he was already nearly bald, but had strands of grey-silver hair slicked down at the sides. In the 1930s and 1940s he had borne an uncanny resemblance to the contemporary crooner Bing Crosby. He certainly had the largish ears to carry this off. Later on, in his sixties, when there were folds of skin around his cheeks, he could turn into Alfred Hitchcock when he happened to wear a dark suit or smoke a large cigar at Christmas time. But in my childhood, in the 1950s, he looked more like a prosperous little bank manager if he was pink, scrubbed and wearing a jacket, or again if he had put on a dark suit for a wedding or a funeral.

Coming back from work at the garage every day, though, he wore brown overalls with a Shell badge on the top pocket and the addictive smell of petrol and engine oil. His banana fingers would be tipped with fingernails black with grease and dirt from working on engines, and his near-bald pate would often be scarred with cuts from collisions with a sump, an exhaust pipe, or some other object protruding from the bottom of a car.

While Dad lived for coming home, putting his feet up and retreating into another world behind the paper or a historical novel, in the 1950s Mum was still hankering for adventure, or at least some more change. If the main image of Dad was of a disembodied voice coming from behind the raised *Daily Telegraph*, the defining image of Mum was of a woman in her early fifties laughing at something ridiculous. She could be holding yet another sunken sponge cake, for instance, chuckling, with her eyes closed, and wanting everyone to laugh with her at the absurdity of baking cakes.

Dad had pink cheeks and a complexion that reminded you of a nice piece of bacon, but Mum had a browner skin, softly wrinkled and covered with a light, almost undetectable down. There were crows' feet at the corners of her eyes, which were of a grey-brown colour. Her hair, which had been thick and strong and a reddish-brown when she was a girl, now had plenty of grey in it. It was usually curled with the help of tongs that she left next to the open coal fire to heat up. And while Dad looked like a typically English mild-mannered man, Mum in summer, with some extra brown in her cheeks, could almost pass for a wiry South Sea island woman.

Mum was basically cheerful, and had an infectious laugh, but there was no mistaking the fact that, as the 1950s went on, eddies of discontent sometimes swirled into her moods. At the same time, there were always strongly positive interests and traits in her character.

For instance, she had a very strong love of animals and all living things, which stemmed in large part from her upbringing. There had been a small menagerie in her family home in Tarporley, and she would often talk fondly about the eccentricities of a parrot that could tease the cat, a huge and loyal dog ("Chief"), and a placid donkey.

She made sure I knew how to rescue a trapped wasp or bee buzzing up and down a window. By gently placing a tumbler over it, sliding a postcard between the base of the glass and the window (and under the insect's feet), you could then lift the glass away from the window with the bee or wasp securely trapped by the card. Then it was just a matter of walking a few steps to an open door or window, pulling the card away smartly and watching the freed insect soar into the sky.

A similarly protective attitude was extended to spiders trapped in the bath. And for years Mum acted as the fond guardian of a large brown toad that lived under a damp mop in the outdoor wash house, by the back door. The bottom of the wash house had rotted, affording the toad a convenient miniature doorway of its own, so that it could go out at night to do toadish things, then come home in the daytime to sleep. There was a shriek, and much consternation and amusement, one winter's day, when Mum absentmindedly forgot about the toad and plunged the wrong mop into a bucket of hot water. The poor toad leapt, literally, from winter hibernation to volcanic heat in three seconds, landing about seven feet away, in the back yard.

Fortunately it was unharmed, and plodded back into the wash house, a reproving look in its eye.

A sense of humour and a philosophical attitude therefore underpinned my mother's character and kept her interest in life going. But after I was about 9 years old I began to piece together the regrets and disappointments she felt. Life had been more exciting and full of promise in the past, and now she seemed to be in something of a cul-de-sac.

To jump ship or not to jump

"I liked him because he seemed a bit different," Mum once explained to me, a note of doubt entering her voice, as she explained why she had married Dad.

Judging from the old brown-and-white photos Mum showed me, Dad certainly did a good presentation job, at least to begin with. With his motorbike, pipe, tweed jacket and matching tweed cap, he cut a figure that was, if not entirely dashing, sufficiently distinctive to be interesting.

Also, to someone like Mum who was of an imaginative disposition, Dad probably appealed on the grounds that he could spin yarns and talk of other worlds and possibilities. And at least she didn't have to pick a man who was one of the run-of-the-mill local farming types, heavily involved in messy relationships with cows or obsessed with dairy products of one kind or another.

However, there was also an erosion factor. "He just wouldn't go away," she once explained, sighing. "Weekend after weekend he just kept turning up." Tiring of a courtship that smacked of a leisurely medieval siege, she eventually resigned herself to Wilfrid. They agreed to a wedding on 3 September 1930, at St Helen's church in Tarporley.

But Mum had agreed to get married because their wedding was to be immediately followed by a much bolder adventure. A year or so earlier she had met Mr and Mrs Inglis, a kindly, open-hearted pair from New Zealand who had stopped at her father's garage in Tarporley. They were on a touring holiday around Britain. Mum was not only impressed by their friendliness but also by their down-to-earth enthusiasm about the good life in New Zealand. Mr and Mrs Inglis insisted that if ever Mum and her fiancé were to come to New Zealand, they could start off with them on their sheep farm.

It was a telling sign of Mum's own character, her own desire to do something different and to take the initiative, that this spark of an idea became a real adventure. Also, she was able to call Dad's bluff. He had been full of stories about travel and doing something different with life, so what about this?

Their bold plan led them from wedding bells in Tarporley to a six-week journey on RMS *Tainui* westward across the Atlantic and Caribbean, through the Panama Canal, and then across the Pacific Ocean via the Galapagos Islands and Pitcairn Island to Auckland, New Zealand, by 20 October 1930. Then

101

they caught a train for a slow, puffing twenty-four-hour journey to Onga Onga, a settlement near Napier on the North Island.

In today's world of instant communications and air travel it's hard to overestimate the significance of Mum and Dad's decision to go and settle in New Zealand, and the enormous impact it must have had on their families, as well as upon their own feelings about each other. When someone left to live on the other side of the world in those days, it was quite possible that you would never see them again — especially if you were getting old, as were Mum's and Dad's parents.

The shock and consternation that greeted Beryl's announcement that she wanted to go to New Zealand are poignantly evident in a letter to her from her mother Evelyn in 1929. The fact that my mother carefully kept this letter in an old, battered brown suitcase, and carried it with her to New Zealand, shows how much these words must have rung in her ears as she thought long and hard about her decision to break free. Mum dearly loved her mother. She was, above almost everything else, an intensely loyal person. And yet the desire to do something different, to seize the initiative, still won out against this letter:

The Garage, Tarporley
Telephone No. 21, Beeston Castle Station

My dear Beryl,
We received your letter this morning, which we have carefully thought about. You and Wilfrid are

not worried, because you don't quite realize what you are doing, there is too much haste about it.

We don't want to stop you going (if we could), but Father says, go in a few months' time, give us time to get used to it . . .

It's too serious to go, as if it's only the South of France or even America . . .

I should be worried to death really, when you go for a week it's a jolly long time but when it's for years, perhaps, you want to go a bit slower, and look before you leap . . . Perhaps I'm considering my own feelings, too, but I want you to really realize what it will mean, like Wilfrid asked you if you had considered it thoroughly . . .

Best love to all from all,
Your loving mother Eve.

Once they were over in New Zealand, though, there was more than a hint of honeymoon and happiness in the photos that Mum and Dad kept from their first months on the Inglises' farm. Early November spring gave way to a sunny December summer, as dense masses of heavily perfumed roses bloomed outside their bedroom window, and my mother was able to enjoy a dip in the cooling river on the hot New Year's Day of 1931.

Unfortunately, Mum and Dad, like almost everyone else at that time, did not realise that the sky was about to fall in. It didn't occur to many that the Wall Street Crash in 1929 was going to be more than a single serious economic setback. People woke up gradually to the fact that the whole world was sliding into an economic depression. The ever-widening ripples of unemployment and business failure spread out slowly but remorselessly, washing across New Zealand just as Mum and Dad were starting their new life together.

Dad had been helping with general farm work on Mr Inglis's ranch, but he'd also made himself useful with his skills of tinkering with farm machinery and mending diesel and petrol engines. At some point, probably before going to New Zealand, he had taken a training course in engine and vehicle maintenance. When the economic crisis bit, though, and the lay-offs came, there was nothing to be done.

Mum told me that Mr Inglis had suggested to Dad that he took the train to the end of the line, stopping off at every halt and station to ask for work. For whatever reason — and it might have been a sensible one, because if thousands of men were doing the same thing it was probably a pointless search — Dad didn't do this. Nor did they use their nest egg of money to buy land, which was being sold for next to nothing at that time, such was the severity of the economic crisis.

Some friends of theirs did, however. They bought land and decided to stay on. "But that meant they had nothing to live on," Mum explained. "Except bread and jam." There was an admiring tone in her voice when she told me about these friends. Eventually the ones who hung on did make good. When I was a boy I was puzzled by the arrival, every Christmas, of a large brown cardboard box marked "A Gift From New Zealand". It was from the friends who'd stayed on.

Inside the box was block after block of golden New Zealand butter and cheddar. It was like unpacking a consignment of dairy bullion. It was a gift that was welcomed, but also seemed slightly silly and made us smile. Mum especially greeted the box as if the friends themselves had walked into the room. She exclaimed, "Well, I never!" and "Good *heavens*, look at all this!" and never failed to be surprised and pleased by the annual gift.

But it was also a reminder to her of the prosperity that might have been, or of what might have happened, if they'd become New Zealanders after all. It always prompted the bread and jam story and "if only we'd stayed on", and how well they must be living now, over there.

When their opportunities on the sheep farm seemed to dry up, Mum and Dad thought they'd make a go of it in town — in Wellington, the capital city, in fact. Things began promisingly, if slightly weirdly, with their decision to make tennis racquets.

They put their nest egg of money into this venture with another couple, a Mr and Mrs Watson, on 11 May 1931, and grandly launched it with the name of the Southern Sports Manufacturing Company. Apparently, racquet-stringing was in its infancy in New Zealand at that time. An old brown photograph Mum used to show me, of Dad and Mr Watson holding armfuls of tennis racquets they were going to string, has remained

105

SUNNYSIDE DOWN

with me since childhood as a symbol of misguided optimism.

They worked hard at the new business but it was an amateurish venture. They wanted to start off sales in a gentle way, building up a steady demand for racquets in this new and still only partially developed country. But they were both amazed and unable to cope with a sudden and surprising demand for tennis racquets. It was as if lean, bronzed New Zealanders all over the country, men and women alike, suddenly arose from their sheep-shearing or sizzling of lamb chops, or whatever else they were doing with sheep, to satisfy a burning, pent-up desire for tennis. Orders flooded in, but the new little racquet-making venture was caught completely unawares, a paper boat in a commercial typhoon. Apparently orders were mislaid, or delayed, or muddled — and unfortunately the business folded. Experienced racquet-stringers and business types quickly moved in to satisfy demand.

And so that journey around the world didn't lead to the outcome they expected. The whole venture — not the experience of New Zealand itself, which Mum loved — ended in a kind of defeat, or at least, a big disappointment. They had to come back. Mum did so because Dad wanted to and also out of a sense of family duty — and perhaps a large dash of guilt — because her mother was becoming seriously ill.

But she had very mixed feelings about coming back. In fact, there was a brief moment when

106

everything hung in the balance and she almost didn't. When the ship docked in Sydney harbour, on the return journey, she was torn by a strong desire to jump ship.

Leave Wilfrid! There were no children yet. Seize your chance! Walk up the busy street with its clanking trams that led up from the docks, and find a new life in the big Australian city.

There is probably at least one moment in everyone's life when we come to a fork in the road like this. Have you experienced one yet? It's this way or that — a clear choice between one life, one set of clothes, and another.

The difference between our time and my mother's, at least for women, is that now people are much more likely to act on the choices that loom up in front of them. There almost seems to be *too much* choice. This school or that one? This or that brand of coffee? That DVD player or this one? This person to live with or that one?

But in Mum's time, getting a divorce was almost impossible, particularly for people without a lot of money. And separating, going off on your own, was shameful, almost unthinkable for a woman. But millions of people, women especially, must have rehearsed this thought daily. You wouldn't have known because, on the surface, they just carried on and made the best of it. Mum had thought seriously about leaving. The interesting thing is that she told her son at the tender age of 9 about the second thoughts she'd had.

THE FRAGILE RADIATOR

Dad had a small-scale, struggling motor car service and repair business in the 1950s. His undoubted skills and talents with engines and cars developed accidentally in his youth in the early 1920s. The accident was a literal one — a broken arm that resulted from a motorbike accident. To build up strength in his arm, once the break had begun to heal, the doctor prescribed electric shock therapy to the affected limb, something that would increase Dad's immunity to enormous voltages passing through his system, up to the capacity of a medium-sized nuclear power station.

The doctor also advised physical work for a few months. Dad went to work on a farm, where he began to discover his knack for fixing farm machinery, vehicles and engines.

But at the time all this was seen as a secondary activity, almost a hobby, in Dad's main career plan to be a tweed-jacketed-gentleman-with-pipe. After all, he was from a professional, middle-class family living in Hyde, near Manchester. His father was a successful veterinary surgeon with a large practice. My grandfather (long dead by the time I had been born) was a rotund, imposing man, judging from the old photographs. With his bulging waistcoat and his watch chain, he looked like an old First World War general. Dad's next-youngest brother, Fred, followed in their father's footsteps by succeeding in veterinary science, and eventually he became the first professor of the subject

108

in a new department that he established at Bristol University.

Dad's attempt to stay in the professional middle class didn't work out, though. A bright lad at school, he had been started at the bank as a junior employee just before the First World War, when he was 16. A solid and prosperous, if unexciting, future beckoned, and it was assumed that Dad was starting off on a path that in time would lead to a senior position in the bank. That's why, when he put on a jacket and tie, or a suit, he *looked* like a solid bank manager nearing retirement.

But then along came the First World War. After a year in the army he returned to the bank in 1919. But he found that he couldn't have his former position back. He was expected to start again on the bottom rung. He flatly refused to do this.

"He always was so *stubborn*," Mum said, telling me this story. "It wouldn't have mattered for a year or so. He'd have been back to his previous position and been able to carry on, I'm sure. But oh no, he just wasn't having it."

After resolutely refusing reinstatement at a lower level in the bank, Dad spent much of the 1920s helping his father, in what seems to have been a fairly leisurely way, with the veterinary practice — mostly by driving his father from place to place. Then, when he and Mum came back from New Zealand, he gradually transferred his energies to helping out at the Swan Garage, Tarporley — the business begun and developed by my maternal grandfather, William Henry White.

When, in the 1940s, Dad was faced with having to run his own business — or find some other kind of paid employment — it must have seemed a natural choice to start up a little motor car servicing workshop. He did this by renting a workshop in a filling station run by a Mr Wilcox, which was near a busy road junction in a beautiful area of Cheshire near to Tarporley, Delamere Forest.

The business never took off in the 1950s, despite an unprecedented growth of car ownership and burgeoning demand for mechanics to fix the untrustworthy, eccentric British vehicles that coughed along the roads at that time. It almost looks, in retrospect, as if Dad took conscious decisions to try to stunt his business: "Mmm, if I'm going to stay ahead of the competition and keep the regular customers, I'll need to invest in some new equipment, perhaps get a bank loan. Must make sure I *never* do that."

Also, as the prospect of money being spent — not just his own, but anyone's — was profoundly unsettling to him, I think he often tried to dissuade potential customers from having work done on their cars. Much as a surgeon might advise an elderly patient not to go in for invasive surgery, Dad would do his best to make the job as minimal, and as light on the customer's pocket, as possible. As long as the car could stagger round the corner and live to see another day (or two), he thought that was far preferable for everyone concerned.

Underlying this approach to his work seemed to be a refusal, deep down, to countenance the idea that fixing cars was really his livelihood. He described himself on

110

official forms as a "motor engineer" (never a "car mechanic"), but all along he refused to accept that the garage and all that went with it summed him up. He remained the tweed-jacketed, pipe-smoking gentleman who knew about classical music and read books, and had travelled round the world.

Planet Wilfrid looked quite different from the actual world we lived in, and he did his best at all times to remain on Planet Wilfrid by retreating behind the *Daily Telegraph* or reading fiction.

Dad's diffident attitude towards the garage extended to his own car. There's a saying that no children are worse shod than those of a cobbler. This aptly applied to the family saloons we were dangerously transported around in during the 1950s. For instance, the pram-like black Austin saloon we had then was treated as if it were a dangerously fragile exhibit from a museum, which, in a way, it was. We were regularly told off if we approached the running boards as if we were going to stand on them because the slightest weight would have made them drop off. And on the occasions Dad took me in the car to the school on the other side of the village, I would have to hold on tight to the door handle. Letting go would have meant the door swinging out dangerously. Any child passenger such as me could easily have been sucked outside, unnoticed except for a small brief scream, if the car happened to be rounding a sudden right-hand bend. Indeed, this very thing had happened to Jay, my sister, years before I was born. Dad had been driving the car slowly, along the stretch of country lane leading up to Sunnyside, when Jay fell out through the unreliable door and bounced along the road, sustaining grazes and cuts but fortunately few other physical injuries.

Not only was Dad reluctant to maintain the fabric and safety of the family car, but he was also extremely unwilling to expose it to any unfamiliar journeys. Dad rightly saw the Austin as an unstable, organic thing, very liable to fall apart or have a crisis if it was exposed to a range of different road surfaces, slopes or unexpected gear changes. A lot of gear-changing was usually necessary in order to substitute for the rather tokenistic brakes.

He was willing to drive back and forth to Delamere every day, a round trip of about 18 miles, and to Chester (13 miles away) most Saturdays, and perhaps to coast gently around nearby country lanes on Sundays on family outings, for a walk or to visit a pub. All these journeys were acceptable, because — much as a seasoned sailor can predict the tides, dangerous currents and hidden reefs of a familiar sea journey — Dad could plan ahead where all the likely danger spots were going to be and work out how to minimise frivolous brake use. He could also foresee where he could let the car roll along in neutral without using valuable petrol.

No wonder, then, that an innocent request to take us for a day trip to the seaside on a sunny weekend would invariably be greeted by a look of horror and incredulity on Dad's face. Rhyl, the resort on the North Wales coast, for instance, was more than *40* miles away! Did we realise? The prospect of a round trip of 80 miles in one day usually sunk Dad into a minor depression. Not only would there be the sharp economic downturn caused by having to spend much more on petrol than anticipated (exacerbated by the extra weight of four or five passengers), but, above all, there was the huge and frightening uncertainty of how the car and its fragile radiator would cope, on a hot day, with all that the A55 could throw at it.

All being well, his tactic of communicating the sheer foolhardiness of a trip to Rhyl would prevail. Further attempts to make him change his mind, along the lines of "Oh go on, Dad" were always met with an exasperated expression, as he lowered his newspaper. This hostile glare would be followed not by words but with a snarling sigh. In that moment he would emit a sound very like a cornered wild animal might utter when stabbed with a sharp stick.

But sometimes he did lose the battle to preserve common sense, the defences were breached, and — with no one, not even himself, knowing quite why he had decided to relent this time — we were told that there would, against his better judgement, be a trip to the seaside after all.

The journeys there must have been agony for him. Each red traffic light in the distance was greeted with a mournful sigh, as if news of the death of a dearly loved relative had just been relayed to him. Any unexpected impediments or delays of a more serious nature — road works, a traffic jam, a diversion — elicited even louder sighs and tragic statements, with a doleful emphasis on one word, such as, "By the *hearty*, look at this!" We would all hold our breath, because going on — just for the highly unnecessary reason of visiting the seaside — was now being portrayed as a particularly reckless venture. Would we have to turn back?

Once there, Dad's mood would gradually lighten. There was always a serious but optimistic look in his eye as we set off on the return journey, often completed in the enveloping warm darkness of a late-August evening. As the car neared its familiar tracks, Dad sometimes permitted himself a light-hearted hum, as he steadied the wheel and indulged himself with a light touch on the accelerator.

Mum remarked one day that Dad always drove faster on the return journey. On the way out gloom and pessimism slowed him down, much as Columbus's sailors, crossing themselves and muttering mutinously, must have climbed the rigging with snail-like reluctance to adjust the sails on the outward journey across the unknown Atlantic. On the way back the promise of safety and familiar terrain made him speed up. The Austin's engine sang, Dad hummed and we had had a day out after all.

What really exasperated Mum about Dad's relation-ship with the car, though, was not only his reluctance to use it for any other purpose than completely routine ones, but something else that happened during several consecutive winters.

When the temperature dipped below freezing point at night, as it tended to do from early November on, the fragility of the car's radiator was exposed. But Dad refused to put antifreeze in it. This was not particularly because of the cost, though that would certainly have caused a sharp jab of pain to the wallet, but mainly because the active chemicals in the antifreeze would have instantly penetrated the radiator's corroding interior and caused it to burst. The radiator's health was probably on a par with a patient with advanced tuberculosis. Any sudden strain or shock, and certainly a dose of antifreeze, would finish it off.

Dad's way round the problem of nursing the radiator through a cruel winter was to drain out the hot water every night when he returned from work, especially when a hard frost was predicted (hence his obsessive concern with weather forecasts). Then the following morning, much to Mum's irritation, he would trudge to and from the car with steaming saucepans of hot water to refill the radiator. It didn't take all that long, and nor did it happen every winter morning, but it annoyed Beryl very much. It seemed to sum up all the limitations of Dad's approach to both his business and to life in general. Mum was the daughter of a man who had started up and developed a large garage business in the local area — a man who, despite some faults, had in his time been enterprising, had vision and had not been afraid to spend money when it was needed.

However, Mum wasn't the sort of woman to "say anything" about her husband's irritating behaviour, especially in front of me or the teenagers. But I remember one particular winter's morning when she almost seemed ready to shout at him. It was exceptionally cold, there was snow on the ground and Dad had trudged back and forth with his bucket, trailing wet snow over the carpet, spilling hot water in the hall and letting icy blasts of air into the house as he went to and fro.

"Oh, for heaven's *sake*," I heard her mutter under her breath. She didn't say any more, but just stood, glowering at him. He was dressed in his brown grease-stained overalls, as usual, but was also wearing a red woollen bobble hat that had effectively turned him into a Christmas tree decoration. He sensed her exasperation, and there was a charged and awkward silence between them at that moment, until I heard Dad say, defensively and lamely, "I see they're predicting it'll be milder next week." Then he sighed his long, uncomfortable, embarrassed sigh, cleared his throat and staggered into the snowy garden with the second saucepan of hot water.

Mum, her sisters . . . and Aunt Annie

I didn't know it then, but there was a lot on Mum's mind at the time. She wasn't just annoyed at Dad's attempts to stretch the life-span of car radiators far beyond any limits known to science. There were deeper feelings than just anger about the car or about Dad himself.

First, she shared the general sense of disappointment that was felt by many of the housewives trapped in domesticity in the 1950s. She hadn't been one of the millions of women who had been swept into the paid labour force during the Second World War, only to be rejected in favour of the returning men shortly afterwards. But it had been an exciting, busy time for her — she often remarked that the war years had been the most fulfilling ones of her life — and now life seemed much more limited.

Secondly, she had the worry of trying to make a low, unpredictable family income stretch a long way, and of seeing a frightening amount of debt at the local grocer's shop mount up, week by week.

At the same time she was coping with all the emotions and turmoil that an elderly cat, a dog, three adolescents and a child can stir up in one small house.

Despite all this, she was a cheerful mother to me, and she managed to communicate a lot of enthusiasm and sparkiness. However, the underlying sense of disappointment and regret did seep through, even though she tried to put a cordon of optimism around me. Perhaps this was partly because she had two sisters — my Auntie Ruby and Auntie Lu (Beulah) — who had also somehow lost their place in the world, and the sense of purpose they had started out with.

From all three sisters' point of view, their own childhood and youth would have seemed better, more golden and full of promise than the present that they were living in during the 1950s. They were Edwardian girls (Beryl was born in 1901, Ruby in 1904 and Lu in 1908) and this meant that they had been young women together in the 1920s. For a while the family home in Tarporley must have seemed like a pulsing beacon of eligible, attractive women — a glamorous group, even, because this was a family associated with cars and new,

117

urban things. Their father's business, one of the first garage and motor vehicle servicing centres in the area, on the main road, must have seemed a hub of new technology.

But by the time I was a small boy both Auntie Lu and Auntie Ruby had lost their husbands, and all three sisters had also somehow lost their status or standing in the surrounding community. Their parents had died, and the family home and business were sold at the end of the war. They seemed to have little to show for having belonged to a family that had enjoyed prosperity and a certain social position in the best days of the Swan Garage. Mum and her sisters emanated an understated feeling that everything now was second-best. An air of gentle regret settled over my childhood like fine, penetrating dust.

On Tuesday afternoons Auntie Lu would slowly cycle over from Tarporley to see Beryl. On sunny afternoons they would sit quietly in the dark, cool front room over long cups of tea, surrounded by the smell of polish and of a hall floor freshly mopped. Their voices would sometimes descend to whispers as they talked, aghast at some latest news of illness, lack of money or ill-advised behaviour of other members of the family. And sometimes, if I came into the room unexpectedly, the talking would stop dead. After a pause they'd smile at each other slightly and ask me something innocuous about school.

Much later on — after I'd left home at the age of 18, in fact — I gradually began to appreciate some of the things they had had to come to terms with. These included painful illnesses — for instance, Mum had a stomach ulcer when I was about 9, something I was completely unaware of then — and being widowed (Auntie Lu), or separated and then widowed (Auntie Ruby).

The Auntie Ruby that I got to know in the 1950s was an intriguing person who carried about her an air of mystery, sadness and faded elegance. My mother told me once that Ruby was the most attractive of the sisters, though I don't know whether this was agreed as a matter of common consent. She certainly had a touch of the pensive beauty of Lauren Bacall about her.

She lived in a flat perched on the city walls in Chester — the address was 16A City Walls — with a view of the River Dee and the gentle, persistent roar of the weir in the background. The bay window of her sitting room jutted out over the pavement that topped the city wall, so that if you sat in or near the bay you could hear the footsteps of people passing underneath, and snatches of muffled conversations as they clattered past.

Three other special things about Auntie Ruby lodged in my mind:

1. She had ice cubes. Not many people had fridges in those days but she did. To have a glass of orange squash at Auntie Ruby's, with two or three ice cubes in it, seemed luxurious but also self-evidently better than any other kind of drink. I took my hat off to Auntie Ruby, when I was a boy, for having pioneered this breakthrough in physics.

119

2. She had a television set. In the early 1950s TVs were only just beginning to enter people's houses, and we certainly didn't acquire one (a cast-off from Auntie Lu) until much later. Auntie Ruby's television seemed to prove that most programmes, like endless droning commentary from Wimbledon on a hot Saturday afternoon, were rather boring. But the *possession* of a set was really interesting because you could say, like Auntie Ruby did, "Er, television?" and go to put it on, then say with classic indecision, "Oh perhaps not," and not switch it on.

3. Auntie Ruby spoke differently from Mum and Auntie Lu. Her Cheshire accent had been gently dropped in favour of a posh one that had, I realised later, been a necessary change to cope with social life in India, where she had lived with her husband in the 1930s and the war years. This meant, for instance, that she could easily come out with "I *say!*" trilling her voice in an exaggerated way. Or she could drawl her voice in a low tone, saying "Well, *re-ally!*" And one of her favourites, when offered anything, was to make her voice go high in a mock bleating shriek, and say, "Oooh-noooh, I couldn't *poss-ibly!*" Even the offer of a small piece of cake could elicit this exaggerated response. She felt that it was very polite and important to obscure from others whether or not she actually wanted anything — an almost Japanese desire not to offend anyone or be obliged to them in any way. It was her version of the "don't make a fuss" gene. However, the thing to do was to keep pressing the offer of cake, cup of

120

tea or small mint at least five times, through a sequence of "oooh-nooohs" and "I couldn't possiblys" until her actual feelings about the proffered object could be ascertained.

Later on, in old age, Ruby rather neglected her diet. She was actually quite hungry sometimes on visits to family, but she would still go through the same shrieking routine of "oooh noooh, I couldn't *poss-ibly*" when offered a second sandwich or another portion of trifle. However, only a split second after the "oooh noooh" there would be a sudden change to a gruff, John Prescott-like voice saying "Oh, all right then" as the proffered food was hastily taken on board.

In contrast to Ruby in later life, I like to imagine her as a young, rather glamorous woman motoring into Chester on shopping trips or hurtling around the country lanes in an open-topped car. I could, as a boy, picture the kind of car they might have had in the 1920s, with running boards and big headlamps, and Auntie Ruby in a cloche hat, driving with her silk scarf flapping in the slipstream.

The reality, of course, might have been slightly different. For one thing, Ruby was not always the most decisive of drivers, and the indecisiveness she showed in driving illustrated a more general air of indecision that hung around her.

For instance, on one trip to Chester the young Ruby drove hesitantly towards a fork in a busy road, playing for time as she discussed with her sisters which way to go. In those days traffic indicators on cars were those yellow illuminated arms that shot up and down like little fascist salutes. But the indicators on the car Ruby was driving had been designed with two separate controls. Therefore it was possible to work them independently, and to have both little arms sticking out at the same time. To hedge her bets and, helpfully, to warn other road users of her state of indecision, this was the indicating experience Ruby eventually opted for.

The car slowed to a snail's pace, both indicators popping up and down as if the car was a flightless bird flapping its wings in panic. The car drew to a halt at the junction and, as Ruby extended her discussion over directions with Beryl and Lu, she left both little arms up. The car now communicated an air of melodramatic surprise, like an Italian footballer appealing to the referee. Suddenly, against a background of other cars hooting, horses neighing and bicycle bells tinkling, a large policeman hove into view. Approaching a flustered Ruby, he enquired sombrely, "And which way are we going *today*, madam?"

Indecisive as she might have been about many things, Ruby, like Mum, was to go on to take one big decision. This, like her older sister, involved both marriage and travelling to a life in another country — in Ruby's case, to India.

In 1927 Ruby married Harry Lawton, a sailor with a Master's Certificate who was to become a ship's pilot on the River Hooghly at Calcutta. This prestigious and skilled occupation brought with it all the trappings of the colonial lifestyle — servants, a large bungalow, days by the swimming pool or playing tennis, and a new social life in the hill station of Ootacamund ("Ooty").

Sadly, after two children — a daughter called Brenda and a son called Buckley — had been born and spent their childhood in India, Ruby and Harry's marriage did not survive. I eventually learned that Harry had "taken up with" an Indian woman and Ruby had returned to live in Chester at the end of the 1940s.

Auntie Lu, the youngest sister of the three, made less impression on me. This was mainly because in the early 1950s she lived further away, in Rhyl. She had one daughter, Thelma, who was nearer in age to my sister and therefore already in her late teens when I was a young boy.

Lu's husband, John Meredith, father of Thelma, died tragically in an accident at the end of the war and this meant that, like Ruby, the Auntie Lu I knew when I was a boy carried with her a vague air of sadness and loss. Like Mum and Auntie Ruby, she often saw the funny side of things and liked to laugh, but the default setting in her eyes, so to speak, was a thoughtful gaze.

Auntie Lu's eyes were the first thing you noticed about her. Unlike Mum's and Auntie Ruby's brown-grey eyes, hers were a piercing china-blue, flecked with black. They were friendly, almost impish at times, but astute and knowing too.

As a boy I had the impression of Auntie Lu as a more substantial figure than either Mum or Ruby — not a taller person, but rounder and fuller like a small brown bear. Before her hair went grey Lu had a lot of dark

123

hair that seemed frizzier and more touchable than Auntie Ruby's or Mum's.

Then there was her voice — remarkably soft and penetrating, and with none of Auntie Ruby's mock shrieks or exclamations. It was a voice that could instantly hypnotise animals. When Lu came into a room, a dog or a cat, a budgerigar or pet mouse would instantly stop what they were doing and look up, transfixed, as if the voice they had always been waiting for had spoken to them at last.

The dog, for instance, would prostrate himself at her feet, his ears completely flat, his stubby tail wagging furiously and his eyes full of devotion and welcome. And when Auntie Lu came, the cat (Patch) would instantly set aside his natural feline wariness to purr and rub his back against her legs. My pet mice in their tea-chest cage would stop whatever they were doing, their big metal exercise wheel humming slowly to a halt like a factory turbine in a sudden industrial stoppage. Then they would gather round, a small group of workers, craning their necks to get a view of Auntie Lu, the visiting star. The goldfish would flip a somersault out of the water, a kind of naval salute. Later, when we had two budgerigars, these birds would stop twittering when Auntie Lu visited. Uttering strange, hypnotised cooing noises, they would hang upside-down from the top of their cage, staring at her.

In early 1956 Auntie Lu left Rhyl and came to live in a small semi-detached cottage in Tarporley, where all three sisters had grown up. Therefore, from the age of 8 I began to see her more often, and it was from then that she started to cycle slowly from Tarporley to Bunbury every Tuesday afternoon, to see Beryl.

It's funny how, when I was a child, no one in the family seemed to talk to me about the peculiar qualities of adults, like Auntie Lu's magnetic effect on living creatures. Maybe it was because I was growing up as the only child in a household of people in their late teens or late middle age.

But just as they didn't sit down to chat to me about what they thought about Auntie Lu or anyone else in the family, nor do I remember asking why this or that adult was living as they were. Why, for instance, didn't either Auntie Lu or Auntie Ruby have husbands? Why weren't there any uncles to go with them? Perhaps girls are more likely to ask these questions than boys are. But whatever the reason I was a good example of the way kids just tend to accept as natural whatever they are presented with. In my case this taken-for-granted family universe just happened to include aunts who lived on their own, one on a Roman wall who said "oooh-noooh" a lot, and one who could hypnotise the dog.

The family also included another aunt who appeared without an uncle — Aunt Annie. She was a much older aunt than Ruby or Lu, possibly in her late seventies or even her eighties when she came to stay with us at Sunnyside for weeks on end.

Aunt Annie's predicament, that of finding herself in the awkward position of being dependent on the willingness of relatives to take her in — was not unusual in the 1950s. I am not exactly sure why Aunt

Annie did not have her own place to live, even though she had been an elementary schoolteacher for many years and presumably had a teacher's pension of some sort in addition to the state retirement pension. It had certainly been much more difficult in the past for single women to find the means to purchase their own house, and perhaps this was the reason.

Another might have been the fact that Aunt Annie also needed a certain degree of care and attention, and was not shy in asking for it. "I have trouble with my water, you see, Beryl," I once heard her say to my mother in a loud, patient voice. "Therefore you must be careful to offer me lots of cups of tea."

This was said in a pronounced Lancashire accent, because Aunt Annie came from my father's side of the family, not from my mother's Cheshire stock. She had the same large, flap-like ears on the sides of her head that most of my father's family had, the same light-blue eyes and the same stern expression that gazed out of the fading Victorian portrait photographs of my father's ancestors.

It was rather sad that, in her old age, this proud, rather domineering and independent spirit found herself having to perambulate between the home of Auntie Irene (my father's cousin) and Uncle Arnold, where she spent most of the time, and our home.

However, Aunt Annie did not allow her dependence on us for bed, board and companionship interfere with what she saw as her natural duty to comment, correct or pass judgement on our behaviour when necessary.

126

"Wilfrid, what is that book", pronounced "bewk", "you are reading?" she inquired one evening. Dad was, as usual, reclining in his armchair in front of the fire, a historical novel held barrier-like in front of his face. Without saying anything, and with an annoyed expression but also a trace of guilt on his face, Dad held the book cover up for Aunt Annie to make it out.

"Mm," she continued, "I should have thought you should be reading bewks or manuals concerning motor vehicle maintenance, not time-wasting bewks such as that, Wilfrid."

It took me a while to realise that Aunt Annie was treating my father — the old man who was more like a grandfather to me than a dad — as a *child*. I rather liked Aunt Annie for that. In fact, for the six or so weeks at a time that Aunt Annie stayed, everyone in Sunnyside, except Aunt Annie the elementary schoolteacher herself, became children.

"Henry, do not torr-ment that dog," she instructed my brother one day, as he played a game of rough and tumble with Kim. And on gentle walks along the lane that led to the main road she would point out various items of interest to my mother, using a large knobbled walking stick. Sometimes I would stroll along with them, because I found Aunt Annie quite fascinating at times.

"Beryl, ob-serve that rose," she said once, pointing so vigorously with her stick that the unfortunate flower caught it in the neck and was almost knocked off its stalk.

127

Although Aunt Annie was domineering and could be rather frightening, I had a lot of respect for her. So one day, when I wrote, "Go Home, Aunt Annie" on my little blackboard in the living room, this was done for rather different reasons than my actual feelings about Aunt Annie herself.

I used to love looking through the Giles cartoon collections, which had become a firm family favourite. I had noticed the frequent appearance of slogans and graffiti such as "Go Home, Yanks" or "Go Home, English" in the cartoons dealing with American and British military bases in various parts of the world. In trying to tap into this vein of humour and apply it to my own family, who else but Aunt Annie could I refer to? Perhaps I had sensed the strain and ambivalence in the family atmosphere that arose after about the fifth week of her stays, and realised that it would raise a laugh (which it did, later) but basically, as a 9-year-old, I had not really thought that one through.

Fortunately, and just in the nick of time, my mother swooped on the blackboard just as Aunt Annie walked slowly and stiffly into the living room. Mum erased the rebel graffiti with one swish of her apron, glancing at me with a wry smile and passing the time of day in a light-hearted way with Aunt Annie.

Thank goodness Aunt Annie never saw that scrawled message from the boy who liked the way she told him exactly what she thought about things, and sometimes commanded him to complete spelling tests and arithmetical sums on that blackboard. It would have put a splinter in her heart, if it had not been broken already, because of course she had no home to go to.

DAD AND HIS BROTHERS

Wilfrid, the eldest of four, outlived all his three brothers. In descending order they were Uncle Fred, Uncle Kenneth and Uncle Harold. They all died prematurely, in their fifties or early sixties. I'm not sure about Uncle Fred's smoking habits, but the consumption of vast quantities of untipped Senior Service by Kenneth and Harold — who were, in my memory, chuckling volcanoes constantly wreathed in blue smoke — can't have helped much on the longevity front.

Uncle Fred, the university professor who set up the first department of veterinary science at Langford, for Bristol University, died of a heart attack when I was 6, and I only have one clear memory of him. By all accounts he was both extremely well liked and successful in the university (I came across an obituary many years after his death), and a very active and happy father and husband. He had become something of a family hero.

I remember the importance of Uncle Fred's coming to see us at Sunnyside being impressed on me, when I was about 4 years old, and how excited I got at the prospect. It was a summer evening, still warm and light, when he came. I had been made to go to bed with the promise that Uncle Fred would come up to see me when he arrived. Sure enough, with the evening light still showing through the thin curtains and a lot of loud cheerful adult voices downstairs, Uncle Fred did come. He had a red, smiling face as he bent over me, a man looking like my father. I have a memory of a green tweed jacket, or perhaps he was wearing a suit, a few moments of kindness, and he was gone.

Uncle Kenneth was the one who made the biggest impression because he and his wife, Auntie Hilda, regularly came over to Sunnyside for Sunday afternoon visits. But Uncle Harold and his wife, Dora, were much less frequent visitors. I don't know why we hardly saw Harold and Dora, who had a friendly, rectangular face like a horse, but even as a boy I picked up a feeling that Dad looked down on Harold in some way. Perhaps it was the feeling that the youngest sibling doesn't count for much — something I could identify with — but I'm really not sure. Certainly it was not because Harold or Dora were standoffish. I could tell that Harold was from the same mould as Wilfrid and Kenneth — the same chuckling laugh and enthusiastic loud voice with a proper northern, Lancashire accent, the same wispy grey hair and pink bacon complexion, the same love of a good story. My uncles didn't look like Eric Morecambe, the famous comedian, but to me they *sounded* like him. They had just a little of that gift of capturing both the disastrous and funny sides of life at the same time.

If the mood in Sunnyside had slumped a little over Sunday dinner it would always brighten up when Uncle Kenneth and Auntie Hilda arrived. They would drive over in their van from Hyde, where they lived in the parental Blakemore home, and stay for a walk on the nearby Bickerton Hills, Sunday tea and sometimes long talks and stories that went on into the evening.

Uncle Kenneth was a vet who had picked up the family business from Grandfather Blakemore, though he hadn't taken a degree course or fully qualified in veterinary science. He was a licensed veterinary practitioner, however, and continued to run the practice from the cavernous gloomy house in Hyde with its surgery and waiting room.

Uncle Kenneth and Auntie Hilda both provided good family entertainment. Without it being at all contrived or thought out they had become a sort of light comedy duo, always ready to tell a funny story. They complemented each other wonderfully in the way each one intervened in the story. These stories often involved small fierce animals in some kind of compromising situation.

Auntie Hilda, a sparrow-like woman with sparkling blue eyes, a Liverpool accent toned down by a dash of refinement, and short, pepper-and-salt hair, knew just when to cut in with an "Oh heck!" or "You could just imagine it. There we were, stuck half-way up the chimney . . ."

Many of the stories involved animals and their owners because of the veterinary practice. However, Kenneth and Hilda, a childless couple, had plenty of animals of their own. For instance, there were seventeen cats, at one point, in the house at Hyde. This was because Uncle Kenneth could not bear to put an animal down if there was hope of repairing them in

131

some way. From time to time injured stray cats would be brought to the surgery by well-meaning passers-by, and Uncle Kenneth would do his best to put them on their feet again. One brave cat struggled for months in splints and bandages of various sorts, hardly able to move a limb. Eventually it recovered and, to show its gratitude, it struggled out of its cardboard box and weakly raised its front right paw in a full salute — something it must have been taught to do, Uncle Kenneth solemnly informed us with a trace of a smile, by its previous owner. Almost certainly a sailor, he added.

All of the cats that Kenneth and Hilda looked after had something wrong with them, and they were altogether a peculiar and visually challenging crew, sporting a motley collection of re-engineered jaws, amputations, missing eyes and ears, and curious listing movements. Some didn't seem quite right in the head. Perhaps they were recovering from post-traumatic stress disorders or the equivalent of shellshock after being blown up by a firework.

I remember being taken to Hyde once, and being allowed to throw darts at the board in the living room. I really wanted to hit a double twenty and I anxiously tracked the dart with my eyes as it soared away from my hand. In the split-second afterwards the dart was nearly intercepted by a flying cat. It whizzed across my field of vision like a fighter plane, a black-and-white blur, leaping spectacularly from a window sill on the left to a large sofa to my right, where it landed with a cry of pain and a cloud of cat hairs.

"Oh heck, he's always doing that!" chuckled Auntie Hilda, drawing on her cigarette. "It's the feathers on the darts that attract him. Mind you, it's a wonder really, because his front legs were in splints and he was on a drip till last Tuesday."

As darkness settled on the large Victorian mansion, permeated by the smell of cat pee and surgical spirit, the cats would start to play. Sudden bumps and crashes would be followed by frantic scurrying and the occasional feline scream. "There they go again," Auntie Hilda would say. "Playing tig!"

"Kenneth will be up there with them for twenty minutes every evening, you know," she added, chuckling. "Being daft with the cats!"

"But then," she said disarmingly, "We haven't got any kids, and you've got to be a bit daft with something, haven't you?"

I'm fairly certain that Kenneth and Hilda's regular visits to Sunnyside, as well as giving them a chance to see Wilfrid and Beryl and to get out in the country air, also gave them the relationship with a growing family that they sorely missed. Kenneth and Hilda both badly wanted to have children, but an operation following a miscarriage meant that Hilda was unable to conceive.

For us, though, it meant that we had an aunt and uncle who took a lot of interest in us, and communicated various enthusiasms and interests. They loved going on holidays in various parts of the UK that, from a 1950s perspective, involved travelling stupendous distances — for instance, to the Highlands of Scotland, to Cornwall and the Scilly Isles. Their adventures certainly put our grudging trips to Rhyl in the shade.

Uncle Kenneth was also a keen photographer and sometimes brought his latest camera on their visits to us, an object that Henry in particular was keen to pore over. They would also bring colour slides and a projector, and we would sit round in the darkness after Sunday tea to look at dazzling photos of banks of flowers in the Scilly Isles, or of Hilda wearing tartan trews, perched on a rock in Inverness. It was fantastic.

As well as photographs, travel and stories, Uncle Kenneth and Auntie Hilda also brought other excitements. They once donated an enormous, ex-service brown rubber dinghy, which looked as though it had been used in the Normandy landings. It was adopted enthusiastically by the twins, and became very useful as both a floating amusement centre and supply vessel on seaside trips to Rhyl.

Later on in the 1950s Uncle Kenneth introduced yet more technological breakthroughs, such as a reel-to-reel tape recorder. We all had to endure the embarrassingly trite re-plays of our voices, recorded in turn around the fireside, followed by a more interesting recording of the dog breathing.

It was yet more interesting to hear Uncle Kenneth's edited tape of the voices of the pet owners who had been (unethically) recorded in his waiting room. This tape included the old lady complaining about her budgie catching the common cold from a spiteful neighbour — a rambling discourse in a broad northern accent that should have become a radio comedy classic.

134

And when it was time for them to go Uncle Kenneth would insist on shaking my hand. For some reason I never expected this, and always forgot it was going to happen. But when you shook hands with him, and took your hand away, there would be a half-crown nestling in your palm — roughly equivalent in its emotional effect to being given a £20 note today.

By the time I reached my early teens Uncle Kenneth had died. It was a shock and, as far as I could tell, a death that had occurred after a short illness and a botched operation in hospital. "Mind you, his stomach and his innards were never the same after he'd been in the Far East, in the war," explained Dad mournfully.

A few weeks after the funeral my parents took me to the house at Hyde for the last time. The dark rooms with their yellowing wallpaper and brown furniture seemed emptier than ever. The smell of cat pee had receded. Auntie Hilda was going to move and she couldn't cope with the cats, so all seventeen had been put down, like the servants of a Pharoah slaughtered to accompany their master into the next world.

"D'you really think I could ask £3,000 for the house?" asked Auntie Hilda. She was standing in the kitchen with Dad and Mum, by the large table with the scrubbed top.

There were no tears. She was being brave — no longer the chirpy sparrow but a nervous, uncertain and frail bird on the edge of migration. On the table I saw the short column of figures on a piece of paper in blue ballpoint: the undertaker's fee, the house price, and so on — all written, literally, on the back of an envelope.

Dad got the grey Austin van with windows that Uncle Kenneth and Auntie Hilda had used for holidays, and had driven to see us in Bunbury so often. How willingly Auntie Hilda parted with it we'll never know, and whether Dad should have had it is also uncertain. However, Hilda couldn't drive and perhaps it made sense. Rather insensitively, though, Dad didn't pick it up on his own, saying his thanks to Hilda and driving away discreetly. He combined the pick-up with the last family visit to Hyde (presumably our own car just about made it to Hyde and expired at the kerbside) and that meant we all waved goodbye cheerfully to Auntie Hilda as we drove off in her and Kenneth's familiar van. Not surprisingly, Hilda's lips were trembling and there was a tear in her eye as we drove out of sight.

The van itself had a defect, only slight at first, in that the front suspension had begun to sag. Uncle Kenneth hadn't been able to get it seen to in the last weeks of his illness. Needless to say, Dad never fixed it — the spares would have been far too expensive. Consequently the sagging and rolling of the front end of the van got worse and worse over the next couple of years. Every hollow or bump in the road would make it rear up and then sag down again, rolling like a small boat in a storm. Even after the van had come to a halt it would continue to yaw up and down for several minutes before it settled down.

Once, on a drive through the Peak District in Derbyshire, I hopped out of the van at a bedraggled tourist car park to dash to a toilet for a pee. I ran back

136

to the van in the grey slanting rain. Mum and Dad were sitting in the front, staring straight ahead with expressionless faces, looking smaller and suddenly much older than I had noticed before. I saw them rising and falling with the van, which was nodding solemnly up and down in remembrance of its previous, and proper, owners.

Mum goes to Calgary

I got the impression — even as a small boy — that Mum never really took to the idea of living in Bunbury, or to the small, draughty semi-detached house in which I was born. After the independence and homesteady feeling of living in a wooden bungalow in Delamere Forest during the war, the irritatingly named red brick Sunnyside, must have given her a closed-in and watched-over feeling.

She once vented her frustration by saying that she was fed up with being the one who had to cook for the family day in and day out, week after week. "Why on *earth*," she said crossly, "don't they organise a big canteen in the village hall, where we could take it in turns to cook for everybody, and every family could just come down and take what they needed?"

So through my childhood in the 1950s I had a mother who was, in one way, a natural anarchist and free-thinker. But in another way she was a constant, traditional parent who loyally voted Conservative — more out of tribal loyalty than out of conviction — and had lunches ready for me when I walked the few steps back from the school gate to the kitchen table. She was anxious to make sure none of us were hungry, or needed for anything. For instance, there might be a delicious extra snack of something on a plate if Henry came home late, starving hungry, or a delicious piece of something savoury, such as cold liver. She was gentle, relaxed, humorous and loved to chat for a long time after meals before clearing away.

These things — and the realisation of just how important she was in holding the family together — hit me when Mum went to Canada. I was 9, coming up to 10, that summer of 1958. I was vaguely aware that Mum was going away, on one count because she had to have a smallpox vaccination and her arm swelled up alarmingly. For two days it looked as if a separate creature had attached itself to her torso — a mottled, blushing seal, perhaps.

And secondly, she told me she was going to be away for a while and, smiling in a way I hadn't seen her smile before, she pressed a brown 10-shilling note into my hand. "If you're hungry while I'm away," she said, "go to the shop and buy yourself some bridge rolls and some ham." For some reason I had recently latched on to the soft, doughy texture of bridge rolls as being the most delicious thing ever.

Mum was going to Calgary to help Jay get ready for her wedding in early July. After only a year working as a nurse in Canada my sister had met the man she wanted to be with, Don MacArthur. The joke was that, as a patient in the hospital ward Jay was nursing in, and immobilised by injuries, he hadn't been able to get away.

As we were perennially short of money it was decided that only one parent could go — and of course, in those days especially, it had to be the mum who would do that, to lend a hand and support her only daughter.

It struck me even then that this was Mum's chance to escape. Would she ever come back? This question hung like a cloud over Sunnyside, not spoken about but casting a gloomy shadow over Dad and the rest of us. I fretted about Mum's non-return as a child does, and would have worried whatever the likelihood of her coming back. The awful possibility that she might not return affected Dad badly, making him scowl most of the time. Only Fred, who was spending his last summer at home working on a nearby farm and anticipating university, was resolutely cheerful. He even had one or two goes at making hot meals with strange combinations of corned beef and tinned peas.

Otherwise, though, the domestic arrangements in the house more or less collapsed. The fire wasn't lit, so there was no hot water. Dirty plates, bowls and dishes piled up in the little kitchen. I don't remember there being anything much for breakfast except soggy cornflakes. For tea there was soggy toast with Marmite and a concrete egg, or perhaps one of Fred's experiments in food science. Patch, our elderly dignified cat, got thinner and thinner, and Kim, our corgi with the barrel chest, began to resemble a miniature stripped-down greyhound on short legs.

139

But for me there was one thing above all that represented the unsettling collapse of the edifice of family life. It was a tiny thing, but it inserted the first knife of disillusion into my trust in Dad, as well as Mum. I noticed, after the first few days, that Dad kept using a *wet* teaspoon, after stirring his tea, to lift white sugar from the bowl back to his teacup. Soon an ugly circle of tea-stained, brown crust had formed in the middle of the bowl. It was only a matter of days before the whole lot had turned into a good imitation of a mud-spattered snowdrift by the roadside.

I surprised myself, even as a young boy, at how quickly I had begun to shift my mind to prepare for the possibility that Mum might not return. This was when Dad drove down to the local station to meet the train on which he thought she would be coming back. I went with him, standing on Beeston Castle station platform, disconsolate as the train pulled out with no Mum on the platform. "Oh well," Dad said gruffly, "we'll have to come back later. She'll probably be on the next one."

But she wasn't.

Later that evening, in the bright July light, we watched as another train headed out towards the sunset. I had no tears but a sad realisation that a dad who could carelessly stain sugar in the bowl could just as easily be wrong about his wife coming back. Memories of Mum saying that she'd always wanted to stay in New Zealand stirred uneasily in my mind, as I drew parallels with her trip to Canada.

So I was startled the next evening, when I turned the corner into our little front garden, to see Mum standing on the lawn, smiling and chatting animatedly to our neighbours over the hedge. She was smaller and browner than I remembered, and she chuckled rather nervously when she saw me.

"It's Kenneth!" she exclaimed.

"Hello," I said, standing still, consciously deciding not to run up to her, as Mr and Mrs Shore, the neighbours, looked on, smiling benignly.

CHAPTER
FIVE

Food and Drink

THE SUNNYSIDE DIET

In the 1950s we saw dramatic changes in food and drink. The last of the post-war food rationing and restrictions were abolished in 1954, which made a big difference. But the changes were also a reflection of other things such as rising living standards and better advertising.

There was also that 1950s obsession with space-age science. New food products were colourful examples of miraculous technology. They were portrayed as biochemical agents to help you boost your energy. Fantastic new foods or magic ingredients could help you have "regular habits", sleep without "night starvation" and be full of zest without dangerous loss of "nervous energy".

Thankfully, not all of these strange innovations made much of an impact on Sunnyside, which — largely because we didn't have much money — had to chug along in its usual culinary way. But imagine whizzing today's children or young people back in time to spend a week on the "Sunnyside Diet". What on earth would

142

they make of it? Here are some of the things they'd notice straightaway:

- No "supermarket" food or frozen food, no supermarkets or fridge. No frozen chips or peas, no burgers, no fishfingers. In summer, milk would usually be slightly warm. There might be ice cream, occasionally (a Wall's "family brick"), but it would be melting around the edges and had to be eaten quickly. "Wrapped in a newspaper before you leave the shop," the advert optimistically claimed, "Wall's stays firm for two to three hours". As an extra treat you could lick the soggy cardboard edges of the box to mop up any little bits of ice cream that had been left over.

- Only one person — Mum — did the cooking, and nearly all the eating was done together at regular mealtimes. You could perhaps make a late-night snack for yourself, like cheese on toast, but otherwise there were no convenience foods like pizzas to throw into the oven at any time. There were a few exceptions, though, like Dad getting his own breakfast on Saturday mornings. Mum had her one lie-in of the week, while he went downstairs before going to work at the garage. (He walked around with half an orange stuck in his mouth, sucking loudly and making himself look a bit like the pig's head at a medieval banquet, while pieces of bread burned under the grill.)

- All meals meant home cooking. We never went to any kind of restaurant, right through the 1950s, either as a family or in any pair/combination, unless you count Hignett's fish and chip restaurant in Chester, an occasional cup of tea and a cake at a department store, and, very occasionally, a wedding breakfast. In July 1956, for instance, we went to a wedding reception for Thelma (Auntie Lu's daughter) at Beeston Castle Towers, a large, sprawling mock-Tudor hotel. I can remember overdosing on meringues at the end of the meal and then, later, walking down to the railway station to wave off the happy couple as they left for their honeymoon.

- There was never any alcohol in the house apart from the odd stray bottle of British sherry or a miniature or two of spirits used exclusively for setting fire to the Christmas pudding. In many 1950s households alcohol belonged to the world outside the home.

- "Shotgun fresh" probably wouldn't catch on as a slogan for meat today. But we occasionally did eat animals and birds — rabbits, pigeons, pheasants — that had been passed on to Dad from a gamekeeper friend. This meant extricating little bits of lead shot from your mouth while you ate. Actually, this *was* a bit weird, even then.

144

A typical teatime, *circa* 1955, will give you an idea, not only of the sort of food we ate, but how it was prepared and eaten.

5.30p.m. Mum is getting the evening meal underway. She is standing in the small, galley-like kitchen, which is really nothing more than the hall turning into a kitchen as the corridor from the front door reaches a halfway point to the back door. We didn't call it a kitchen; it was "the scullery". The contents of three misshapen aluminium saucepans are beginning to bubble on a small, grey electric cooker that has one larger solid heating plate, glowing red, and one smaller one. Mum is wearing a "pinnie" with a faded flower pattern on it, and frowns as the cooker gives her a painful electric shock when she touches one of the knobs. She inserts some lamb chops under the uncertain grill.

5.35p.m. The back door opens and Henry, now an apprentice, scowling, pale and tired, enters. He is wearing blue overalls. He complains about the general injustice and unfairness of the world. Mum hands him a piece of bread and butter. He mutters a few words and goes upstairs to take off his overalls. I'm outside in the back garden, halfway up the apple tree. Fred is sitting at the table in the back living room — confusingly called "the kitchen" — next to the scullery, concentrating on his homework. The table has already been laid with a tablecloth and cutlery, but Fred has put an exercise book between knives and forks, and is writing rapidly and methodically. He doesn't pause or

145

look up when Henry passes by in the hall, but continues writing.

5.40p.m. Enter Dad, through the front door. He is carrying a rolled-up *Daily Telegraph* and is whistling, partly to announce his arrival and partly to show that he is pleased to be home. He doesn't say anything to Fred, in the sunny kitchen, but leans for a few minutes against the doorway where the scullery space begins. He talks to Mum, running through his day. Each news item is preceded with the phrase "I see", as in, "I see there's been another horrific accident at Fourways." She responds appropriately, but looks distracted as she checks the chops, pokes the potatoes and washes some sprigs of mint under the tap at the sink. Dad's daily bulletins nearly always seem to include a report on the latest tall story from someone called George Eyes, and these reports clearly bore Mum. She chuckles now and again, but her heart isn't in it. "You'll never guess what George Eyes said today — he's off for a holiday to *Spain* of all places!" (This is clearly incredible, and Mum chuckles half-heartedly.) "Hee hee," continues Dad. "You can't believe a *word* he says, y'know, like the time he claimed he'd won all that money at a casino." Mum chops the mint furiously with a large blunt carving knife.

5.55p.m. As the weather forecast for land areas starts on the radio in the kitchen, Dad, on cue, makes his way upstairs to wash. A school of dolphins are unleashed in the bathroom, splashing, snorting and squeaking. When he has finished you can hear him shouting "Brrr-bah-hah-hah-hah!" with his face in a towel.

146

6.00p.m. The news headlines follow the Greenwich Time Signal on the Home Service, and the radio is switched off. Mum calls me in from the garden. Henry looks balefully at Fred, who is still writing at the table. Dad appears, wearing trousers and a short-sleeved shirt, looking pink and scrubbed.

6.05p.m. Everyone is now sitting at the table except Mum, who is serving up each meal on plates in the kitchen. She brings plates through, starting with Dad's first, apologising as she does so for the way she's cooked the food. Each plate has on it a lamb chop, a number of boiled potatoes, peas (picked from the garden) and carrots. "I don't know if you'll really like these chops," admits Mum. "They weren't very good to start with — that Tony's a real twister — but I've burned them a bit as well." No one responds to these apologetic remarks; we're used to them, and also know that the chops will be delicious. Fred is still writing though, speeding up as he nears the bottom of the page, and he has to be physically separated from his homework. He gives the impression that he might continue writing on the tablecloth, or the wall, as his exercise book with the crest of Nantwich and Acton Grammar School on it is prised out of his hands.

6.08p.m. We all start eating, except Mum, who hasn't sat down yet nor brought a plate of food for herself. No one comments on this. We know that, about half-way through the first course, she will bring a much smaller, scrappier portion of food into the living room for herself. I have an uneasy feeling, looking back on this, that, like a lot of women in low-income families,

147

Mum was regularly cutting back on her own food so her children and husband could have enough. She would eventually sit down reluctantly and say things like, "You don't really fancy the food you've cooked yourself. I'm fed up with looking at it." Until then she hovers about making sure that we're all right, while we eat. She's forgotten the mint sauce, made by adding a little bit of hot water and vinegar to the mint that has been chopped up with grains of sugar. She brings it through. Curiously, none of us drink anything with our meal.

6.20p.m. The first course is over. Dad has left two boiled potatoes on his plate, a small gesture to signal that he had been given more than enough and is satisfied — a pointless gesture that annoys Mum. I like it, though, because when Dad has finished I sometimes scoff his tepid, unfinished potatoes, made tasty by drops of Worcestershire sauce that have soaked into them. Henry has been told off for scraping up a mixture of mint sauce and gravy on to the edge of his knife, and then inserting the knife cross-wise in his mouth, like a pirate, to lick off the delicious juices. He is frowning and sighs in a depressed way. Fred says something cheerful about physics.

6.21p.m. Mum, who has hardly touched her food, brings in the second course, which is rhubarb crumble — made with rhubarb from the garden — and Bird's custard. Mum apologises again for the poor quality and the predictability of this pudding idea, and doesn't have any herself. We all enjoy it. No one has "seconds", though — it's understood that the section of crumble

148

left over will reside on a plate in the safe in the pantry, to be plundered later by whoever gets there first.

6.30p.m. The males finish their rhubarb crumble. I notice sunlight on the apple tree, which is calling me back. Mum goes out to the kitchen to put the kettle on for tea. Dad says something about the weather. Mum returns with teacups and saucers, a milk jug and a sugar bowl. She goes back out again, to the pantry this time, returning with a brown loaf, butter in a butter dish and a slab of red Cheshire on a plate, with a small cheese knife. Dad gets up and stretches his arms, then stands surveying the garden, swaying gently at anchor. Fred reaches for his homework. Henry takes a .22 air rifle out of a drawer in the bureau, aims it in a mock way at the Peter Scott painting on the wall, and starts to polish it with a cloth at the table. Mum, who has gone out to the kitchen yet again, comes back in with a large metal teapot. She sets it down, admonishing Henry for putting a rifle on the table. Henry complains that it's clean and why all the fuss, and Dad glowers at him.

6.35p.m. The atmosphere is suddenly more relaxed. Dad and Mum share a joke, then Dad picks up his cup of tea and the *Daily Telegraph* and wanders through to the front room to read, chewing a Rennie's digestion tablet. Fred says something cheerful about chess. We all chat as Mum butters thin slices of bread and we all help ourselves to slivers of moist, red cheese. This is the food Mum likes best. The tea in my cup is strong and brown and has thick Jersey milk in it, with two teaspoonfuls of sugar. The slow, enjoyable chit-chat

149

continues until about seven o'clock, perhaps later if Mum makes a second pot of tea, and then we all get up. Henry goes upstairs. I go out to play. Fred says something cheerful about nuclear power. Mum washes up.

"THE FOOD'S QUITE GOOD HERE, YOU CAN'T COMPLAIN"

When I was in my late teens I came home after a year in West Africa as a young volunteer teacher. I was astonished, one day, by a casual remark that Dad made at the kitchen table. We were waiting for Mum to bring some food through. "Y'know," he said, nodding in the direction of the scullery, where Mum was serving up, "I don't know what you think, but I've always thought that the food here is pretty good, all things considered. And there's always plenty. I've never had reason to complain, anyway."

It took me a while to take this in. It was a comment delivered in a tactfully quiet voice, while Mum was out of the room, so that she wouldn't overhear it. I stared at Dad. He sounded like an old regular who had been visiting this little café in the countryside for years.

Then it dawned on me just how Victorian Dad's and Mum's attitudes to food and cooking had been, all along. It was suddenly obvious, but as a child I hadn't noticed it at all. He went out to the garage every day to be pessimistic and to dissuade people from spending too much on their cars, and she cooked all the food,

150

served it and washed up. Somehow I hadn't quite taken in before just how *separate* this arrangement was for each of them. Buying and cooking the food was Mum's "department", while the work outside the house was Dad's. That was the deal. With adaptations, it's still going strong in a lot of households today.

There was a sort of fairness to it, in a way, because it meant that the husband and wife could respect each other's area of expertise. Also, it was understood that neither party could unfairly "interfere" in the work that belonged to the other, or comment too critically about it. But there were two big flies in the ointment, as far as Mum was concerned.

Firstly, there was the issue of making ends meet. Dad left a certain amount of money on top of the bureau in the kitchen, every week. He seemed to assume that Mum would discover it, with a little cry of pleasure and surprise, as she went about her dusting. The actual amount that was needed to cover the cost of the week's groceries, coal and milk was never discussed. On Planet Dad, it seemed that a full catering and fuel supply service could be obtained by leaving a modest amount of cash like this under an old butter dish. It was not for him to question or discuss how the housekeeping money was put to use. It was enough to see the warm plates appear reassuringly before him each day, carrying bacon and tomato in the mornings, and liver and onions or shepherds' pie in the evenings.

But the problem was this lack of a direct link in Dad's mind between lovely cooked food and its actual cost meant that it was too tempting for him to assume that food costs had stayed the same since about 1934. The money left on top of the bureau was never quite enough, but then Mum didn't feel able to confront Dad about it — that would have meant being too critical of "his" department. As a result, the grocery bills at the local shops crept remorselessly upwards, like clear sea water welling up in the bottom of a lifeboat.

The second problem, as far as Mum was concerned, was boredom. She had been left with all the responsibility of what to make for tea, but basically she had gone off the idea. Much later, in the 1970s and after Dad had died, she once told me that, while she felt lonely from time to time, there were some compensations. "At last!" she said. "No more cooking. I can eat what I really like — *sandwiches!*"

Part of Mum's difficulty was that she wanted to avoid cooking the same thing on a given day of the week — the "cold meat on Mondays, fish on Fridays" syndrome. That would have been just *too* boring, when life was already beginning to seem to be far too restricting and predictable. On the other hand, this was a rural community in the 1950s. You couldn't nip out to a local deli for slices of wind-dried Chinese pork, or a bottle of sesame seed oil. Nor could you consult someone like Delia Smith to find out what to do with an avocado. There weren't any avocados, or melons, or broccoli. Even British produce such as lettuce, cucumber, tomatoes and peas was seasonal, and hard to get hold of in winter months. I only got to see my first cob of sweetcorn when I was about 10 years old. I was with Mum in Nantwich, and she was keen to try some. "I think you cook them like potatoes, a rolling boil for about twenty minutes," the uncertain shop girl explained, hamming it.

Another difficulty for Mum, and probably for many women in the 1950s, was lack of inspiration. Today we've got the paradox of wall-to-wall TV programmes about food and cookery, together with special magazines, fascination with special diets and with celebrity chefs, but we actually want to cook less and less. It's far easier to put a ready-made meal into the microwave. Then, when a lot of real cooking was going on, and just when a lot of new ideas were needed, there weren't many.

However, after 1955 there was a striking increase in food and drink advertisements and menu suggestions in magazines and other outlets. A 1950 or 1951 *Picture Post* or *Everybody's* has hardly any adverts for food or drink, apart from occasional sombre inserts to remind readers of the existence of British sherry. One issue of *Picture Post* in 1950 carried a single advert for an obscure chocolate wafer bar called Banjo. It was a grey-looking object comprising "two creamy, nutty wafer bars covered in full cream milk chocolate" (they must have been kidding) and obtainable for only one point from the ration allowance.

But 1955 and 1956 issues of the same magazines are full of colourful splashes of adverts. Suddenly there are Bounty Bars ("milkier, juicier coconut than even South-Sea Islanders ever knew"), Ribena, Kia-Ora Fruit Squash, and Aero ("a new experience in milk chocolate"). In 1954 came the first full-page advert for

153

Summer County margarine proudly announcing "the first margarine with that **country fresh** flavour" and "the first . . . to be planned after the end of all rationing and restrictions".

Without television and just the occasional women's magazine or the weekly *Everybody's*, however, Mum was often stumped for ideas about how to vary the Sunnyside menu. She had a very old recipe book that looked as if it had been published in the Edwardian era. It was falling apart and had yellowing pages. Some days, after breakfast when the house had fallen quiet, she retired to the lavatory with it to riffle yet again through its well-read pages. Sometimes I could hear a sigh of frustration, followed by a cry of wind from her bowels like the mournful call of a distant blue whale as she slowly sifted through the recipes for an idea.

Later on she would occasionally branch out and make a curry, which, guided by her Edwardian book, meant simmering rice, curry powder, raisins, bits of meat and other interesting ingredients like peas all together in one large pan. I used to think this was delicious, especially when it had gone cold, the day after cooking. Many years later I came across it again, in an old-fashioned Scottish "hydro" hotel in Crieff, where it was served as an after-dinner savoury called a gamecock. It tasted exactly the same as Mum's curry, and might well have come from the same weirdly distorted Edwardian, imperial view of what Indian food was supposed to be.

Dad, however, would utter a low snarl when Mum's curry appeared, which is why we rarely had it. It was one of the few meals he would ever show disapproval of; it was just too "foreign".

The fact that Mum had to stick to a traditional round of old-fashioned English dishes makes it sound as though the food we had was bland and boring, but it wasn't. Somehow, despite very limited equipment and having to work in a tiny kitchen, she always succeeded in making tasty, hearty food.

Also, before the advent of convenience foods and frozen items like fishfingers or burgers made of meat slurry, the traditional British diet did have some strong flavours in it. As a child I was offered — and liked — a lot of these powerful tastes and interesting textures. The most outstanding were a corner of blue cheese from Dad's plate at Saturday teatimes, homemade pickled onions, sliced beetroot in vinegar, kippers. In the runners-up category were pomegranates, roasted sweet chestnuts in the autumn, fresh uncooked peas straight out of the pod, celery, black pudding made by the local butcher (featuring mystery globules of fat), black toffee in November, liver and onions, roast pheasant, rabbit stew and Mum's rock cakes. First prize in the best vegetable category has to go to bubble and squeak. And my nomination for best pudding goes to Mum's citrus suet pudding, though there were lots of other good-tasting things such as lemon meringue pie and apple crumble. For Sunday tea the sweet course might have included jelly made with condensed milk, a pudding that tasted a lot better than its appearance, which was like "one coat" pink emulsion by Dulux.

155

Turn your home into a gay restaurant

A jazzy advertisement in a 1954 copy of *Picture Post* suggested, enthusiastically, "It's fun and easy to transform your dining room into a corner of a gay Paris restaurant!" There is a picture of a pavement café with the Eiffel Tower in the background. "Start on a note of luxury" the advert continues, "with Batchelor's Cream of Tomato Soup!" Then, in a desperate lunge for credibility and in words that tacitly anticipate the gales of laughter that are likely to greet this suggestion, the advertisement lamely adds, "In France, they'd spend hours making a soup like this."

One of the main jobs of the food industry of the 1950s, once rationing restrictions were eased, was to remind people about the convenience foods of the old, pre-war days, and to perk them up with a new image to boost sales. "Old favourites" like this were usually in the kitchen cupboard or the pantry at home: Ovaltine, Oxo, a bottle of Camp Coffee — "the same as pre-war", as an advert in 1949 said — and, after the mid-1950s, a full range of packet soups. Campbell's, for instance, were producing powdered soup mixes in mushroom, chicken noodle and "thick pea".

The other job was to tell consumers about new convenience foods, or new ways of approaching and using "traditional" food items. Some might see this as the beginning of the "Americanisation" of English food and eating habits. I'm not so sure. Much American food is bland, but a lot is delicious and made with fresh ingredients. Despite a weakness for genetically modified

156

food, and eating too much of everything, people in the USA are much more concerned about food quality and ingredients than they are in the UK. So perhaps the tasteless, sometimes weirdly garish products that get sold and bought in the UK are nothing to do with "Americanisation". They're just a sign of a very British evil genius for making foods that are as artificial as possible.

In the 1950s the marketing was certainly homegrown rather than American, in that peculiarly British paternalistic way common then. It showed up particularly in attitudes to women and cookery. For instance, in an advertising campaign to re-launch tinned fruit as the main route back to stylish domestic cuisine in Britain, one advert concluded, "Yes, it all adds up to chef cookery — but well within the scope of even a young bride!"

Some advertisements included real-life vignettes of family life, underlining what women and men each do, in a not-very-subtle way. An advert in 1954, for instance, stressed how crucial a mug of hot Bournvita was to restore the energy, morale and sleep patterns of a Mrs Hilda Wing, worn-out housewife:

Mrs Hilda Wing of Hogsthorpe, Lincs., is **always** busy. She helps her husband do his job; runs a spotless home for him and their two red-headed sons, Peter and Paul, aged 4 and 9; and keeps a general store where you can buy anything from children's frocks to wedding cakes!

157

Perhaps this ad was a little tongue in cheek — at least, I'd like to think so. But no sooner had you seen an advertisement like this than you might spot a magazine feature such as the article in *Everybody's* of 23 October 1954, which crowed, "Women Are So Gullible!" This was a feature on the new marketing techniques that were helping shoppers to part with their money faster than ever before. To be fair, the article corrects the impression given by the eye-catching headline. The research showed that actually men were even more gullible than women in shops. "Men are more likely to bring home oddments which will not be of much use," the study concluded.

The high-handed "let us advise you" tone in food ads and magazine features didn't just emphasise differences between the sexes. There could also be a very paternalistic harking back to the times of food shortage and rationing, even in the "modern" adverts of the mid-1950s. In a Lin-Can ad for tinned fruit and vegetables for example ("Lin-Can fresh is preferable to the staleness of so-called 'fresh' "), a typical housewife shares some hoarding wisdom: "I lay in a stock for winter use. Unless I make sure of them, I may have to do without."

And just in case you were a wayward schoolchild about to carelessly toss aside useful information, a Brooke Bond advert was there to remind you about "The Story of Tea" in "a series of handsome booklets". It went on to say: "Schoolchildren and others collecting this series of instructional subjects on tea should note

158

that this is the last of the series. Do not fail to cut it out."

Even if the advertising now looks clumsy and heavy-handed, the firms that made and sold the products then must have been doing something right, at least in terms of meeting consumer demand, because most of them — like Campbell's Soup, Brooke Bond Tea, Bournvita — remained household names well after the 1950s. However, there were failures too. Some products that appeared in adverts in 1950s magazines are now the dinosaurs of the food world.

One of these, surely a throwback to more austere times of wartime blockades and 1930s poverty, was Ricory. What the hell is that? I thought, as a rather austere, black-and-white advert caught my eye in a 1954 copy of *Everybody's*. "Mmm," suggests the advert, probably written by someone on some sort of hallucinatory drug or perhaps in deep hypnosis, "Let's have a nice cup of Ricory! In moments of crisis someone is sure to say it!"

Studying the advert more carefully, and looking at the main ingredients of Ricory, it seems it was a coffee-style drink made of a blend of chicory and other things. No wonder it never caught on in a big way. "So heartening," the Ricory advert concludes, "Especially the thought that Ricory is so economical!"

KEEP WARM BUT DON'T GET EXCITED

Today, and in more recent times, it's striking how much food is being presented not so much as food but as a sort of medicine. We are constantly being urged to eat this or that, or to avoid eating certain foods, for health and cosmetic reasons — to lose weight or stay slim, lower cholesterol (which I don't think existed in the 1950s), reduce blood pressure, or just look healthy. And it's not just individual food products that are discussed this way, whole diets are being subjected to an onslaught of publicity. But all for the same reason — staying healthy, looking good.

Back in the 1950s, for most people, food was just something you shovelled in. People didn't stop to worry about the health implications of eating black puddings or quaffing pints of full-fat milk.

"Dieting" — mostly a peculiar habit for a minority of young women — meant slimming. There seemed to be only one main type of slimming diet in 1950s women's magazines. They always suggested half a grapefruit for breakfast, scrambled egg on toast for lunch and a seven-course dinner with coffee, cigars and after-dinner mints in the evening.

My sister Jay, for instance, was usually "on a diet" in the years before she went to Canada, though she wasn't overweight as far as anyone could tell. Her diet featured poached eggs on lightly steamed spinach accompanied by Energen Rolls, the small tasteless buns that had the same weight and consistency as polystyrene foam. The only visible effects of the diet on Jay, according to my mother, were that her fingers grew thinner and her moods grew snappier in the mornings.

In the 1950s, as well as the minority interest in "going on a diet", there were, however, two main obsessions about the positive qualities of particular food items and certain kinds of drinks, even though most food was seen as pretty unremarkable. These obsessions were, firstly, about keeping warm and, secondly, a surprisingly modern preoccupation with "stress", or, in the language of those days, "nerves".

The first one isn't very surprising if we remember that this was the age before many homes had central heating, a lot of houses still had outside toilets, and fuel crises and shortages were a recent memory. Also, when it was wet and cold, you often had to trudge or bike it through the weather rather than being able to hop into a nice warm car.

Tinned or packet soups were the most obvious products to market with a "warm you up" tag, but breakfast cereals weren't far behind, especially as nearly all of them were advertised as being best served with hot milk. For instance, Welgar, an ancestor of Shredded Wheat, was advertised in an unsophisticated way with a picture of a shivering butcher hanging by his collar on a meat hook, alongside a row of dead pigs. "I'm in cold storage until I've had my Welgar shredded wheat and *hot* milk!" quipped the butcher, sadly.

Ribena, the blackcurrant cordial, was also pitched with dire warnings of the dangerous effects of cold, dark winters. "Lack of summer sunshine will take its toll this winter," predicted the gloomy advert. "Colds

161

and 'flu are attacking sun-starved bodies, So take delicious Ribena now and strengthen your resistance to infection."

Alcoholic drinks could be sold on a ticket that united the contemporary preoccupations with keeping warm and with avoiding "nerves". However, some — such as Lemon Hart Rum and De Kuyper Cherry Brandy — aimed only at "warmth" appeal. "Moldano" Wine Cocktails, either Damson Cream or "Late Night Final" had "a glow in every glass". And Ind Coope's Barley Wine was also advertised on the strength that it "keeps out the cold".

More often, though, alcoholic drinks — particularly wines — were portrayed as giving a wide range of health benefits, apart from just keeping your body temperature at a nice "simmer" level. Hall's wine, for example, was "enriched with vitamins". And Rednutt "Ancient Browne Sherry", it was claimed, was versatile not only because it could be served as "both an Aperitif and a Dessert Wine", but also because it had trapped sunshine and goodness in it; as well as being able to reawaken the dead.

The winning garland must go, however, to Keystone Burgundy for its loquacious claims to soothe battered nerves and restore general health. Like a lot of adverts of the time, Keystone Burgundy went in for quite lengthy vignettes of consumers' lives to extol the benefits of the product. Incredibly, given what we now know about the dangers of alcohol abuse, one of these adverts featured a bank manager pictured, smiling and with a confident face, at his desk. He is nonchalantly chucking items into an "out tray" as he sits beside his desk lamp, a bottle of "Keystone" to hand: "This bank manager, ill from over-work, took Keystone on his doctor's recommendation, and subsequently always took it when he needed a pick-me-up." . . . "Yes — doctors know the value of good burgundy when you are run down, over-tired, weakened from illness!"

The most melodramatic story was at the bottom of the page. It showed a picture of a young woman in a suburban garden pegging out washing, watched by a young child and a baby in a pram: "Eldest of an orphaned family of nine carrying on the home single-handed, this patient was advised Keystone Burgundy by her doctor and has found it a great help."

Not that alcoholic drinks enjoyed a monopoly over the claims to deal with 1950s stress. Other drinks and foods could do it as well. Ovaltine, for instance, "helps establish a *natural* sleep routine" and "helps relax nervous tensions." Similarly, "Sleep is sweeter . . . with Bournvita" (memories of Mrs Hilda Wing), and even Wrigley's chewing gum (PK, Juicy Fruit or Spearmint) was marketed in the 1950s as a stress-buster. Its main attraction was that it could "relieve strain, soothe nerves".

Even sweets could do it. Fox's Glacier Mints, for example, were for unwinding at the end of the day and "for long evenings by the fire". Somehow, the subliminal message, "you're never going to be stuck for something to do as long as you've got a smouldering fire and a small wrapped mint", seems particularly sad.

163

For boys like me in the 1950s, however, sweets were just sweets. After years of careful rationing and sensible, spartan food, the British confectionery industry cranked itself up to full speed in the mid-1950s, making sure that the vulnerable enamel on our growing teeth was shot to pieces by the avalanche of sugar. They were all there, waiting for us. There were Nuttall's Mintoes (the main culprit as a cause of fillings, in my case), Fry's Crunchie Bars (by 1956), Sharp's Toffees and Quality Street, Mars Bars, acid drops, Barratt's sweet cigarettes, sherbert, Maltesers (a pre-war invention), liquorice allsorts and fruit gums. Also lying in wait were Cadbury's Dairy Milk ("a glass and a half of milk in a half-pound block", just to be absolutely sure you're getting enough saturated fats), Fry's chocolate creams, and Spangles.

"MUM SAYS, CAN WE PUT IT IN THE BOOK?"

Like a lot of sizeable villages in the 1950s, Bunbury had a number of thriving shops and other businesses. Clustered around the triangle of lanes at the centre of Lower Bunbury were the focal points of the village hall, post office and the Nag's Head. But there was also Ravenscroft's fish and chip shop, a newsagent's and sweet shop/tobacconist's, two grocers (one including a bakery) and two butchers, a garage, a part-time bank and a draper's/wool shop. A bit further on there was a Co-Op grocery store and, a bit further on again, a small general store (which had a very liberal approach to

164

selling fireworks to small boys before 5 November), a lumber yard and a blacksmith's.

In the 1950s nearly everyone, whether rich or poor, would have obtained their daily and weekly provisions from the local shops, except for special items and extras from Nantwich or Tarporley. As supermarkets were unheard of, and few people had cars, it was necessary to walk into the village to buy food and household things. There was usually a weekly shop for a larger number of items, including perhaps a joint of meat for Sunday. But also, almost every day, either Mum went down to the village or sent one of us to pick up fresh items (for instance meat or bread) or individual things we had just run out of, like a packet of tea or a half-pound of butter.

So compared to the typical weekly shop at Tesco's, Sainsbury's or Asda today, there was more daily shopping and thinking about food then. It took up a lot of time and employed numerous people. For instance, the pub, post office and shops must have provided, between them, full-time employment for at least twenty-five people in the 1950s compared to, at best, five or six today. It also meant that the village was busier and looked more populated than it does now. During shopping hours there were always people walking about or cycling past, or standing to chat at the roadsides.

For people who couldn't be bothered or weren't able to carry their own provisions home, each shop had a delivery service involving boys like me. When I was a bit older, over the age of 11, I started doing an early

165

morning newspaper round and eventually took on delivering groceries by bike as well, after school. But before I started doing these jobs I'd got used to the sight of older boys panting up the hill out of the village, riding the old black delivery bikes with their small front wheel and large basket in front. On Saturday mornings the bikes' baskets would be full of white packets containing meat from the butcher's, with addresses and contents of the packets scribbled in pencil on each packet.

In the early 1950s, however, Mum relied less on the village stores and preferred deliveries from outside. I think that this must have been a hangover from her Tarporley days. She stayed loyal to Vaughan's, the grocery store in Tarporley, which she clearly thought was a better shop than anything Bunbury had to offer. Also, as long as she could continue to use Vaughan's she could hang on to her former identity as a member of the family that had once run the Swan Garage — she wasn't just any customer.

Vaughan's in Tarporley was one of those old-fashioned grocer's shops that smelled of ham, roasted coffee and cheese. As a small boy I can remember watching, fascinated, as the little metal containers on wires whizzed across the ceiling from different directions, ferrying money in one direction to the central cashier, a silver-haired man in a white coat. Change and receipts whizzed back in the other direction.

Being unable to drive and without a car, however, Mum had to rely on a weekly delivery from Vaughan's.

The delivery man, wearing his brown coat, would come to sit in the kitchen for a cup of tea after he had brought the groceries through. As he and Mum chatted about Tarporley news, he would write down a list of items for the following week's delivery as they talked, so that a phrase like "You'll never guess who's getting married" would be interrupted with "Oh, tea! I've just remembered." It was a leisurely discussion. When the list was complete, the Vaughan's man would brush away the cigarette ash or scone crumbs on his coat, stretch and politely take his leave.

And he wasn't the only one. In addition to Vaughan's, other people called, each one personifying a service or a food. When I was 3 or 4 years old I used to get very excited about these calls. I'd love to shout to announce their arrival, dancing around on the lawn, if I happened to see them first. "It's the Vegetable Man!" or "The Fish Man!", "Coal Man!" and "Dust Man!"

I used to picture each of these men as if they had taken on the properties of the goods they were responsible for. The Coal Man evidently was made of coal, for instance; the Dust Man was dusty from the ash and cinders that filled the bins in those days; and the Fish Man had a suitably white coat and smelled of fish, with cool grey cod-like eyes on the sides of his head. The Vegetable Man was a brown-skinned, cheerful, round-faced giant onion who could talk to the other vegetables and weigh them out from the back of his dark blue van.

One weekly caller, however, couldn't be as easily identified with a product. He was Mr Wade, an intriguing mystery man to me because all he seemed to do was to come in, drink a cup of tea, talk for fifteen minutes and go again. I found out only recently that Mr Wade was an insurance agent who called at houses all around the area to collect weekly subscriptions. To me, though, he was the mystery man in a brown suit, who smiled kindly at me and seemed amused by me, as much as I was intrigued by him.

One December, weeks before the day itself, Mum and Dad asked me what I wanted for Christmas. I was excited and pleased to be asked, but looked sceptically at them, because as a 6-year-old I believed that it was Father Christmas who took all the decisions. I judged that it would be difficult for them to get in touch with Father Christmas and wondered whether, despite their assurances, he would actually have time to listen to them. So I decided not to tell them what I wanted.

When they persisted in asking me I had a brainwave. I doubted that they would ever be able to contact Father Christmas, but I was sure Mr Wade could! He had that magical air about him — a man who travelled, wore a suit, and apparently specialised in talking and taking messages, then disappearing. I whispered my secret list to Mr Wade a few days later. I found out, only recently from his daughter, Hester, that Mr Wade was both very amused and touched by my trust in him, and that I became one of his favourite stories about the many families he called upon.

Later on in the 1950s all the various weekly callers and deliveries began to tail off and we began to rely more on the village shops. This might have been because of changes at Vaughan's in Tarporley, or because the various delivery men gave up. Or perhaps it was because Mum found that it was possible to build up a credit account at the local grocer's and butcher's shop. Bit by bit, as expenditure regularly exceeded income week by week, she found that she was trapped by a debt relationship with the local shops.

I was unaware of the size of the grocery bill, but at its weightiest it reached the £250 zone, or thereabouts — a total that can only be appreciated today by multiplying it by twenty or so. It would be equivalent to the sort of credit card debt that it's all too easy to fall into today.

Luckily for us, the family firms that ran the grocer's and butcher's shops were understanding enough not to demand immediate repayment and to continue supplying us. However, there was an emotional cost in loss of pride and a feeling of guilt and humiliation, if not the financial cost of a high interest charge. I didn't have to pay the shame and embarrassment cost, though, because I was relatively young when I was sent to pick up the shopping. Unaware of any "atmosphere", I would cheerily ask, "Mum says, can we put it in the book?"

But Henry, being older, did very much notice the glances and sighs of impatience when he said the same thing. When the amount "on tick" reached its alarming level, he would have been at the self-conscious, adolescent stage. He had to face the pert, knowing glances of the shop girls (all of whom would have known our family), or the condescending glance of the grocer or one of the other men who worked in the shop.

Also, this was the era before self-service. It added to the tension and uncomfortable nature of the shopping event, because each item had to be asked for individually. The shop assistant would have to walk off to a shelf or a back room somewhere before returning with the requested item. It would go something like this:

"A packet of cornflakes, please."

Sound of shop assistant's shoes clacking on the wooden floor. The sound recedes as she goes into a back room. Shop assistant comes back: clomp, clomp, clomp.

"Er, half a pound of White Cheshire please."

Clomp, clomp, clomp. Pause. Sound of cheesecutter. "It's just a bit over, is that all right?" Clomp, clomp-clomp again. "Yes?"

"And, er, a jar of strawberry jam."

Clomp, clomp, clomp (to the same area that the cornflakes came from). Pause. Clomp, clomp, clomp. "That all?"

"Er . . . Mum says, can you put it in the book?"

A sharp intake of breath and a stony glance followed by another sigh.

If there were twelve or so items, it might take at least ten minutes for everything to be assembled and for the torture to be over. This was because the shop assistant needed to insert momentary scowling time, as well as needing a minute or so at the end to tot up each item

170

(in three columns for pounds, shillings and pence) on a piece of paper, before ringing up the total on the till.

Still, it wasn't all bad. Somehow the food kept coming. Thanks to Mum's ingenuity in the kitchen and stoical attitude to making do in other ways, we not only didn't starve but actually enjoyed good food. Also, as nearly everything was home-cooked, this meant that the tastes of convenience or manufactured food were very unusual, almost mystical experiences.

For instance, I can still remember the first time I was able to buy a sixpenny packet of chips for myself, after Cubs, on a summer evening. Ravenscroft's, the little fish and chip shop, had just got into its stride that year. I took the first chip into my mouth and tasted the unbelievable saltiness of it. It tasted so wrong, yet so daringly right — the searing salt on the outside, the crunchy coat of the chip and the moist neutrality of the potato inside. No chip or potato in any form had ever assumed such divinity, as far as I could tell.

Tasting Sugar Puffs for the first time was another unforgettable moment. Sugar Puffs, in my mind, will for ever be associated with the fair. Every year, in a small field behind the part of the village with shops, ramshackle fairground rides and stalls were erected by strange, piratical-looking people. When I was 7 or 8 I was allowed to go down to this fair with two or three other kids to watch people being spun round in waltzers or on a creaking, dangerously tilting merry-go-round. We spent most of the time running around the merry-go-round platform, shouting hysterically and trying to catch each other. We were daring each other not to fall into the gap between the hastily assembled planks and the whirring, grinding machinery, until an old pirate with a scarred face told us to bugger off.

Arriving home, hot and excited, I told Mum all about it. She smiled and pushed a box towards me. It was a new cereal she had heard about — Sugar Puffs. My fairground money hadn't stretched to include candy floss or sweets, but the bowl of Sugar Puffs more than made up for it. As with the chips, they tasted deliciously illegal, as if no one should actually be allowed to eat such things. The 1950s food technologists and scientists had done their job well. Here was a product that probably contained less nutrition than the box it came in, but it tasted *so* good. It was 1955, and a whole new world of food lay before me. In time there would be fishfingers and neat pieces of cod cut, apparently, from oblong fish. Soon there would be Vesta curries. Eventually, there would even be Ski Yoghurt in little plastic pots. But before I could get to those things, there were still going to be a lot of Sunnyside meals to look forward to.

CHAPTER
SIX

Fun, Films and Fêtes

THE GERMANS!

A 1950s village childhood meant being in the village most of the time — you didn't get taken very far beyond it. So almost everything that was supposed to be fun — school trips, the fair, summer holidays, the Beeston Castle fête on 1 August, fireworks on 5 November — had a "homemade" local feel, and the fun things mostly happened at a particular time of year.

But there were three main exceptions to this. One was Chester Zoo, and the second came into the category of special events such as village festivities to celebrate the Coronation in 1953, or occasional concerts and amateur dramatics in the village hall. And the third "non-seasonal" kind of fun was going to see films.

The first, the zoo, was like a mind-expanding drug. It wasn't just the sight or smell of the various animals and birds, it was the idea that these exotic creatures had come from all over the world. It made the zoo feel a bit like a huge international airport. As a kid, I was hooked on places in other parts of the world and the idea of going to see them. The animals themselves were fairly uninteresting travellers from these places, who yawned a lot and looked a bit fed up with their seemingly endless wait in Departures.

The only time I remember them being lively was on a particular winter's afternoon when every animal attempted to get out of its enclosure in order to kill Henry. He'd been to a funeral, and was still wearing a dark suit. True to form, lions, tigers and other fierce beasts roared, their eyes darkening as they focused on his throat. But it was a surprise to see normally placid, shy animals such as reindeer, otters and tropical birds throwing themselves against their fences, snarling or tweeting angrily at my inoffensive brother.

Whatever the animals were doing, I could always look at the world map next to each enclosure, where the regions the animals had come from were coloured in green or black. The information about these places just clicked into my head, like a computer hard disk being loaded up. Click, click, click, whirr, whirr . . . Bolivia, the Congo, Siberia . . . it was a strangely pleasant feeling. My brain was just aching for knowledge.

Any day might just turn out to be a "zoo day", though perhaps two years might elapse before anyone agreed to go. I just had to keep myself in a state of zoo-readiness. If by any chance the conversation of adults trailed in a desultory way into "What do you think we should do this afternoon?" I could be ready to strike like the Blue Streak missile with "Why don't we go to the zoo?" (And be prepared to try to foil a negative response such as, "By the time we get there it won't be worth going round, the animals will be going to sleep".)

The second exception to the "everything's-fixed-in-seasons" rule was the special or unusual events. The Coronation of Queen Elizabeth, when I was just 5 years old, was memorable to me because it was the first time that I can consciously recall seeing a television set. Three or four TVs had been placed on tall stools in the village hall, so that the mainly television-less village population could troop down there to sit solemnly on hard wooden chairs to watch grainy live pictures of the royal coach trundling along grey London streets.

Outside the hall there was a much more life-like life-size replica of the coach, with Mr Fred Burrows (the butcher), his wife and two local worthies, Mr and Mrs Cookson, to lend dignity to the royal event. Without the coach and top-hatted driver and footmen, however, Mr Burrows and the little group standing outside the grocer's and butcher's shops looked more like provincial stalwarts from Republican France than from a deeply pro-monarchist English village.

While the Coronation was a one-off, historical occasion, opportunities for dressing up and play-acting occurred more frequently, though not with absolute regularity, when local people got together in the village hall to put on a fund-raising concert or a play. The concerts were home-grown attempts to stage comedy reviews, so a large number of participants were roped in to do a turn.

For some reason the Cubs — which included me — were also expected to appear on stage, or to run about backstage carrying things for the nervous and excited cast. Therefore, from the age of 7, I would occasionally be able to watch the astonishing antics of adults backstage as they burst into tears, quivered with nervousness or fooled about.

For instance, on one occasion I was able to stare for several minutes at the huge expanse of the thighs of a young woman as she sat in fishnet stockings on some wooden steps. I'd never seen thighs before. The woman was weeping inconsolably about what she thought was her inadequate singing voice. "Oh, you're not singing out of tune, it's fine," chorused several men standing around her, trying to comfort her, though even as a 7-year-old I could tell from the politeness in their voices that there probably was something a bit wrong with the voice, if not the legs.

Actually, the concerts and village plays were more entertaining to a young boy backstage, and revealed more than they did when you were looking at them as a member of the audience. This was certainly true when you couldn't pick up on the adults' in-jokes, or understand the tortuous plot of a whodunit. But even if the meanings of the productions weren't very understandable, they revealed a flash of eccentricity in the normally staid and reserved adults in the community. There were also a few who seemed to be completely bonkers, and naturally this characteristic came into its own on the village stage.

Like the zoo and village drama productions, films were nearly always mind-expanding, and the chances of going were much greater. Unlike urban kids, though,

176

for us there was no nearby cinema for a weekly trip to see Saturday-morning films. Most of the films I saw as a child were matinées, on occasional weekday afternoons in Chester when Mum would take me after a torture session at the dentist's.

A lot of those 1950s films must have been junk, with silly romantic comedy plots that were incomprehensible to a boy of 7, 8 or 9. However, they were almost always in colour, usually had some foreign locations (Arizona, China, the South Pacific — click, click, whirr, whirr . . .). Also, if you were lucky, someone got shot or at least had a nasty accident.

A few stood out as being really good, like *Twenty Thousand Leagues Under the Sea* — a film that was ahead of its time in special underwater effects. The title foxed me, though. At school, I told Lloyd Passey how terrific this film was. He looked at me sceptically. "A league's about half a mile, isn't it?" he said. "The sea isn't *that* deep. It would be thicker than the Earth if it were that deep. It's rubbish, that film."

Another way I might get to see a film was with the whole family, though these outings were very rare. However, I can just about remember seeing the knights in *Ivanhoe* charging at each other in Technicolor when I was perhaps only 3 or 4 years old.

Ivanhoe or *Inn of the Sixth Happiness* would have been in a proper cinema in Chester, but it was also possible to see films one evening a week in the village hall. Again, it was a rare occasion for all of us to go, but once in a while we did — for instance, to see *Reach for the Sky*, the Second World War aerial combat drama starring Kenneth More as Douglas Bader.

There was a buzz of excitement in the hall. A lot of people brought packets of fish and chips in from Ravenscroft's across the road. It's not popcorn but the pungent reek of vinegar mixed with chips and batter that will for ever be associated in my mind with old movies.

The projectionist who brought the films to such small rural outlets as Bunbury mounted a proper programme, including a newsreel, advertisements and a shorter "B" movie as well as the main feature — all in black and white.

In the days before many people had television, it was somehow stimulating and relaxing at the same time to see moving images, especially in your own rather static and peaceful village. When Roy Rogers leapt in one bound on to the back of Trigger, he was doing it in your very own village hall! (Trigger was a horse, by the way.)

No wonder, then, that the relatively unsophisticated Bunbury audience couldn't help interjecting, murmuring or sometimes exclaiming loudly when particularly dramatic or striking moments occurred, because it was happening in their own backyard, and the gap between reality and appearance had closed.

There is such a moment, for example, in *Reach for the Sky* when a complete line of German bombers and fighter planes appears, close up, with a deafening roar of engines. The reality and directness of the German planes were particularly striking because they looked like real flying machines. Perhaps the Bunbury film audience had resigned itself to expecting little cardboard models suspended from threads of cotton, but no, the film-makers had used real planes. Hey, they were real *German* planes piloted by real Germans — look at the markings on the wings!

As the villagers stared with rapt attention and fear at the line of planes, one of which had been responsible for dropping incendiaries and a land mine on Bunbury, a lone adult voice said, in the darkness, "The fokkin' Germans." And instead of others being shocked by the expletive and shushing him, telling him not to swear while there were children about, most of the adults in the hall breathed the words in unison, as if hypnotised, "The Germans!"

To me, a boy about 8 years old, it seemed as though this film was from a long-ago era. After all, the war had been over a full three years before I was born — it belonged to ancient, pre-historical times which had nothing to do with me. But of course to most of the audience that night in 1956, the war was a recent event. Just eleven years had passed since the war had ended. Today, in the early twenty-first century, it would be like referring to something that had been going on in the mid-1990s.

CHRISTMAS AND EASTER

In the 1950s there was, as Joan Bakewell put it, "a general awareness of the church year, Sunday observance [and] banks that closed at 3pm".[1] These

---

[1] *The Guardian* (Review), 11 March 2005, page 12.

familiar routines and rules structured time — the pattern of each week, month and year — in a way that has largely disappeared now. But in the 1950s the weekly and seasonal routines were a fact of life whether you liked them or not, and even if you were not a churchgoer, or particularly religious.

Neither Mum nor Dad was a churchgoer, or that interested in religion. They were probably in a majority in my home village of the 1950s, though the church was pretty full on most Sunday mornings, and packed to capacity on significant occasions such as Christmas Eve and Easter morning. Bunbury church is huge, relative to the size of the village, so filling almost all the pews must have meant that a high proportion of villagers attended on those special days of the year. The congregation in the 1950s was led by a very well-liked vicar, Maurice Ridgway, who swept around the village in his long dark robes, and there is no doubt that his popularity boosted church attendance.

Also, even though many people in 1950s Bunbury weren't particularly religious, the general atmosphere surrounding the big holidays of Christmas and Easter had strongly holy overtones, especially in a traditional rural community.

But as far as I was concerned, this meant that Christmas was more like a "super Sunday" than anything else. It wasn't exactly low-key, but on the other hand it certainly wasn't the mass exercise to cultivate shopping hysteria that it's become now. Today the Christmas shopping adverts start their offensive early, pounding away relentlessly like howitzers from early October onwards. Then, it didn't seem as though anyone thought much about Christmas until a week or two beforehand.

For instance, there was always indecision at Sunnyside about the Bird. Unfortunately, the task of buying the Christmas Bird regularly fell between two stools. Dad thought that Mum would be buying or at least ordering something because it fell under the jurisdiction of "food" or "housekeeping". And Mum thought that Dad would be doing it because she had never been given enough money to manage the regular grocery bills, let alone an expensive bird, and in any case it was a special item that lay outside the jurisdiction of normal housekeeping.

The other complication was that neither ever seemed to talk to the other about this ambiguity. Perhaps they didn't argue because there was a risk that whichever one raised the issue might lose his or her case.

There always *was* a bird, but on some Christmas Days the bird that appeared at the table was patently some character that had been drafted into the play at the final moment. One Christmas, for example, a brace of pheasants appeared — obviously a last minute deal between Dad and his gamekeeper friend. They were tasty, but they did look a bit like unfashionable, wrinkled old repertory actors who'd been signed up for the wrong production.

There were other signs that Christmas was supposed to be a fairly low-key event. A Sunnyside Christmas, for instance, didn't have to involve a Christmas tree, and nor did it involve either Mum or Dad giving anything

181

significant to each other. And we weren't expected to give them presents — presents were just something for the kids.

In fact, Christmas presents to adults were an embarrassment and an irritation to Mum (Dad never bothered to think about it). This was mainly because she didn't have much spare money to buy presents for relatives or friends. Yet a few awkward, unthinking relatives would persist in sending Mum and Dad presents. "Oh, drat," she'd say with a sinking heart, as the postman delivered yet another parcel. "Who the heck's this from? I wish they wouldn't."

One year, a couple of days before Christmas Eve, our living room temporarily resembled a small postal sorting office. Mum was undoing parcels and unwrapping presents, re-wrapping them with swapped-over wrapping paper, and re-parcelling them for re-posting to different relatives. The key thing was not only to avoid sending a present back to its original sender, but also to avoid sending it to a third person or family member who might compare notes with the initial sender about what Mum had sent them. Any question of the present actually being appropriate to its actual recipient therefore had to be a secondary consideration — but isn't that what the fun of Christmas is all about?

I used to worry about this recycling of presents, though. What if our rather whiskery, elderly Aunt Annie had been sent aftershave, instead of her usual eau de cologne?

182

Despite Bird Uncertainty and Present Uncertainty, Christmas Day itself was a good time in Sunnyside — at least, from the point of view of my childhood experience. There would be presents to unwrap in the bedroom's morning darkness, with Fred and Henry in their pyjamas looking on and chuckling, helping me to get the wrapping paper off.

One year (was I 7 or 8?) I was genuinely astonished and fantastically pleased to find that I'd been given a *new* Hornby railway set. It had a gleaming, black clockwork-powered locomotive. I was young and unsophisticated enough not to know about electric train sets, and this present seemed to confirm that the universe was basically a positive place to be in. Later in the day I was able to lie on my back in the front room, staring at the engine and its rolling stock on its track. I was totally absorbed in it. And I had a very clear, conscious thought that I was the luckiest person in the world, just at that moment.

Coming downstairs that Christmas morning angels were signing on the radio. The tired old friendly Christmas decorations were strung up across the ceilings and deposited along picture rails. On Christmas Day there would be a fire in the front room as well as in the kitchen. Sunnyside felt warm throughout for once, and we basked in the glow of two fires and the smell of roasting Somebird.

After the heavy Christmas dinner had been eaten, it would be time for Dad to light up his annual Havana and for the radio to be switched on for the Queen. We all had to be quiet for ten minutes and tolerate the incomprehensible, high-pitched voice. I wasn't sure it was actually the Queen, though. The Queen I knew was a human being. She was that disappointingly small, unsmiling, waxy-faced woman in a huge black car who I had once been taken to see in a school party, standing at a roadside near Crewe. But this voice wasn't even of a human being. It sounded as if the leader of a distant, once-powerful species in another part of the universe was broadcasting to us.

The wonder was that adults seemed to be able to understand these incomprehensible, high-pitched sound patterns. When it had finished Dad would say to Mum something like, "I didn't think it was quite as good as last year, do you?" This implied that they had both understood the alien sounds. But the fact that neither ever referred to anything specific in the Queen's speech — such as "My corgis are doing well this year, I've got sixteen now" — suggested to me that they were pretending.

After Christmas came the long slog through dark winter months, which brought snow, slush, ice on the inside of the bedroom windows, fog, flu, colds and wheezing chests, and the need to nurse Dad's car radiator through all this.

Not surprisingly, then, Easter usually coincided with a time when your spirits could begin to lift. I wouldn't wish 1950s rural winter discomforts on anyone today, but in one way I'm glad I experienced that seasonal shift. Now, the change from winter to spring seems to be much less evident, less sharp, in people's lives. Shivering in your house in February and huddling round a fire is something that most people in Britain did from prehistoric times up to the mid-twentieth century.

There were some really cold winters in my childhood, though nothing to compare, I was often told, with the blizzards and intensely cold winter of 1946–47, more than a year before I was born.

That was the winter in which Henry nearly drowned. He'd been playing next to the stream at the bottom of the hill near the church, launching a little model of the *Queen Mary* into a large, brown, swirling pond that had been formed by meltwater. Bending as far as he could to rescue his boat, he'd fallen in and then got sucked beneath the surface and carried all the way through a culvert under the road, his head bumping along the bricks of the top of the culvert as he sped through. Luckily he was spotted, alive and spluttering, by a woman pedalling a bike with a sidecar — she delivered milk around the village. Throwing the milk canisters out and the shivering Henry into the sidecar, she pedalled furiously up to Sunnyside to deposit him on the doorstep. (No milk today, just one son, please.)

Now, winters don't seem quite as cold as they were — they seem to be changing into a sort of mild monsoon season. And once the bite of "real" winter has gone, the coming of spring and of Easter doesn't seem to have quite the meaning it once did. It wouldn't be right, though, to say that in 1950s Bunbury we were bound into the agricultural cycle in some mystical way.

It's just that we often got freezing cold in the winter and felt a lot better when it got warmer.

Also, just like Christmas, the arrival of Easter wasn't a particularly religious occasion at Sunnyside. Neither parent went to Church on Easter morning, though Jay would usually put on a smart dress and go, and Henry and Fred would attend because they were in the choir.

However, a kind of religious aura did spread over the village in the run-up to Easter. It didn't amount to anything approaching religious fervour, and most people in Bunbury probably didn't bother much about Lent. But there was definitely a grey stillness in the air, in those mild, moist early spring days leading through Lent up to Holy Week, when the primroses and the daffodils start to show up.

The closest parallel now, and the best way to recapture it, is to go in Easter week to a rural area in a country where Catholicism is still fairly strong, such as Spain, Portugal or Ireland. You can watch an old farmer in a black waistcoat in one of those countries, plodding through a field sprouting green shoots. Or you can lean on a fence to see a young man ploughing, and be back in the quiet Easter air of Bunbury *circa* 1955.

So the Easter holiday wasn't exactly *fun*, like Christmas, more a marker in the year that gave a sense of relief from winter, and from the sad, solemn Lenten thoughts of suffering that the Anglican Church then had the strength to waft all over the country. We got our palm-frond crosses at Sunday school on Palm Sunday, a week before Easter, ate our hot cross buns (it was highly immoral to have them before Easter, we were told) and broke into our hollow Cadbury's eggs on Easter Sunday.

Not that it was all easy. About this time of year it was "Bob a Job" week — the week set aside for Cubs and Scouts to pester every household in the village for simple jobs to perform around the house or garden, in return for contributions to the Scout movement.

Lloyd Passey and I usually worked together, trudging from house to house. But we always seemed to find that we'd made the error of going to the stingiest, most slave-driving, mentally warped people in the village. While other kids had the sense to work out that if you were quick you could get to the doctor's house next to the church and get 10 shillings for doing nothing, we got saddled with endless tasks for a whole afternoon, and were rewarded with a bare shilling. At one house on Bunbury Heath we spent a whole afternoon laying a gravel drive (preparing and levelling the surface, ferrying bags of gravel in wheelbarrows, fixing brick edging) without even a bottle of pop to keep us going. Before the shilling (one between us) was bestowed, the ungrateful householder asked us to take his dog for a walk before sunset. It was a nice dog, and that was what stopped me and Lloyd from tethering it to the railway line.

FAR-OUT TRIPS

Once summer approached you could begin to think about preparations for the annual school trip. I

187

remember going on three of these, the first being a trip by train to the Lake District and Morecambe, just before my eighth birthday. At this stage the village school still "taught" the older boys aged over 11. So it must have been quite a large group, perhaps forty or more boys aged between 7 and 15, who joined the special train at Beeston Castle station early that summer morning. Mr and Mrs Steventon, the village schoolteacher duo, accompanied us.

It would have been a steam train, of course, and, being a holiday "special" for school trips, it had particularly dingy, maroon-coloured coaches. The train was already thronged with noisy children from other schools, but the Bunbury contingent soon managed to colonise a section of one of the coaches.

The journey to the Lakes took a very long time. After heading off in the general direction of Warrington, the train was side-tracked into a meandering tour of the railway sidings of the north-west.

About midday, following a four-hour trek, the train pulled into an isolated siding that was surrounded by overgrown weeds and tall pink flowers. It was hot, with the June sun beating down on the carriages. In the distance there was an unchanging view of a gasworks, some tall chimneys, a row of grimy redbrick houses and a crane. After a quiet five minutes in which bees buzzed outside and everyone talked quietly, there was a sound of chains and of couplings being uncoupled.

Our locomotive chuffed off into the distance. There was complete silence now, as everyone looked at each other with questions in their eyes. Where were we going to be sent next? Warsaw? Vladivostok? We were beginning to get hungry and thirsty. Everyone had eaten their sandwiches and drained their last bottle of Tizer or Dandelion & Burdock.

Eventually a relief locomotive turned up, but that period of waiting left a lasting impression on me. It was a tiny insight into what thousands of refugee children must have experienced before and after the Second World War. We had had just an hour's sample of their endless days trundling around, with inexplicable zig-zag journeys and long waits on foreign sections of track surrounded by wild flowers and feelings of being forgotten and lost.

After the long train journey everything seemed to speed up by about a hundred miles an hour. We were quickly herded from the train at a station somewhere in the Lake District into a yard full of brightly coloured little buses. These buses — turquoise, red, deep purple — had aggressive little bonnets and streamlined fronts with bright silver grilles glinting in the sunshine.

The amazing thing to us was that the bus drivers lounging laconically next to the buses were sun-tanned, trouser-wearing, smoking *women*. Ours was middle-aged, with greying hair in a 1940s-style perm. She grinned at us, flicked her cigarette end out of the window, gunned the engine and, with a powerful jerk to the neck, we were off.

I can honestly say that, to this day, that coach journey through the twisting lanes of the Lake District is still the most frightening, exhilarating, dangerous ride in a road vehicle I have ever had. I would give my

189

rush-hour taxi ride through central Rome seven points, and the trip on unmade roads through the hills of southern Ghana, in a truck with no brakes driven by a sick man suffering from malarial delusions, eight points. But this bus ride definitely reached the full ten points of adrenalin.

The sense of thrill and danger were amplified for me because I was on the seat just behind the front passenger door, which had been left open. Bright sunshine and fresh mountain air surged through, as the driver jammed down the accelerator and we sped into the mountains. When the bus hurtled over a hump-backed bridge at 50mph, soaring into the air like a tigress, I had that spiritual, floating, near-death experience that people who have had heart arrests report. Luckily I had that metal bar to hold on to, the one just forward of the front seat, as my body rose up towards the bus roof and I experienced weightlessness for the first time.

And when she approached a downhill bend at 60mph, with an expert racing change to swing the bus round, I had a whole half-second to observe the cattle truck coming the other way. There just didn't seem to be room for both vehicles, but our driver didn't even bother with brakes. No, it was the lupins for us.

She twitched the steering wheel just slightly to the left, aiming the bus dangerously close to a solid earth embankment that came almost to the side of the road. There was a minuscule space to spare, and it was filled with large clumps of lupins. As our bus raced into the gap between the cattle truck and the embankment, a

190

Wordsworthian host of purple, red and blue lupins were harvested at full speed. Bunches of dark green lupin foliage and thousands of confetti-like lupin flower-cups flew into the coach, dancing in the rush of air from the open door. We cheered, and the She-Driver laughed maniacally in response, as we grazed past the oncoming truck with an inch to spare. Then the bus went into a final, wailing, Stuka-like dive towards the peaceful, unsuspecting streets of Windermere.

At the lakeside there was little time to draw breath or notice how damp our palms were before we were stampeded up a ramp on to a large white pleasure-steamer. All the other children trooping off the other buses looked equally pale-faced but astonished and excited, as if they too had been on the most dangerous fairground ride ever. Clearly, all our reckless women drivers were in love with death.

The boat was casting off even as the gangway was lifted up, the propellers threshing the calm blue waters of the lake into a turmoil. I saw several teachers, including Mr and Mrs Steventon, anxiously counting heads to check how many of their charges were on the boat and how many had been strewn across the grass verges of the Lake District during the dangerous bus journey.

What was it about this part of the world? It wasn't a city, it was as rural as where we'd come from, but everyone in it seemed to have a complex about speed. I looked over the side and, on the wooden pier that was rapidly receding from view, saw several teachers who had not kept up with their pupils dancing about, waving and squeaking.

The steamer charged around the lake like a last-minute Christmas shopper. There was a bracing breeze. It was good to be alive in the sunshine, to have survived the bus trip. Excited, we saw how the boat created immense waves in its wake, causing several rowing boats to yaw and pitch dangerously. One man tried to stand up in his nearly capsized little boat, but was forced to half kneel, clutching on to the side with one hand and waving his other fist angrily. We cheered and waved back.

In no time the steamer was being reversed expertly against another pier at the far end of the lake. We had hardly been able to take in the magnificent views of the grey-green mountains and the startling blue of the lake. But what were waiting for us, lined up like racing cars on the starting line near the pier? You've guessed it: the aggressive little buses had been driven round to pick us up! The sun-burned, trousered women-drivers leaned nonchalantly against their vehicles' radiators, smoking and permitting themselves the occasional daredevil smirk. We were scrambling for a lightning raid on Morecambe.

I can't say I remember much about Morecambe. Don't forget, I was only 7 years old, still dizzy from the bus journeys and I hadn't eaten anything since the refugee train. By now it was about five o'clock in the evening. We staggered off the buses on to a promenade.

And then I walked into a lamp-post. Reeling and in tears, with blue, yellow and red stars circling against a black background in my mind, I saw Mrs Steventon coming up to me, wreathed in smiles. She tried to comfort me by telling me how silly I'd been. "Ho-ho-ho," she chuckled. "It's just like you, Kenneth, isn't it, to walk into a lamp-post?" Then she put an arm round me and pulled me towards her for a moment. I felt the full weight of her sizeable, overhanging bosom. The daylight disappeared. Luckily her breasts were held in place by the straining, creaking, high-tension metal hawsers of some brassiere-like structure. But it still felt as if two sailors in a hammock were sitting on my head.

I followed up the blow to the head and the decidedly Freudian encounter with Mrs Steventon's breasts with a candy floss. This might not have been the wisest idea, but I was getting really hungry. It was probably even less advisable to have gone on from the candy floss, with its dramatic impact on mood and blood-sugar levels, to several experimental spinning fairground rides. These, and the overall effect of all the day's experiences added together, were to temporarily uncouple me from my personal identity.

I wandered lonely as a cloud through a host of fairground amusements, noticing eventually that they were less busy than they had been. I looked around, checking in an absent-minded way for familiar faces. There were none. Who was I, anyway? Where was I from? Oh well, I thought, I might as well wander off to the railway station to pick up some clues. I had a distant, pre-concussion memory of being told to go back there . . . some time. But where was the station? Remaining calm, but with a strange, disembodied feeling in me, I stared at three long, straight roads that fanned out in different directions. Eeney, meeney, miney, mo — that meant I should take the left-hand one.

Luckily, it was the correct road. I sleepwalked through the station yard on to a platform, noting that a red-faced Mr Steventon was standing by an open carriage door, gibbering and hopping up and down. Whistles were blowing and green flags were being waved. A lot of kids' faces were staring out of the carriage windows at me, grinning and with their mouths making shouting expressions. When I was pulled on to the train I found that they really were shouting, and I got a large round of applause. I blushed and raised my arm weakly. The station platform began to move sideways, and Morecambe slid back into a forgotten world.

You can't say that about Heathrow Airport, which was the destination of the school trip the following year. Heathrow is the opposite of a forgotten world — it's now a kind of persistent headache located in west London. These days it sounds a bit weird to have taken a small posse of rural schoolchildren to wander about an international airport. But in the 1950s Heathrow, and air travel in general, had a lot of glamour and exclusivity attached to it. Just to wander about the hallowed temple of air travel was considered to be both exciting and highly educational.

Despite the potential fascination, however, no school trip ever lived up to the first one, the Lake District and Morecambe trip, for sheer thrill, danger and the fear of being left behind. For one thing, the group of children from Bunbury was now only a small band because the older boys had transferred to the secondary modern.

As there were more spaces, the Steventons encouraged parents to go on the trips. To my surprise — because he had never done anything like this before — Dad decided he'd like to come. It was probably because aeroplanes held something of a fascination for him. Every September he liked to go to the Farnborough Air Show, and the Heathrow trip, with its promise of soaring jets and modern technology, fitted in with that fascination.

It was a grey, drizzly summer's day. Once we'd established that an airport was just an airport, and we weren't flying anywhere or meeting anyone, it got a bit boring. The sight of the radar mast with its rotating arm, or of the control tower with its green glass, had given us village kids an initial shock of excitement. The highest form of technology most of us had seen before was a combine harvester or a muck spreader, and neither of these types of equipment seemed to have been fitted with rotating radar arms. And few of us had ever been to London before — I certainly hadn't.

But again, it didn't take long for the space-age gloss of these strange new sights to wear off. The most interesting bit for me was when Dad pointed out the passengers walking down on to the tarmac from a plane that had arrived from India. It was the first time I had seen people wearing bright colours such as lime-green and bright orange. There were brown-skinned women

195

in saris, wearing gold jewellery, and men with turbans and long floppy shirts.

"They're very wealthy people," Dad said, pointing them out. "They must be, to have come by air," he added, with an admiring, fascinated tone in his voice.

The following year there was a coach excursion to Snowdonia, and this was the last of the three primary school trips I went on. It was during the early stages of this trip that Lloyd Passey vomited into a biscuit tin.

Mothers, including mine, seem to predominate on that trip, rather than fathers, so the whole outing had a rather sedate, homely feel. There was a lot of chatting between Mums, and of staring out of rain-streaked coach windows by us kids, as we slowly turned green on the switchback mountain roads.

Once we'd all been sick there wasn't much else to do. The North Welsh rain became more intense as the mountains grew higher, so that all we could see were mist-enveloped, black hillsides with waterfalls chucking yet more water everywhere. Drenched, disconsolate sheep huddled in little groups beside remote stone shelters, as if waiting for the local vet to bring them their next batch of anti-depressants.

We eventually stopped at a rain-lashed resort somewhere to glance at the grey, white-capped sea and a few solitary people, bent double against the wind, walking along the sea-front with their umbrellas blown inside-out. We drank a brackish cup of tea in a new invention, a plastic cup. Then we all piled back into the coach. There were another few hours of "Your Hundred Best Cumulo Nimbus Clouds" to get through before we could drop down to the welcoming dry hedgerows of the Cheshire plain.

The August Fête

Summer fun in a 1950s village didn't really have many great peaks of enjoyment. My birthday was in July, and it was nice to get a present, such as the amazing clockwork-powered submarine Dad gave me once. But I don't remember any birthday parties as such, except one when I was 8.

Apart from my birthday, there were a few other low-key summer events, like a day trip to Rhyl, but mostly, like William Brown's Pirates, we rambled aimlessly around the village, breaking small things.

So it's not surprising, given the rather slow tempo of 1950s summers, that the August Bank Holiday Fête at Beeston Castle (held at the beginning of August in those days) stood out as a high point.

This really was a day when the social life of the village was transformed. Thousands of people came for the day at the castle — buses met every train arriving at Beeston Castle station — and some exciting things happened. On 3 August 1959, for instance, for a mere shilling (adults) or sixpence (children) you could enjoy the following:

Motor cycle hill climb (organised by Nantwich Motor Club at 5.45p.m.)
Acrobatic and combat flying display (Chester Model

Flying Club)
Archery display (Chester Archery Club)
Punch and Judy show, baby show, children's sports
and competition
Numerous stalls and sideshows.

Beeston Castle stands, an enormous broken molar, on a dramatic rocky outcrop that rears up from the Cheshire plain about 2 miles north of Bunbury. It's mostly in ruins, though the walls of the central keep and the gatehouse are fairly intact. Steep slopes run down from the castle itself. They are covered in bracken and are criss-crossed by paths, some of which enter deep ravines in the red sandstone. In one place there are damp mossy caves to explore. At the bottom of the slope, on the southern edge near the gatehouse and perimeter wall, there is a flatter, grassed area, and this is where most of the fête took place.

It's the smells of that summer excitement, as much as the sights and sounds, that stay with you, such as the pungent smells of bracken and wet grass trodden by hundreds of feet. Add to this the steamy aroma of tea in large urns and of egg sandwiches in the big marquee, where Mum and other village ladies toiled over mounds of cut-up bread, spreading butter furiously. And best of all there was the acrid masculine reek of motorbike exhaust, as, one by one, daring riders tried to climb to the top of the western flank of the near-vertical castle hill.

There was no doubt in our minds that this last event, the grand finale, was what the fête was all about. It was

198

good to throw darts at cards to win a coconut, or to see if you could find lost coins in the bracken, snatching (as Lloyd Passey once did) a half-crown from under the feet of the milling crowd. It was also good to let the anticipation build by wandering around the spot where the model flying club were expected to launch their planes into the air at any minute.

Except that they never did. Maybe I was always in the wrong place at the wrong time, but in at least seven years of fêtes I never saw any of those model planes airborne. Why was that? It wasn't as though there was any lack of public interest — we kids were *desperate* to see the exciting and realistic-looking planes take to the air, zooming this way and that by radio control.

But the members of the flying club had a curiously listless, almost despondent air about them. Men and women, they lay on their backs smoking cigarettes and looking up at the sky. When, for the tenth time, we asked them when the flying would be starting, one of them would say something meaningless. For instance, I remember a young woman with blonde curly hair and a disdainful look in her eyes probably wanting to say, "Fuck off, little kid." But actually she said something like, "Geoff's working on the radio thingummy." Or (on a still, hot day) "It might be too windy." Or "Come back in half an hour."

What was it about these people? Looking back (I would never have thought of this at the age of 10), I wonder if perhaps the Chester Model Flying Club had spawned within itself a series of steamy, overlapping love triangles? Gradually, perhaps, the trivial pursuit of

199

flying flimsy toy aeroplanes had taken a back seat to the much more substantial agenda of shooting moody, jealous or meaningful looks at other members of the group, or of suddenly expelling cigarette smoke in an exasperated way and walking off?

Whatever the reasons for this tension-building inactivity, the Non-Flying Model Aeroplane Non-Event certainly played its part in making the hill climb at the end of the day superbly exciting. There were no moody adults lying around in the grass; here were determined riders who went straight for it, no messing.

Each one emerged from a small knot of people far down below, at the bottom of the steep hill, with a motorbike engine revving and straining, soon blocking out the fanfare of announcements from a loudspeaker van. From a vantage point at the very top, the rider far below was a tiny toy figure, a medieval knight in leather armour. He'd dash up the first slopes, weaving his gallant horse up the precipitous slope to dodge boulders and steep mounds in the bracken.

If the bike neared the top the engine would be straining desperately. No one in the crowd on the craggy outcrops at the top spoke, and everyone leaned forward to get a proper view of the rider who was still so far from the summit, anxiously transmitting a telepathic thought, "Yes, you *can* make it!"

Very few did. More often than not the desperately rearing bike would emit one final scream of tortured engine and jet of blue smoke, bits of bracken and mud flying out behind the rear wheel, before it threw the rider backwards to the ground. The fallen rider would then (usually) stand up, hot-faced and spattered with mud and vegetation. Defeated, and uttering a few expletives diplomatically muffled by polite clapping from the crowd at the top, the stricken knight would putt-putt disconsolately down a gentler slope to the bottom of the hill.

Every year, though, one or two heroes did make it. Against all the odds, and twisting his bike through the narrowest of fissures, the grimacing rider would burst over the top ledge. Suddenly the heady smell of burning oil and petrol would surround you, mixing again with the odour of earth and torn roots. The victor would be framed against a dramatic backdrop of blue sky and, a mile or two away, the silhouette of Peckforton Castle's keep and battlements on its neighbouring forested hill.

Applause surrounded the sweating, helmetless rider. But it wasn't the done thing in the 1950s to acknowledge this applause. There was no post-modern whooping, excitement or tears, as there might be today, just another terse grimace and a toss of the Brylcreemed head before plunging the bike down a slightly less precipitous slope to the bottom again.

FIREWORKS

The key to understanding the joy of the motorbike hill climb, at least for a boy like me, was danger. I didn't want anyone to get seriously hurt, but a bit of injury and drama was the seasoning that made the survival of the bike riders worth admiring.

The same thrill of danger and risk accompanied the last big item of fun in the calendar year: Bonfire Night on 5 November. I'm sure we would have thought differently about this if one of the small band of kids in Bunbury had been seriously burned or blinded by a firework. But, as far as I can remember, no one suffered this fate, despite everyone handling lots of fireworks before the big night, and stockpiling as large a supply as was possible with limited pocket money.

There was almost as much fun to be had in admiring and poring over each other's unexploded fireworks as there was in Bonfire Night itself. Lloyd Passey, Clive Bevan and I would read with growing excitement the lurid, inflammatory descriptions on the multi-coloured sides of the fireworks. Bangers, rip-raps (jumping jacks), flying demons and rockets were our favourites. Each year, the claims about what the fireworks would do seemed to get a little more adventurous, a little more dangerous.

In the 1950s America, Britain and the Soviet Union couldn't resist the temptation to explode nuclear devices in the open air, so neither could we.

However, letting off a banger became a predictable and unexciting activity. It was imperative to up the arms race. Thus tying a banger to a rocket to "see what would happen" became an essential part of nuclear testing, as did tying four or more bangers together, putting them into a jam jar and igniting them. After taking cover and listening to the stuttering *crack!* we could go to inspect the scene of the explosion, admiring the shards of glass impaled in a nearby tree trunk.

A real breakthrough in explosive technology came when Henry lit a banger in the bath at Sunnyside. I can honestly say that this was not only the loudest explosion I have ever heard, but also the loudest and most penetrating sound of any kind that I've been exposed to. When it happened, the expected *bang!* was magnified tenfold by the sides of the bath. This combined with a resonant and deeply troubling metallic clanging noise, which echoed not only throughout the village and beyond, but also within our very souls. Flocks of rooks flew upwards, croaking with alarm, and herds of cows, tails up, ran across fields like maddened wildebeest. For years afterwards, all the cats and dogs in the neighbourhood walked cautiously in the shadows, a haunted look in their eyes. And Henry got into a lot of trouble with Dad.

A year or so later I was able to find confirmation from other kids that yes, just as Henry had demonstrated, you could combine a lit firework with water. The recommended way was to stick a banger into the neck of a small bottle that had been filled with water up to about a third of its capacity. You could then stand on a bridge over the canal, light the banger and drop the fizzing bottle from the top of the bridge. We saw the bottle sink like a stone, with foam and bubbles appearing on the green-brown surface immediately. They increased with exciting ferocity until there was a dull boom from the depths and a sudden spout of muddy water.

I was able to add my own scientific refinement to this, in the form of a large roman candle. Taking a milk bottle (which in those days had wide necks) rather than a puny ketchup bottle, we weighted it with water as before and jammed in the heavy firework. We were rewarded with not one but three large, satisfying underwater booms as the roman candle shot its meteors successively upwards from the depths. And then a dramatic new sight among the strands of underwater weed floating to the surface: one small, stunned grey fish. We rubbed our hands. This was scientific progress indeed.

Thus Bonfire Night itself was a culmination of mounting excitement among boys like me. It was a thrilling combination of gunpowder, fire, increasingly dark early evenings and the first really cold weather.

The difference between now and then is that in the 1950s — in Bunbury at least — no fireworks were let off after 5 November. Now, the high-pitched whingeing noises of puny little rockets and the bangs of fireworks seem to start at the beginning of October and last until the run-up to Christmas. Then, almost all the fireworks were saved up for the night, and they all had to go in one glorious festival of bright lights and loud bangs.

It was particularly glorious on one very memorable 5 November at Sunnyside, when I was perhaps only 7 years old and when a spark fell into the large box of fireworks lying on the garden path.

As Henry and Fred admitted later that evening, perhaps it hadn't been such a good idea to leave the box, which had the largest arsenal of rockets and other fireworks ever assembled before at Sunnyside, with its lid off, so close to the crackling bonfire. Typically, Dad was only just emerging from the back door, having reluctantly put down his *Telegraph* on the chair by the warm fireside, when the munitions dump began to explode in all directions.

The bonfire, Fred, Henry and the fireworks were all at the far end of the back garden, just in front of the ramshackle little garden shed and the apple tree. I was standing nearer the house on the lawn with bewildered parents, spellbound by the pyrotechnic display that this year had decided to come to us rather than remain at the bottom of the garden.

To begin with, the angry box seemed to concentrate all its fire on Henry. Fred ran towards us, giving a terse briefing on the current situation. Henry had taken cover by squeezing into the tiny gap between the back of the shed and the hedge, peering out occasionally and grinning because he was pinned down by a relentless barrage of red, blue and green mortar-fire from a dozen roman candles. Golden rain bathed all the neighbours' gardens in an eerie glow, as if bombers were to return again from the Second World War, attracted by the guiding incendiaries.

With a sudden *whoosh!* six rockets took off at once in wildly divergent directions. *Oooh!* we all cried, as they each split the dark night, heading towards various, very local, targets. Two were lodged in the thick garden hedge, where they spurted fire and then their final starbursts, making a deep-red glow inside the mass of dark-green privet. Another bumped horizontally along

205

the lawn like a sturdy off-road vehicle, causing Mum to burst into hysterical giggles and shout, "Oooh, look at *that*!" before it burst its stars at the bottom of the orange blossom tree. Two more raced at a low angle towards the school roof, just two doors down the road — leading me to whisper to the god of fire, "Please, please, yes!" — and the sixth caused us all to breathe in suddenly with shock.

This was because, with only a foot or so to spare, it whizzed past the enquiring, worried face of our ponderous neighbour, Mr Shore. At just that moment he had decided to pop his kindly, Mr Toad-like head over the top of the garden hedge to see what on earth was going on. Mr Shore was a naturally cautious man who liked to do take things at a steady pace, following proper procedures. On this occasion, though, the usual stolid calmness was jettisoned. With a whinny of terror Mr Shore scuttled backwards to the safety of his back door. Mum and Dad looked at each other, concerned but unable to stop chuckling behind the backs of their hands. A rather guilty outbreak of laughter about this incident was to be enjoyed for years to come in Sunnyside.

Within a few minutes the entire box had gone up, leaving only vivid red, green and bright tracks on the backs of our retinas. The fizzing and hissing of the fireworks stopped. Just a few spent cardboard pyramids and cones continued to flicker with ordinary flames.

The stars and the moon switched on their lights again, and gradually the bonfire subsided to a red glow. Some black toffee was suddenly put into my hand — a

206

dark, burnt taste with an edge of vinegar — and I breathed in the pungent smell of spent gunpowder and wood smoke.

I was not to know that this was to be almost the last of those Bonfire Nights at Sunnyside. Fred and Henry were already teenagers and would find other things to do on 5 November. I'd have to find someone else's bonfire and fireworks to watch, usually at Lloyd Passey's house, but it was never quite the same as the night all the Sunnyside fireworks went off at once.

Luckily, though, any glimpses of that future would have been completely incomprehensible to the 7-year-old me, standing there sucking shiny black toffee by the dying embers of a 1955 bonfire. A chilly breeze from the inky black field beyond the garden blew across our faces. The November night began to envelop me in dark folds.

"C'mon in now!" I heard Mum's voice and turned reluctantly from the glowing ashes to see her silhouetted in the yellow light of kitchen doorway. "Come on in, Kenneth, or you'll catch your death. It's winter now!"

CHAPTER
SEVEN

Getting Around

FLYING THROUGH THE AIR

My first experience of flight was on — or should I say *over?* — the handlebars of a bicycle. I was 12. It happened on a dark winter's night just after the 1950s had finished. I was cycling home in a snowstorm. It was a Saturday, early evening, and I was going to be late home for tea. When I'd left a friend's house in Nantwich, 8 miles away, it had been cold and, windy, but dry. Then, about 5 miles from home, the first flakes wetted my eyelashes. The snow came thick and fast, soon covering the country lane with a white carpet that sighed under the bike's wheels. There was no other traffic — I was coming home on the back lanes — and looking behind, I saw that my track was the only one on the lonely road.

It was hard going but I was determined to get home as quickly as I could, before the snow got too deep to cycle through. I was riding Fred's bike, a blue Raleigh with drop-handlebars and four-speed Sturmey-Archer gears. As I pushed hard on the pedals to gain speed on the last mile into Bunbury village the snow came down even faster, millions of cold white feathers racing

208

horizontally out of the black night. The bike's dynamo lamp, fastened low on the right-wheel fork, was rather feeble at the best of times, emitting a soft yellow glow. But now even those mellow rays were obscured by thick snow accumulating on the lamp's glass.

There were no streetlights in Bunbury then. Still, I could see where I was going — just. The road was a broad, blue-white band in front of me. To my left, as I whizzed down the steep dip into Lower Bunbury, was the pool of light and the comforting smell of Saturday fish and chips from Ravenscroft's — the only sign of life in the snow-hushed village. Secure in the knowledge I was nearly home, I blinked the relentless flakes out of my eyes and pushed hard to get the extra momentum downhill towards the brook. I would need as much speed as possible to make the final climb up to Bunbury Heath, and Sunnyside at the top.

And then, without any effort or inconvenient pain being involved, I found that I was airborne. The haunting words of *The Snowman* theme, "I'm Flying Through the Air", always come back to me when I remember that experience. I was like the boy in the cartoon just after he takes off, holding hands with the Snowman himself. Momentarily I was hanging, at one with the snowflakes, as the white landscape whizzed past below.

Somehow I had become disconnected from the bike. But how? I had had a fleeting impression of glissading up a broad, light-blue slope. It had launched me at a 45-degree angle into the night sky like a light aircraft. That slope had been wonderfully well designed —

209

smooth and rubbery on the surface, to minimise friction, and yet sufficiently soft and yielding to absorb the shock when I connected with it at the bottom and glissaded up and away at the top.

Fortunately the landing was almost painless, too. Arms outstretched, I did a banking turn and glided down at a low angle on to the road. The surface was softened by snow, and, as I taxied gently along the road surface I could observe the blue-grey stones in the tarmac passing by until my head hit the kerb with a slight, reassuring bump.

Looking back, bewildered, I tried to piece together what had happened. The snow was still coming down thick and fast, making it hard to see. I stumbled back to where I thought the bike was, only to find a large moaning mound in the middle of the road. "Ooo-ooh," said the mound, which now lifted a face with its eyebrows, nose and mouth covered in snow, as if it were a clown and someone had squirted it with shaving foam. "Ooo-oh, I'm ever so sorry, Kenneth, I shouldn't have been walking in the middle of the road."

Well I never — I'd cycled into Akela's backside! The smooth, firm, yet somehow yielding launch pad had been Akela's broad back, upholstered in a light blue mackintosh. Without realising, I had cycled the bike's front wheel straight between Akela's ample buttocks. That was why I had no recollection of colliding with anything terribly resistant.

Heaven knows what emotional or psychological damage Akela sustained as a result of this incident. However, she seemed to be finding it more embarrassing than physically painful. Her rear defences seemed to have protected her, to some extent, from the sudden intrusion of the bicycle wheel.

And the large consignment of fish and chips she had been carrying home for the family considerably softened the impact as she fell face down on them. In fact, the fish and chips were the only serious casualties. The whole package had been squashed flat by Akela's substantial chest.

Nevertheless, showing an extremely generous spirit, she invited me into her house to recover with a hot cup of tea. She clearly thought that she had been in the wrong, walking along in the middle of the road in a snowstorm camouflaged by a light-blue, snow-covered coat. Perhaps she had a point. I wasn't going to relieve her of that feeling of guilt, I decided. However, I did feel as though I had been at least partially to blame. Her children seemed to think so, too. They glowered at me, munching extremely thin pieces of battered cod that looked like small, ironed orange shirts.

BIKES

Akela hadn't expected a young lad suddenly to toboggan up her back, but getting run over by a bike wasn't unknown. It had nearly happened to me once. It was an early evening in winter, and pitch-black outside. Suddenly, halfway across the road, I was surrounded by looming "sit up and beg" bicycles, the screech of ancient brakes, lights from bike lamps, and farm workers shouting "Whoa! Hey!" They were scolding and concerned rather than angry, and they managed both to miss me and to avoid falling off, but it was a near thing.

Bikes were everywhere then. Although it was the age of public transport, in a rural area like Bunbury you often had to use a bike to get to a railway station or to a bus route. Also, although rural bus services were better then than they are now, and there was a railway station at Beeston Castle, a mile or so away, public transport could be patchy and infrequent. So kids like me would think nothing of cycling the 8 miles to Nantwich to see a friend, or riding the few miles to the main road at Highwayside, where we could catch the hourly bus to Chester.

Bikes were a near-universal form of transport. To appreciate this, the best comparison would be with China or South-east Asian countries in more recent times, where rural roads always have a few peasants cycling by. Bunbury had a low-density population, so the roads weren't exactly thronged with cyclists, or with anything much (unless you happened to come across a herd of cows being driven to milking).

But perhaps the number of cyclists was particularly high in the area because getting around on a bike was easy. Much of Cheshire, and certainly the area around Bunbury, is fairly flat. If you didn't venture into the Peak District to the east, or into the mountains of North Wales to the west, it was surprising how far you could pedal on a bike without really noticing the effort. For instance Fred and Henry, when they were young teenagers, once cycled to Rhyl — over 40 miles away on the North Wales coast — in about two and a half hours. They left early one summer's morning, expecting the journey to take until well after midday, but arrived at 9 a.m. to find a yawning Auntie Lu at home, just getting up.

Almost everyone you knew appeared on a bike at some time or another. There were stately old ladies ticking slowly along on bicycles with extra cushioning on the saddles, and flowery plastic covers over the back wheels to prevent their coats from getting tangled in the spokes. There were farm workers, men in long dirty greatcoats, riding old black "sit up and beg" bikes, with small metal containers dangling from their handlebars, creaking steadily past like galleons of the road.

And there's Roger Ryder, the small boy from Ryders' farm just up the road, whizzing past on a small bike with a basket in the front. The wiry face of a small Yorkshire terrier peeks out of the basket, while on Roger's shoulder is his tame magpie. And along the main road comes a group of young people in shorts, on drop-handlebar bikes from a riding club in Crewe, Chester or even Manchester. They puff and strain, taking the occasional sip from a bottle as they scan the horizon for landmarks like Beeston Castle.

BUSES

Whenever I see a country bus today it always seems to have just one or two passengers on it. I don't know why, but I *always* seem to see the same two fat teenage girls sitting at the very back of the bus, whether it's a bus in rural Wales, Yorkshire or the south of England. They're always giggling and doing disgusting things with long fronds of pink gum. And once today's bus has gone by that's it for public transport until the next third Tuesday in the month (excepting Tuesdays following a Bank Holiday).

All this creates a feeling of despondency in me, perhaps because I'm as addicted to using the car as anyone else is. I have no moral right to criticise the grudging, limited notion of public transport in the countryside today. Rural bus services now are a reminder of the decline of villages as living communities where, before car ownership became so widespread, a lot of people caught buses to local market towns or just to the next village.

In the 1950s Crosville Buses ran the rural services around south Cheshire and the surrounding areas as well. They were green buses, mostly single-deckers with rattling engines under large front bonnets. If you could get to the main road between Nantwich and Crewe, to the east of Bunbury, you could catch the lumbering, double-decker C84 that went to Chester in one direction and in the other to Nantwich, Crewe and eventually to Newcastle-under-Lyme. At Newcastle the Crosville empire gave way to Potteries Motor Transport, a name for a firm that had obviously been coined before anyone had heard of the other kind of PMT.

214

People could smoke on buses then, though on the single-deckers the smokers tended to gravitate towards the back of the bus. On the back of the next seat in front of you there was always a small ashtray made of metal with criss-cross ridges on it, which you could pull out from a vertical position. It was usually stuffed with old bus tickets and chewing gum-wrappers, as well as dog ends.

Bus journeys in the 1950s seemed to involve a lot of human contact and talking, whether you wanted it or not. As a child travelling with grown-ups on the bus to Nantwich or Tarporley, I heard a lot of greetings and explanations.

"Hello, Mrs Cowap."

"Morning, Mrs Cheers."

"I'm going to get something for these bunions. They're killing me. Our Brenda's getting married next month and I've got to get into those new shoes."

"That girl in Boots is very good."

"I know, that's where I'm off to."

Village people on the bus seemed to feel as if they had to admit straightaway why they were going to town. It was much better to confess immediately than to be quizzed by someone. This sometimes led people into talking about quite intimate or personal things, and if you were lucky you could tune into these conversations.

One Saturday afternoon, when I was 9 or so, I was on the bus home from Nantwich when I began to overhear a mystifying conversation between two middle-aged women sitting behind me.

"They soon learn, don't they?"

215

"Yes, they soon become *aware*, you know?"

"Mmm. Our Janice was asking for a bra only last week."

"Never!"

"Oh yes. She won't have a liberty bodice now."

"I don't know how they pick it all up so quick."

"I know, finding out that they're a girl. Our Christine was just the same."

This was totally mystifying to me. Bras and liberty bodices sounded faintly worrying. But I couldn't work out the connection between these exotic items of clothing and the startling fact that many girls apparently did not *realise* they were girls. But they seemed to stumble upon the discovery, by accident, sooner or later.

This is the problem with conversations overheard in buses — they are often left dangling, and you don't always hear a satisfactory resolution of the story. However, in the 1950s — and in most places for a couple of decades after that — there was a third party on the bus who could occasionally help to tie up the loose ends of a conversation, much to the relief of eavesdroppers. This third party was the bus conductor. Depending on how busy they were, or how nosy, they could sometimes conveniently interrupt with a probing question, or remind two discussants of the need to get back to the main point.

Sometimes, the more bold or cheeky bus conductor would proffer a comment. Once, I overheard two mature women passengers complaining to each other in reserved and polite voices about the shortcomings of a local painter and decorator. "Yeah, but he *is* a twat," commented the conductor, as he calculated their fares, and briskly turned the handle of his ticket machine in front of the open-mouthed ladies.

The ways in which bus conductors interacted with passengers very much depended on which type they were, and as far as I could see from our local bus services there were only two categories. Both types were men. I never saw any women bus conductors in the 1950s, except on rare bus rides in big cities such as Liverpool.

Firstly there was the "rock 'n' roll" category. They could be any age between 17 and 50, and were distinguished mainly by having greased, slicked-back hair, impressive sideburns and insolent, challenging grins. Their basic function was to add noise to the journey and to make it as much like a fairground ride as possible. They would do this by breaking into song at any moment, and at any position in the bus: "Lallipap, lallipap, ooh lalli-lalli-pap . . . LALLIPAP! Oooh!"

They also brought verve and excitement to the journey by dangling out of the front door of the single-decker bus, hanging monkey-like by one arm on a rail, to shout friendly insults to mates or to wolf-whistle at young women. They could also add drama by appearing to forget to board the bus at the start of a journey. They could then sprint alongside and leap aboard when the bus reached about 15mph. This manoeuvre, the "driver playing a trick on the conductor" game, usually led later in the journey to the well-known reverse trick, "the conductor playing a trick on the driver". The rock 'n' roll conductor would do this by ringing the bell inappropriately, many times, sometimes while singing, "We're gonna rock aroun' the clock ternight, we're gonna rock [bell dings] rock [ding] rock [ding] till broad daylight" [ding, ding, ding].

On some single-decker buses, the driver sat in a closed-off cab, which cut down on these types of exchange and banter between himself and the conductor. But on the buses in which the driver sat in an open area at the front a free-flowing conversation between the two could take place. This was especially the case when a rock 'n' roll conductor was paired with a rock 'n' roll driver. On these occasions there would be a lot of guffawing, showing off, revving of the bus engine and dangerous sudden braking.

No doubt the bus station supervisors did all they could to prevent this kind of pairing, but on some occasions there must have been no alternative. The problem, when this happened, was that the driver and conductor were far more engrossed with shouting at each other, and jeering at pedestrians or other vehicles, than they were with road safety, or with when passengers wanted to get on or off.

Sometimes this was to your benefit, though. I remember one rock 'n' roll conductor who developed a healthy disdain for the whole concept of fares. From kids he would take the (correct) money, flamboyantly turn the handle of the ticket machine, drop a few coins

218

into his leather pouch, but then give you back most of your money with a ticket and a large wink.

However, rock 'n' roll conductors were much less concerned with talking to passengers than they were with singing, combing their hair or talking to the driver. This cannot be said of the second category of conductor, the "pipe and slippers" variety.

It was not as though they actually wore slippers or smoked pipes. They put on the same grey or beige jackets that other Crosville Bus employees wore. But they acted as if they'd decided to come downstairs in their dressing gowns to have a nice little chat with you before bedtime.

Unlike the rock 'n' roll conductors, the grey-haired, pink-cheeked pipe-and-slippers men were kindly and solicitous to a fault. Whether talking to a young boy like me, an elderly gruff farm worker or a teenage girl, there would be the same polite enquiries as to fare, reasons for travel, likely time of return, mother's maiden name and so on.

And this was the drawback with these conductors. They were unobtrusive and so easy to talk to, but before you knew where you were you'd been drawn into divulging almost every bit of personal information there was to know. Even worse, this type of conductor's self-appointed role as conductor of conversations would sometimes prompt him into throwing open a customer's information or difficulty to the floor, a sort of prototype for daytime TV chat shows.

"Guess what, this lass here's expecting a happy event — her first baby!"

From surrounding passengers: "Congratulations, love." "Good gracious!" "Ah dunna believe it." "I didn't know that Jacqueline were married yet."

"I'm not!" Young, blushing female passenger bursts into tears.

The oddest thing about the pipe-and-slipper conductors was that they all appeared to be about 60, whereas the rock 'n' roll category had an age range. I sometimes wondered whether the rock 'n' rollers suddenly mutated into pipe-and-slippers. Perhaps they went up to the mirror one morning to apply the Brylcreem, only to find — as in a horror movie — that their sideburns and Marlon Brando toughness had suddenly been replaced by an amiable round face, an unobtrusive little grey moustache and a balding head.

But no, I don't think so. They were separate species, and remain so today in quite different occupations such as attendants at leisure parks (the rock 'n' rollers) or ageing weather forecasters (the pipe-and-slipper men).

When I eventually left Bunbury at the age of 18 I was away for a year in West Africa and then came back to the village by the back roads bus from Nantwich. It was early Saturday afternoon on a cloudy summer's day in 1967, and nothing much seemed to have changed on that rattling country bus. I was excited to be coming home after a whole year away!

It was all reassuringly familiar, and yet I was able to see the fields and the people through the bus window with different eyes, having been away for so long. As the bus stopped every half-mile or so I watched the passengers get off — mostly stout women with stolid faces, dressed in floral-print cotton dresses and carrying heavy shopping bags. I began to see that this could be a typical rural bus journey anywhere between the green plains of Ireland to the west and the green plains of Poland to the east.

In fact, some of those solid, thick-armed Cheshire women with their head-scarves looked decidedly East European as they stepped off the bus and looked placidly towards their houses down little lanes. They were going home to cook sausages, with loud TV football commentary coming from the living room where their husbands would be drinking beer and watching the match — a sleepy Saturday scene happening here, or in Portugal, Italy or Ukraine.

Suddenly I realised that the bus was taking me to a different place. It was still going to Bunbury, this was still south-west Cheshire and I was still going home, but because I'd been away I was seeing it with different eyes. It had become a different, more exotic place.

TRAINS

I get the same feeling, looking back at local journeys as a child in the 1950s, when I remember travelling on trains. Probably this has a lot to do with the fact that every rail journey involved steam trains.

I always felt a tingle of excitement at the age of 7 or 8 years old, waiting on the platform at Beeston Castle station for the train to Chester. When I was impatient Mum would reassure me by saying, "Yes, of course it'll come. Look out for the white smoke at the bend in the track."

That single white plume in the distance called to mind people living far away, in remote areas like the steppes of Russia. They too would have longed to see the white plume that would spell escape, the sight of birch trees in spring rushing past the carriage windows, the intoxicating prospect of going to Moscow or St Petersburg.

I didn't realise then, as a small boy, how lucky I was to be living in the last decade of steam trains, which established a link between us and nineteenth-century iron, power and steam. When the huge black locomotive pulled into Beeston Castle station, it darkened the sky for me. The platform trembled as it passed, its solid flagstones turning for a second into shaky jelly. I loved to stand near the platform edge to be enveloped in the huge clouds of steam and sulphur smell as the engine thundered by, with Mum shouting at me to stand further back and to come here.

Sometimes we'd nearly miss the train (I can't remember ever actually missing it). But if you could get to the top of the stone steps, panting, and be in sight of the guard standing anxiously on the platform, he'd blow a whistle but keep his green flag down, waiting for you to scramble through a carriage door.

Once inside, the train always seemed incredibly quiet after the noise of the platform, almost like walking into the tranquillity of a church. The corridor of the carriage smelled faintly of polished wood, of a tang of disinfectant and coal smoke. In the background you could hear a distant chuff-chuff-chuff as the train began to move and pick up speed, and glimpse a lot of white smoke and vapour scurrying past the windows.

Then you'd walk down the corridor to find a compartment that was empty, or at least a compartment without too many weird-looking people in it. It was a bit like walking past a line of aquariums at the zoo. You'd look through the glass to decide. This aquarium's nearly empty . . . but no, there's a conger eel lurking in the darkness there. Reject the next one, it's got three grouper fish in it with grotesque teeth. Here's one — just a normal-looking middle aged trout, knitting, and a small pilchard — that'll be OK.

It would still be quiet inside the compartment, unless two or more passengers (or one mad person) were already engaged in a conversation. Apart from those discreetly murmured words, and the odd cough, the only other detectable sounds would be from the under-seat heating, which would sometimes make metallic crinkling noises, and perhaps a repressed giggle or two from a child such as me.

Train travel is much noisier today than it was then — particularly on today's rattletrap "Cross Country" services — and people seemed to talk to each other more on trains in the 1950s than they do now. The amount of talk seemed to be less than on the buses, and it always took a cough or two and an awkward smile for people to be able to break the silence. But once it began conversation seemed to flow better in 1950s train compartments than it does in the open layout of train coaches today. Oddly, compartments make people

223

friendlier. Also, if you didn't like the look of a particular fellow-passenger, you could always pretend to be getting out at the next station and go to sit in another compartment.

The short train ride from Beeston to Chester involved a gentle glide through the green, park-like Cheshire countryside with two stops at quiet rural stations, Tattenhall and Waverton. As the train approached Chester station it passed through a marshalling yard, and this was always fascinating to me. I'd often stand at the compartment window at this point to get a good view of the acres of criss-crossing railway tracks, the signals and signal boxes.

From a small boy's perspective it looked like another world, though the vast marshalling yards outside Crewe station were even more impressive. Lone black locomotives and smaller tank engines stood here and there. Some had white smoke and steam pouring out them and a driver leaning out of the cab, ready to go. Others looked as if they'd been left alone for too long, and had just a few wisps of steam escaping from around their wheels, while others had been abandoned altogether — they were rusty and steamless, and stood in sidings with weeds growing around their wheels. I used to wonder when the latter ones would be woken up, perhaps for a last run to Wales or across the Pennines.

As the train rumbled into Chester station we could troop into the corridor and wait for someone to open the door. This meant releasing a vertical leather belt just below the window. It was held in place with a brass spike that fitted into a hole in the belt. As the belt was released from the spike it disappeared downwards inside the door like a tongue, and this allowed the heavy window frame to come down. Then the passenger could reach through the open window space to find the door handle on the other side and open the door just as the carriage was trundling to a halt.

Before we left the station, if there was time, I'd ask to go for another look at the engine at the front. I'd run forward and then stand for a moment, gazing into a secret world of the foot-plate with its dials, handles and shiny little control wheels. Sometimes the door of the firebox would be open, and you could see the glowing orange redness inside. Sometimes the fireman would be standing on the foot-plate, sometimes on the very top of the tender, a Satanic figure without a shirt, completely covered in black coal-dust, his reddened eyes smiling down at me.

The magic of train travel didn't stop there because there were often strange sights in the station itself. As you walked along the grey-flagged platform there might be some large cane baskets to look at, with destinations written crudely on labels that were attached to them: Sheffield, Uttoxeter, Cheltenham. If your mother didn't pull you too abruptly by the arm you could stoop down to look at the shadowy figures inside — gently cooing racing pigeons.

There were other animals to observe as well. These were the days when livestock was still transported on a large scale by rail, and occasionally there would be a silent line of cattle trucks by a platform inside the

225

station. The animals would be unexpectedly quiet (perhaps they'd given up protesting and become fatalistic). If you put your ear to a slat in the side of one of the trucks you could hear calves inside, rustling in their straw.

CARS

I hadn't appreciated that cars were far more than just a means of getting around until one sunny day when Dad drove home a large, ultra-modern sky-blue saloon. It belonged to a customer, and he'd been working on it. The beautiful car with its chrome grin and superb futuristic fins stood outside our little red brick house, a gleaming shark from some faraway, tropical ocean.

Lloyd Passey noticed it. The next day it was all over the classroom (not very difficult, with only six or seven children in it) that my dad had bought a new car. I couldn't believe the amount of admiration that was in the other boys' eyes and voices. Evidently a big flashy car could give instant status even though it might not be warranted. No, I had to inform them regretfully at break-time, our old car was still with us — the dull black 1939 Austin 8 that Dad had bought years before I'd been born.

On the other hand, having *any* car in the 1950s household was still unusual. Lots of families didn't have one, but for most people that didn't matter too much because there was public transport to get around on.

226

Personally, I always felt jealous of kids whose families had a motorbike with sidecar. Firstly, I liked the idea of having parents who were young enough to ride a motorbike, and secondly, I particularly wanted to be a Spitfire pilot sitting in the front of the sidecar's cockpit.

Our old car was the ultimate in being unglamorous, though I wasn't aware of this at all until the comparison with the new car with fins was made. Dad's Austin had worn, torn leather seats that had aged to a very dull brown-red, and a whiff of neat petrol when you clambered inside. The controls were spartan and rudimentary, and one dial, "Oil Pressure", had a needle that was permanently unemployed. The whole thing creaked, groaned and squeaked as it rolled along. Riding in it felt as I imagined Thor Heyerdahl's balsa wood raft would be — a sense of something that was about to fall apart, but also of an underlying organic resilience and flexibility. Moss and the occasional miniature fern grew in the front footwell. The running boards sagged. Spiders (whom Dad treated affectionately, as long-term friends) took up summer residence in various parts of the car, where they would spin ambitious webs across the interior and out to an external mirror.

The old Austin, with its dowdy black exterior and its small, old-fashioned windows, might have been unglamorous, but riding in it could be interesting, even mildly exciting, at times. This was for two reasons.

Firstly, there was always that "centre might not hold" feeling. Gripping the front passenger door handle tightly in your hand, to stop the door flying open suddenly, heightened this sense. And when Dad decided to take us for a Sunday walk on the Bickerton Hills, a few miles away, there was always that anxious moment when it seemed as though the bronchial old Austin wouldn't make it up the steep one-in-ten slope near the top.

Secondly, dramatic tension entered most journeys because Dad liked to smoke his pipe while driving, and this meant not only lighting it and puffing away as he drove along, but also concentrating on loading it with tobacco. To be fair, he never tried to do this while carrying out complicated manoeuvres. He'd wait for a straight bit of road, then steady the wheel with his knees and put the car into neutral so that it could taxi along at a gently declining speed. Then he could reach with one hand into his jacket pocket for the pipe, and with the other hand bring out the small round green-lidded tin of "Whiskey Flake".

It was all finely judged. With occasional narrow-eyed glances in the rear-view mirror, Dad would methodically tamp down the tobacco with the butt end of a penknife, replacing the tin lid carefully before putting the pipe to his mouth and reaching into his pocket again for a box of Swan Vestas. By now the approaching hairpin bend or hump-backed bridge would be getting dangerously close. Calmly observing the Centurion tank about to lunge on to the road from his left, or the hundreds of wildebeest thundering towards us from the opposite direction, he'd nonchalantly strike a match. Then there was a brief moment of pleasure to inhale the smoke.

228

After that, there would be several swift impresario-like movements just as the Austin was about to hit the bend. A lightning twist of the right hand to wind down the window would be followed by a sudden jerk as the smoking match was passed from left to right hand and thrown out. This happened so quickly that it was a blur of movement. His left hand shot back from match relay to gear-stick to throw the car into gear, while his right resumed control of the steering wheel and his knees disengaged. Thus was the magical change effected — nonchalant pipe-smoker to responsible driver — in about two seconds.

Dad's knee-steering manoeuvre added a dash of dramatic tension to journeys in those days, but it didn't seem particularly dangerous. On the quiet country lanes of the 1950s, the same confidence that led Akela to walk along in the middle of the road on a dark, snowy winter's night allowed Dad to fiddle with his pipe while driving, without a second thought. No other vehicles would be coming, or if they were there would probably be plenty of warning. So light was the traffic on the back lanes in those days that it was quite an event to see another car or a truck hove into view, as if it were another sailing ship on the horizon.

It's made me wonder, since then, what on earth other drivers in the 1950s got up to while trundling along in their slow vehicles? Was Dad's elaborate pipe-loading the rule rather than the exception? Were other drivers sneaking a quick glance through the morning paper, perhaps, or catching up on a bit of knitting or re-mounting stamps in their albums?

Just as train travel in the 1950s represented a bridge back to a misty world of steam and clanking engines, so did many of the cars in the 1950s provide a historical link back to a pre-war world of motoring. Of course, an increasing number of cars in my boyhood were new. But even the newer ones (in the early 1950s at least) had the same straight up-and-down lines and the same limited range of colours (black, grey, dark green) as the pre-war ones. Their engines often sounded like exaggerated petrol lawnmowers, and they were prone to sudden mechanical failures, with dramatic escapes of steam, oil or blue smoke.

These were the cars that, like cavalry in the First World War, were going to perish in their hundreds, if not their thousands, on the first motorways of Britain in the early 1960s. Many were under-powered and had engines that weren't used to getting all that hot. These were old cars accustomed to their drivers stopping for a cup of tea every half-hour. They simply hadn't the stamina to cover mile after mile at over 60mph. Faced with this unexpected challenge they restored to blowing up or catching fire.

But all this was still a world away from Bunbury in the 1950s. The very idea of a motorway would probably have been completely unimaginable to my maternal grandfather, Mr White, the man who had established the Swan Garage in Tarporley. However, he had been one of the pioneers of early motor vehicles. In the early 1900s, before settling in Cheshire, he had lived in Coventry and Birmingham, working with others in the first engineering workshops to push ahead the

230

development of the motor car. At home there was a large sepia photograph of him sitting at the helm of an early Daimler. My grandfather, someone I had never known, looked down at me with his impassive face every time I climbed the stairs (the large brown photograph was mounted on the wall facing the landing), his hand forever resting on the tiller at the front of his small horseless carriage.

Both Henry and Fred seemed to have been inspired by this family history of engagement with the early combustion engine. They set about acquiring ancient, pram-like vehicles as soon as they were able to do so. For instance, while he was a student, Fred bought for £5 an old 1930s Morris, a small bathtub on wheels, and drove it as far as Scotland on a youth hostel holiday.

Henry experimented with larger vehicles, including a Humber Snipe and a heavy 2.5 litre Jaguar. But perhaps the most memorable was another small car, a 1935 Morris 8, which had a canvas top and spotlights. This little Morris had a jaunty look, in an old-fashioned way, with its small windscreen and its running boards. Like a little street urchin, it communicated a kind of skeletal cheeriness. When the formidable Aunt Annie was confronted with a 30-mile journey in it, she boomed, disbelieving, at Henry with her strong Lancashire voice: "Does that vee-hicle possess brakes, young man?"

It certainly did have effective brakes, as the young Henry found one wet afternoon in Chester's rush hour. Skidding to a sudden halt at a red light, he became aware of a considerable weight pressing down on his head. It was so heavy that his head was forced down in a hangdog position over the steering wheel as the canvas roof bulged downwards. Alarmed, and despite the change of the lights from red to green and the tooting of other cars behind him, Henry pulled his head from beneath the bulge and got out of the car. There, on the roof, was a winded cyclist, gasping for breath like a stranded fish. In the road behind the car's rear bumper lay the man's bicycle, its front wheel bent into a near-rectangle. The little Morris's brakes had been so sharp, and the car had stopped so abruptly, that the unfortunate man had ridden straight into the car's rear and had catapulted himself on to the soft roof.

Much to Henry's disgust, Dad took to "borrowing" the Morris and gradually took it over for daily commuting to the garage in Delamere. Long before, our old family car, the Austin, had developed terminal tuberculosis of the radiator. Dad let it be known that he simply had to have a car of some sort to get to work and Henry reluctantly agreed to lend it to him.

Unfortunately, Dad didn't look after Henry's Morris very well. It soon developed all kinds of faults and began to disintegrate. When nothing more could be done for it, even by Dad — a past master of bodging and making do without any spare parts that were actually new — he proposed to take the poor old car to a scrapyard a few miles away.

Henry wasn't altogether surprised to be asked by Dad for the money to cover the cost of the petrol to get the Morris to the scrapyard. Sadly, it was true to form.

232

But Henry was aghast when, after neatly pocketing the few shillings' petrol money, Dad said that he'd rescued the spotlights from the car.

"No point in them going to waste," he suggested. "I don't suppose you'll be wanting them, will you?"

The bitterness between Henry and Dad over that car went over my head, as a young boy at the time. But in the late 1950s I had begun to notice some larger-scale changes. The rather down-at-heel, tawdry world of limping second-hand cars and arguments over old spotlights was beginning to give way to a more colourful world of mass car ownership.

It struck me forcefully one Monday morning, when I asked Clive Bevan what he'd been doing the previous weekend. "Oh, me and my Dad went to sit on the bridge to watch all the cars on Saturday," he said.

The main road, the A49, was at the top end of our lane, and it also passed through Beeston, where Clive lived. And yes, without me consciously realising it up to that point, it had suddenly become difficult to cross at certain times — always on holiday weekends, but often during ordinary weekdays, too.

The A49 links the industrial north-west, including towns such as Warrington, with the West Midlands. Before the building of motorways, it provided one of the main routes between these busy areas. In fact, about half of the traffic that would eventually use the M6 was throbbing in slow procession along the main road a quarter of a mile from Sunnyside.

On a Bank Holiday evening the traffic on that road reached levels of congestion that were unprecedented, and which soon became a talking point in the village. In the glint of the setting sun, a great long ribbon of cars, vans and trucks laced up and down the gentle hills leading towards Beeston and Tarporley in one direction, and south towards Shropshire in the other.

The cars were no longer just black, grey or dark green. They were all shapes and sizes, old and new, but now included cars that were pink, sky blue and navy blue, white, turquoise and red. Some had fins and new-style indicators that could flash on and off, a miracle of modern electronics. And inside each car were hot, tired-looking families with bored or frustrated faces, willing their cars forward as they edged along in single file to the next junction. We sat on the grassy bank above the main road to watch, pity and satisfy our curiosity.

The drivers of all those cars represented a growing population that liked to discuss the pros and cons of taking different routes. In the 1950s slowly deliberating over the route one had chosen was a nationwide obsession, especially among serious-faced uncles and fathers.

One of these men was Uncle Arnold, who was married to Auntie Irene, Dad's cousin. They had two attractive daughters, Kath and Margaret (Maggie). This was the Ainley family who took the main responsibility for looking after Aunt Annie, and when they moved to a town called Stone, in Staffordshire, in the late 1950s, we began to see more of them, particularly on Sundays when we were invited over for delicious afternoon teas.

Uncle Arnold had a craggy, granite-like but kindly face, and was clearly one of those 1950s fathers and husbands who had been much affected by military training. He brought that sense of careful military strategy to motoring, and particularly to the idea of the dawn getaway for the summer holiday. The girls would be woken at 4a.m., just as dawn was breaking, and led sleepily into the car where they could continue to slumber on the back seat. Then, at about 8a.m. in the morning, they would wake to a calm, sunny morning and find that their father had stopped the car in a grassy picnic spot. He would be enjoying a wet shave in front of a camping mirror, while Irene would be preparing their hot breakfasts on a primus stove.

I used to listen to Dad discussing all these motoring manoeuvres with Uncle Arnold. The relative merits of staying on the A51 versus risking a detour along the B5769, bearing in mind the roadworks on each route and the frequency of the lights changing near a roundabout opposite the Nag's Head near Spongleton, were discussed at length. There was always a lot of sucking of pipes and shaking of heads.

The object of the game was to engage in gentle rivalry. It was important for the host to demonstrate to the visitor that the route he *should* have taken (if he were you) would have resulted in a far less arduous, quicker journey. The visiting driver, on the other hand, could win by showing that the route taken was infinitely preferable to any alternative, and that he and his family would still be on the road if they had been foolhardy enough to take any of those. Usually the result of Dad's and Arnold's route discussions was a draw, reluctantly conceded by each contestant.

But, with a twinkle in the eye and a twirling of his pipe, Arnold would narrowly win at the very last moment by getting in one last piece of advice just as we were leaving. This was the Uncle Arnold Gambit. To be unable to counter the last move meant that you'd lost the game. And Dad would have no opportunity to reply. First gear would have been engaged, the car would be moving off, and it would have looked too silly to stop simply to correct Arnold's last ploy. Uncle Arnold had worked all this out.

"Don't forgot, Dad," he'd shout after us, with a suppressed chuckle. "Try the B5769. It'll cut out that queue near the Throngley roundabout." As our old car pulled away, Dad would be snarling and muttering under his breath.

A FOG THAT TURNED SOLID

In the late 1950s the main roads that touched the edges of Bunbury got a lot busier than they had been, but the country lanes stayed much the same. The collision I'd had with Akela illustrated this. Akela had confidently decided to walk in the middle of the road on a dark night in a blizzard because she wasn't *expecting* any cars to come by in the few minutes she had to walk home from the chip shop. Later on, when I was a young teenager in the early 1960s, cars began to speed up and to get quieter, and you had to take a little more care.

However, in a dense fog when visibility is reduced almost to nil, it's fairly safe to assume that any cars on a back country lane at night will have been forced to crawl along at a very slow speed. I made this assumption one warm October night, after an evening of experimental drinking of a large quantity of homemade nettle beer. I had been doing this with Pete Walley (Wol), who lived in a hamlet called Acton, near Nantwich.

As I set off giddily on my bike from Wol's house it was a clear, starry night. An enormous yellow harvest moon hung in the sky just above the large oak trees on either side of the main road. I weaved my way unsteadily across that road into the narrow lane that led in 4 miles to Haughton, and in 2 more miles to Bunbury.

As soon as I freewheeled into a little valley, though, a mist descended. It began to thicken. This is where I made the assumption that no cars would come hurtling out of the fog.

It was a safe assumption, as it turned out. I began to sing and, for some reason, to shout, "Ho-ho-ho-ho-oh!" as I cycled rapidly right across the road from left to right and back again, gambling with the danger of tumbling into the ditch by riding on to the uneven grassy roadsides.

By now the fog had become so thick that it was impossible to make out any features ahead of me, by the sides of the road, or behind me. Visibility was down to about a yard. I was enveloped in a dense white eiderdown of fog. Hedges, trees, stars and sky had all gone.

I began to feel very disoriented, but not at all concerned. This was liberating. Feeling happily in limbo, I slowed the bike down to a wobbling walking pace, holding an outstretched arm in front of me in case I might collide with another Akela or some other unsuspecting pedestrian in the dense white fog.

And then, just a mile or so after I'd turned off the main road into this narrow lane, the fog turned solid. It had already acquired a peculiarly dense feel, as if I was cycling through mashed potato. But now there was no mistake — I could go no further. I got off the bike and put it to one side. Kneeling down on the road surface, I pressed the warm, milky fog in front of me and yes, my hands met with solidity from right to left. I moved a few paces to the right and pressed the fog again with both hands. It was still as solid and dense as a wall, but warm and pleasant to touch.

A few seconds later, and further to the right, my fingers came into contact with an ear. It was an incredibly soothing, silken ear. I realised then what had happened, especially as the ear's owner breathed out a hiss of air through its nostrils like a surfacing whale. It was a white cow lying in the road right in front of me. I peered through the mist beyond, and could vaguely make out other bovine humps and mounds. A whole detachment of cows must have discovered a hole in a hedge or fence somewhere. On a cool autumn night, following a sunny day, the road had retained warmth

238

that the cows had noticed and decided to take advantage of.

Laughing to myself, I moved from cow to cow, whispering gently into each silken ear, asking them to get up in case a car came. Incredibly, they understood. They didn't need to be shouted at or kicked. Philosophically, they rose to their feet, chewing the cud and breathing heavily, like dinner guests who have sat too long at the table before lumbering across to an armchair for a coffee. I opened a gate to a nearby field and ushered them through, smiling at each one's face as they passed.

It took me a few minutes to find my bike, which wasn't in the middle of the road where I thought I'd left it, but lying on its side on a right-hand verge. I almost gave up looking for it in the all-enveloping mist.

The nettle beer and the mystical experience with the white cows made me drowsy and gave me an almost irresistible urge to lie down on the road myself. It would have been so good just to stretch out on the warm tarmac where the cows had lain, breathing in the smells of sweet cow manure, bitumen and harvested fields, with the fluffy duvet of fog enveloping me. Nowadays, when I'm driving late at night along some soulless street-lit bypass that could be anywhere, I have to make a strong effort to push this soothing, sleepy memory away from me.

CHAPTER
EIGHT

"Let Your Requests be Known"

A RADIO CHILDHOOD

Radio sounds and radio voices swirled and eddied in my mind from the earliest days of childhood and from the earliest moment of each day. Sometimes, on a winter weekday, I'd wake at some unearthly time before dawn to the chimes of Big Ben.

It would still be dark and I'd be lying in blissful warmth under heavy blankets. Only my nose would be aware of the cold air in the room. I could hear Mum moving about downstairs, the tap being turned suddenly to fill the kettle, the clink of cups and plates. If I opened one eye I'd see the surrounding blackness and a rectangle of yellow light coming through the half-open bedroom door.

"Ding-dang-ding BONG. Dang-ding-dang BONG!" The radio was on in the kitchen. But in that small house the sound easily reached the landing and our bedroom.

There'd be a loud whisper from Mum in the hall, "Go on, then!" followed by the clattering of the dog's feet up the threadbare-carpeted stairs.

240

"BONG . . . BONG . . ." Kim would have been waiting at the bottom of the stairs, his fox-like ears erect and eyes bright, waiting for Big Ben. "BONG . . . BONG . . ." The chimes had become his signal to be ready. He would already have put one short front leg on the bottom step and be looking inquisitively to Mum for confirmation that he could indeed race up the stairs now. "BONG . . . BONG . . ."

He'd bump the door wide open with his sturdy chest and, with an excited bounce, leap on to Henry's bed, his stumpy tail wagging. He'd lick Henry's face in an attempt to convince my reluctant brother that it wasn't such a bad day after all.

Henry hated his job at the switchgear factory in Chester, but the ritual of being woken by the dog every morning softened the blow of emerging into a grey, depressing world. Kim would burrow down the bed to the bottom, curling up at Henry's feet.

I was jealous of the fact that the dog would never do the same thing for me. He could only be cued to run upstairs to Henry by the early-morning chimes of Big Ben. No other stimulus would work. Still, I could enjoy basking for another three-quarters of an hour or so, listening to the luxurious sounds of someone else having to get up.

The radio talked in a kindly, rustic voice, warming the house with explanations of the weather and market reports for farmers. Often, the going rate for a hundredweight of early potatoes or sugar beet would subliminally enter my mind while I'd be lying there half-asleep. Later, I'd go to school trying to brush these mental burrs off the surface of my mind. Once I even wanted to tell an irritable Mr Steventon about the shockingly low price of sheep at the Shrewsbury market the day before. Then I thought better of it. It *would* have looked a bit weird, at the age of 9, to reveal a detailed knowledge of fluctuations in livestock prices.

BBC radio not only started the day and gave me my bearings every morning, it permeated my whole life as a child. This was possible in the 1950s because we didn't live in a multi-media, multi-channel world. On daytime radio there were just three choices, or really two and a half, all of them provided by the BBC: the Home Service, the Light Programme or the (part-time) Third Programme.

There was nothing else. As yet there were no commercial, private or "pirate" radio stations, unless you counted the crackling, intermittent strains of Radio Luxembourg in the evenings. As the radio in Sunnyside was switched on much of the time, and as the BBC had thoughtfully structured the universe for us, it was a fairly simple matter for a child like me to latch on to radio programmes as a way of telling the time.

More than that, some regular programmes came to be associated in my mind with the shifting moods or atmospheres of the house, and with certain foods or odours.

For instance, the harp signature tune for *Mrs Dale's Diary* on a weekday morning meant that it was 11.15a.m. and this programme I somehow associated with milky coffee, sunshine (even if it was raining or cloudy outside), and a lightening mood. The same signature tune in the afternoon, at 4.30p.m., evoked the glow of the coal fire and the smell of warm scones.

Music While You Work, a programme of band music delivered at a military tempo, meant that it was between 10.30 and 11.00a.m. or 3.45 and 4.30p.m. This brisk, relentlessly cheerful music flavoured the day with a number of associations: wet, mopped floors in the hall and scullery, the damp wool smell of Monday washing, and the tang of cigarette smoke as my mother tackled drain-cleaning outside.

An episode of a "Sherlock Holmes" mystery on *Children's Hour* (from 5.00p.m.) came to be associated in my mind with black pudding and tomato sauce, while the evening edition of Alistair Cooke's *Letter From America* (7.30p.m. on Sundays) evoked the bonfire-and-plasticine smell of Dad's pipe smoke. As Alistair closed his letter and bade listeners goodnight, Dad used to say, "G'night!" back to him. He did this with a slightly self-conscious smile and a nod of the head to emphasise that this really was a programme worth listening to. Sunday evenings had a serious aroma of dark, polished furniture and current affairs.

If Alistair Cooke had talked about Latin America, that would strengthen the associations I made between his programme and the creased, cream jacket Dad used to wear, along with a Panama hat, when he set off to play snooker. In fact, I developed a whole complex of Latin American associations from the radio. They involved Alistair Cooke's voice referring to Cuba or Mexico, warm Sunday summer evenings, Dad in his stained cream jacket, and a music programme later in

243

the week in which Edmundo Ros and his band played tangos, rumbas and other Latin American rhythms.

Thus radio was much more than the sum of its different parts, more than a string of programmes. Radio was a voice that spoke to me from the inside and the outside at the same time. It told me about an external world that stretched far away but it also helped me to build my own internal world.

It told me, for example, through the beautifully rich, warm and whimsical voice of David Davies reading children's stories, how posh people spoke. For instance, if he was reading a *Winnie the Pooh* story, David Davies would call Piglet "Piglitt". And while I'd never dream of copying that pronunciation, it all added to the fascination. People spoke in radically different ways from the way we did at home, and radio was letting me in on this.

The radio voice often seemed wiser, more knowledgeable, humorous and lively than either I or my parents could be. It took me to places my parents never could, or would. It made me laugh and it made me excited. It even had little faults and caused frustration when it was boring, just like a real person, but it always seemed to make up for any disappointments by coming up with something interesting, funny or mystifying.

I even regarded the actual radio set we had as a mystical object that had to be venerated and treated with respect. It stood in a corner of the kitchen, a large light brown oak-effect box with a round dial in front and a grille for the speaker. The dial had a bent needle that you could touch because the transparent cover had fallen off and been lost years before.

If you twisted a round knob on the front of the set, the needle would turn laboriously, progressing slowly past Leipzig towards Hilversum and Paris. But this action didn't make much difference to the sounds that came out of the radio except that it would add a loud hissing noise to whatever you were listening to.

To really improve reception it was best to turn a diamond-shaped knob quickly to right and left. This had the effect of clearing the radio's throat, so that the volume increased and the voices or music became a little sharper, though this was all relative, because everyone on the radio sounded as if they were talking from the bottom of a deep well.

Every few weeks there was a heart-stopping moment when the radio appeared to have stopped working.

"Oh no, I hope it isn't A Valve," Mum would say. When Dad came home he'd be called upon to squint inside and poke around with a small screwdriver. Fortunately, it never was A Valve. Following Dad's intervention the radio would crackle into life again, though not always immediately.

I'm not sure its recovery was ever the result of what Dad did with a screwdriver. I had a theory that the radio had a life and an agenda of its own, and that little beings inside actually controlled it. Once, after Dad had finished a poking session, I screwed up my eyes and squinted into the back of the box. I was astonished and enchanted. There was a little industrial estate inside! It had streetlights, buildings, tiny towers and squares, impressive cables running alongside roads, a small nuclear reactor and a humming, teeming life all of its own. No wonder the radio's speaker stopped working now and again. Making sounds and delivering radio programmes for us was obviously only a small part of this miniature industrial city's business.

While radio and the radio set possessed a magic all of their own, the same cannot be said for television in our house. This was probably because we didn't actually have television.

At the start of the 1950s not many people had TV sets in their homes, but after 1955 almost every family in Bunbury seemed to have one, and certainly all my schoolmates' families did. A lot of families rented their sets. This wasn't surprising because, even as late as 1960, an average-sized TV set could cost over £60, more than £1,200 in today's money or about a month's wage. Also, owning your own set meant that you had to be responsible for summoning and placating that inscrutable demi-god of the 1950s in a brown workman's coat, Television Repair Man. If you rented, which cost a few shillings a week (£5 or £6 a week at today's prices), Television Repair Man would come out and fix things for free.

Even when TV sets became more widespread, however, a lot of people still preferred radio for certain kinds of programmes. For instance, millions more people preferred to listen to the sports commentaries on the Light Programme on Saturday afternoons (1.15 to 5.58p.m.) than to watch sports programmes on BBC television or, in the late 1950s, ITV. As yet the

246

techniques of television were limited, so close-ups and exciting, rapid cuts from one angle to another were out of the question. Watching a football game on TV in the 1950s was like looking at an aquarium full of grey water, with a few uninteresting small fish swimming slowly back and forth across the glass.

Our first set didn't arrive until about 1961 — a very small brownish box with a 14-inch screen — and, predictably, my parents didn't have to pay for it because it was a hand-me-down from Auntie Lu. The picture was often very bad, giving the impression that aliens with misshapen faces were experimenting with pioneering broadcasts from their distant planet. Sometimes the picture could be improved by turning a knob at the back, but any gain in sharpness and clarity was at the cost of irregular white lines that descended from the top of the picture to about halfway down.

Dad wouldn't hear of having a television aerial — that would have been a frivolity. Until he was eventually beguiled by TV weather forecasts, he regarded the whole idea of television with sneering disgust. Television was "common". It had obviously been designed for the rabble rather than for people of discernment and good taste such as himself.

Though the content of television programmes couldn't compete with the magic of radio, the fact that there wasn't a TV set to watch at home gave television a sort of exotic glamour. As a child I was a bit like an inhabitant of the old East Germany, where everything was threadbare and consumer goods like television sets were somehow officially disapproved of. It was just unthinkable that we would ever have a TV set, so I never campaigned for one or even asked why we didn't have one. I just watched children's TV at Lloyd Passey's house, or Clive Bevan's. Sometimes our next-door neighbours the Shores kindly let me watch early-evening programmes, including the talent show *Opportunity Knocks* and quiz programmes like *Double Your Money*, hosted by Michael Miles ("Take the money!" the audience would shout. "No, open the box!").

One day, while I was watching an episode of *Robin Hood* at Lloyd's house, it suddenly struck me that I just loved the process of drinking up television with my eyes. Any programme would do. *Robin Hood* and *Lassie* were tame, though better than some boring television programme for adults. But the best thing about television, I decided, was the way that those rays came out of the screen and went straight into your brain. It was as if TV clicked some "direct input" switch and then — one, two, three — your mind was hooked, you were soaking it in, bathing in electrons. Watching TV seemed to cancel out the external world. For half an hour or so you could forget all about Mr Steventon and the prospect of more backbreaking weeding in the school garden.

Despite the attractions of the drug-like trance that TV could induce, though, I never got sucked into television in the way that I'd become absorbed in radio. Radio was part of everyday life, and sometimes that meant it was just background noise, but listening could also be a social event. It's hard to believe now, but people in the fifties would actually stop what they were doing and sit around together, listening to a radio in the corner of the room and looking thoughtfully at each other.

Sometimes Dad would be reading a book and Mum would be ironing, but if the programme was good — particularly radio comedy such as *Hancock's Half Hour* — it would hold everyone's attention. We'd catch each other's eye from time to time, chortling and gaining extra amusement from the others' laughter. When *The Goon Show* started, Dad would retire, muttering, to the front room with his pipe and *Telegraph*. I remember Fred and Henry rushing into the house one winter's night, panting, laughing with anticipation and fiddling with the old, eccentric radio to get better reception, desperate to catch every second of this groundbreaking new comedy.

THE HOME, THE LIGHT AND THE THIRD

The BBC used to be referred to, affectionately, as "Auntie BBC". But in my 1950s childhood I pictured the two main radio channels of the BBC — the Home Service and the Light Programme — as two different uncles rather than a single, collective auntie figure.

To me, the Home Service was the uncle with silver hair and a grave face, soberly dressed in a long, dark, comfortable coat. Home Service was well spoken, with a measured voice that sounded like Alec Guinness in his later years. Home Service could have been an undertaker with a sense of humour. His serious expression was lightened by the occasional twinkle of merriment in his eye. There was a dash of eccentricity in his character and sometimes he would say things in a grave tone of voice that were completely tongue in cheek.

The Light Programme, on the other hand, wore a light raincoat made of some up-to-date material spun from artificial fibres. He was the cheery, red-faced shorter uncle with a big smile and a hint of whisky breath, always ready for a larf. He usually wore a striped shirt with a bow tie. Light Programme could have been a travelling salesman who had to stay in seedy guest-houses in places like Doncaster and Luton, or sometimes he was a stand-up comedian familiar with seaside pier theatres and resorts such as Blackpool, Cleethorpes and Margate.

Light Programme knew he was well liked and could always get an audience, but there was a trace of anxiety in his voice that was never present in Home Service's unruffled and measured tones. Light Programme seemed to know that he was past his peak, and over-compensated for this by getting noisier and more desperate to entertain with lots more electric organs, banjos and community singing. Light Programme, at heart, was a more tragic figure than Home Service because there was an emptiness in his soul. He had mislaid his identity somewhere between Scarborough and Torquay.

This showed in the programming. To me, it seemed to be a mess and didn't have many anchors except for a few really well-known slots like *The Archers* (6.45p.m. every weekday). On Sunday mornings from 9.45a.m. *The Archers* omnibus edition always began with a synopsis from Tom Forrest, the gamekeeper character. He would summarise the plot so far ("Hurr, not much 'as 'appened in Ambridge since they'm dropped that nuclear devoice on it larst week") and then add a few shreds of homespun philosophy about respecting voles.

Other Light Programme landmarks included the Sunday at noon slot for *Two-Way Family Favourites*, a widely popular record request programme for service men and women stationed abroad, and their families at home. It was presented by Jean Metcalfe in London and Bill Crozier in Cologne, and always began with a swooning violin theme tune and the lines "It's twelve o'clock in London and it's one o'clock in Cologne . . ."

No other theme tune or radio programme could quite compare with *Two-Way Family Favourites* in its ability to stimulate both the digestive juices and the heartfelt emotions of the nation at the same time. This was because it was timed to go out just as millions of Sunday lunches were being prepared all over Britain. The air was laden with that theme tune and with yearning messages to and from men and women in the British forces posted overseas, the aromas of roast lamb and gravy, and the sounds of new potatoes being scraped and mint being chopped.

Two-Way Family Favourites was, in short, the distilled essence of 1950s family bonding. It did get a

251

bit silly, however, before it was taken off the air in 1965, because Britain seemed to get drawn into a mad, last-minute, post-colonial spree of military projects in the late 1950s and early 1960s. Poor old Jean Metcalfe struggled to keep up: "It's twelve o'clock in London and it's one o'clock in Cologne [violin music swoons along] but it's four o'clock in Cyprus and — phew! — six o'clock in Aden [violin theme getting a bit tired] nine o'clock in Singapore, eleven o'clock in Hong Kong . . . tomorrow in Fiji?"

For me there was just one other anchor in the Light Programme, at least from the late 1950s onwards: the pioneering masterpiece of double-entendre comedy, *Beyond Our Ken*. It went out between 2.15 and 2.45p.m. on Sunday afternoons and included Kenneth Horne, Kenneth Williams, Hugh Paddick, Betty Marsden, Bill Pertwee and Pat Lancaster. Its sexual innuendoes and references to gay pursuits were incredibly daring for the time, but the show's writer, Eric Merriman, had correctly judged that over 95 per cent of the stolid, Light Programme audience wouldn't notice, as they were dozing in their armchairs after heavy Sunday lunches. But although a lot of the double entendres went over our heads, *Beyond Our Ken* was also just plain funny in a saucy, Carry On film kind of way. There was a wide range of comic characters, including the camp pair, Julian and Sandy, and Kenneth Williams's filthy folk singer, Rambling Sid Rumpo.

Apart from this and a few other gems, the Light Programme seemed to be aimed mainly at a middle-aged and older audience. There was the vast army of 1950s housewives to cater for during the day. Daytime programming consisted of patchy drizzles of light music and chat, interspersed with quiz and magazine programmes (including *Woman's Hour* at 2.00p.m. every weekday), comedy and drama serials such as *The Flying Doctor*.

The latter should really have been entitled *Very Unreliable Small Australian Aeroplane*, as every week the plot, almost without fail, involved an "oh no, not again" stalling of the flying doctor's plane. There would be the grim moment when the pilot made a terse emergency call to Wollaboola Base. Then the plane would have to make an emergency landing (usually in a nuclear bomb test zone) just as a groaning woman passenger gave birth, or as the doctor was halfway through conducting a complex heart bypass operation — sometimes on the pilot. I could never fathom out why any sensible Australian patient ever set foot in that flying death trap.

In contrast to the Light Programme's sometimes artificially cheery attempts to entertain, the Home Service communicated an air of solidity and self-assurance. There wasn't disdain for the audience, exactly, because the Home Service took its duty to the listening public seriously. But it was an easier station to listen to because the underlying message was "We're here anyway, and we're jolly well going to carry on, so whether or not you lot listen to us is entirely up to you."

No one communicated the idea of not taking things too seriously better than Jack de Manio, the man who bumbled through *Today*, the morning news and current affairs programme. His mellow, posh voice conveyed a cheery amateurishness that sounded comforting and pleasant. He spoke as if he were halfway through a round of buttered toast spread thickly with Oxford marmalade. There were frequent pauses and a lot of paper rustling, suggesting that neither Jack nor the rest of the studio crew had a complete grasp of what was going on. My mother chuckled as Jack de Manio struggled to read the studio clock — he was notoriously unable to tell the time, and this made *Today* an even more interesting programme to listen to.

Occasionally, the actual news content of *Today* got through to me as well. For instance, there was the day that Ghana became independent on 6 March 1957. I don't know why this particular piece of radio news impressed me. Perhaps it was the sheer exuberance of the sounds of drumming, singing and dancing that were broadcast on *Today* that day. Or perhaps it was the vividness of the report itself, with its descriptions of fireworks the night before, beaches fringed with palm trees and crowds cheering as the Union Jack came down and the new Black Star flag went up. Even Mrs Steventon picked up on the excitement of the story. That day, at the start of class, she remarked on what a special time it was for Africa and that we ought to know how astonishing it was that black people were going to be allowed to run their own country.

Today and other news programmes in the 1950s were all much briefer than they are now. This was hardly because less happened in the 1950s. The Cold War was continually prompting tense incidents and news of rivalries between America and the Soviet Union. And there were numerous other "hot" little wars happening around the world. Also there were colonial rebellions and upheavals as Britain began to dismantle the empire, not to mention political changes and social issues at home.

And yet the main Home Service news programmes in the morning were only ten minutes long, and the later ones (at 6.00 and 9.00p.m.) only fifteen minutes.

The *Today* programme didn't grind on relentlessly as it does now on Radio 4 from the crack of dawn to nine o'clock. Sensibly, there were two editions of just twenty minutes each, with Jack de Manio presenting them, at 7.15 and 8.15a.m.

The Home Service's morning schedule even included a short interlude with records, between 7.40 and 7.50a.m., presumably to allow people time to brush their teeth or go to the lavatory, or for the wife to pack hubby's sandwiches for work without being distracted by news or livestock prices. TV news programmes were also equally brief, with ten minutes at 6.40p.m. and fifteen minutes at 9.45p.m.

All this brevity probably meant that people were less weighed down with news than they are now, and that news bulletins themselves were possibly more punchy and interesting. I can only guess because news and current affairs were largely beyond me as a young lad with the exception of Ghana's day of independence and big events such as the Suez crisis of 1956.

Another whole area of radio — the Third Programme — remained an unknown world to me. It was like Tibet — a lofty, imposing kingdom which was very difficult to get into but, because of its unknown and challenging heights and rarefied atmosphere, it held a certain fascination.

Its inaccessibility was shown by the fact that it was difficult to tune into on our old family radio. Access could sometimes be gained by turning the lozenge-shaped knob (next to the diamond-shaped one) to right and left smartly a few times while simultaneously turning the tuning dial wildly. If you got a certain background hum and silence, followed by an announcer with a plummy voice saying something like, "And now for the eighth in our series featuring choral music from Northern Ireland" you had crossed the mountain pass into the Forbidden Kingdom.

It all remained a bit of a mystery though. Even for a young radio geek like me, the Third Programme was hard going. For instance, just taking one item from a *Radio Times* listing of Third Programme music in 1960 (25 April), the evening's broadcast was rounded off by a Quartet by Rubbra. Earlier that evening there had been a scholarly talk by Cranford Pratt on "Tribalism and Nationalism in Uganda" and a lengthy talk on "Symbol and Image" by Sir Russell Brain.

DRAMA

What bonded me to the Home Service like Airfix Glue, though, was radio drama. There was so much drama on radio in the 1950s, and it seemed to pop up all over the schedules. It's hard to believe now, but *Children's Hour* between 5.00 and 5.55p.m. every weekday often consisted of two short serialised dramas. They were listed in the *Radio Times* with proper cast lists and sometimes with summaries of "the story so far", just like adult serials.

But whether they were plays and serials for *Children's Hour* or everyday dramas in the main Home Service programme, it didn't matter. The magic of radio always did its trick.

Unlike TV or film, which is limited by the visual effects that can be achieved — and the black-and-white TV dramas of the 1950s were often *very* limited, technically — radio can go anywhere and do anything.

With historical dramas I was freed of the constraints of time. I could swoop from Roman Britain to a Caribbean island in the seventeenth century, where I could hear pirates talking, and then on to Dickens's London, with its cries of street vendors and the clip-clopping of coconut shells on the cobbled roads.

Science fiction worked well on radio, too. What stood out wasn't just the way that radio could transport you to fantastic physical worlds but also to imaginary social worlds. For instance, I remember listening to (what turned out to be) a telling short story which explored the concept of virtual reality. It was about spoiled, pudgy young men and women who spent all their time ignoring the real world by staying in large plastic domes in which virtual reality environments had been created. They munched snacks in a zoo-like tropical house and talked pointlessly for hours on end about nothing. How much closer could you get to predicting *Big Brother*?

The other good thing about listening to radio as a child was that all the imagery and excitement coming from it got swept into playing outside. If I'd been following a serial about Viking invasions, or a Second World War spy mystery, for example, with John Vickers or Lloyd Passey, we'd rush inside to switch on the radio, breathless from playing, yearning to hear the next episode. Then, when we'd got to the end and to the inevitable cliffhanger, we'd rush outside again, back to the old wooden plough in the field that was a Viking long-ship, or which suddenly became a large plane circling over wartime France as we got ready to parachute out.

Looking back at that time, it's not just the quantity but also the quality of fresh radio and television drama that's striking. Arguably, as television drama got better in the sixties — more daring and socially challenging, and technically much better than in the fifties — it put radio in the shade. TV audiences for drama such as BBC's *Play for Today* soon outstripped the numbers who continued to listen to radio drama. For this reason 1960 was, perhaps, a key time because it was the point at which radio and television were at level pegging. Radio drama was still at a high point, in terms of popularity and excellence, but TV was on the up.

The incredible richness of BBC drama on both radio and television can be illustrated by a certain week — 24–31 April. That week, I decided, radio probably couldn't get any better than this. So, being a serious-minded 11-year-old, I put the *Radio Times* in my cardboard box of treasures to keep it as a permanent record.

On radio that week there was a production of Chekhov's *Three Sisters*, the first-ever broadcast of Samuel Beckett's *Waiting for Godot* (on the Third Programme, inevitably, but I did listen to it) and, on *Saturday-Night Theatre*, a warm comedy about Italian immigrants, in Australia, *Little South of Heaven*. There was also a *Thirty-Minute Theatre* production on the Light Programme, together with a number of other drama productions on the Home Service, including the first episode in a serialisation of Jules Verne's *Around the World in Eighty Days*.

It looks as though it was a good week for television drama, too, though of course I didn't know because we didn't yet have Auntie Lu's old TV set. But that week Tom Bell and Billie Whitelaw were starring in a TV dramatisation (by Ronald Gow and Walter Greenwood) of the gritty play *Love on the Dole*. And on Thursday there was the start of an ambitious TV trek through Shakespearean drama, *Age of Kings*, that was to continue over the following fourteen weeks.

259

Musical Supression

While radio drama had a hold on me as a child, most of the music I heard didn't. This was partly because we weren't a musical family. The dog sometimes keened in a low, lamenting whine and Mum whistled along to *Music While You Work*, but that was about it. Henry and Fred were in the church choir but I never heard them singing, either in church or at home.

Dad was an astonishingly good piano player, apparently, though he adamantly refused to touch the keys of the battered piano that stood in the front room. Once he was caught surreptitiously playing an intricate opening passage to a classical piece of music, his thick fingers darting up and down the keyboard like dancing piglets. But he stopped, embarrassed, the moment he was discovered. No one knows to this day why he wanted to keep such a skill under wraps.

However, he did like to listen to classical concerts on the Home Service, and this is perhaps another reason I didn't take to listening to music. I liked the beginning bit and the sense of occasion when the announcer described the concert hall and sketched the scene as the conductor approached the podium and the audience applauded. But once the applause died down and the music started I began to lose interest. Serious music seemed to be just that — slow, dirge-like and sad — although sometimes it sounded over-excited, discordant and nerve-jangling. It was usually too loud because Dad was hard of hearing and would have the volume turned up high.

At the other end of the musical spectrum there was a Saturday morning record request programme intended just for children, called *Children's Favourites* and presented by Derek McCulloch ("Uncle Mac"). The problem with this was that when I got beyond the age of 7, *Children's Favourites* was boring. There are only so many times that you can listen to songs about a blue toothbrush and a pink toothbrush, or musical sagas about Sparky and his magic piano, or kings being rumbled for walking around in the nude and exposing themselves.

Every week Uncle Mac would present the same records in a slightly different order, so the only excitement was in guessing what would be next. Only now and then would an entirely new record be allowed in, and this would cause a certain tetchiness in Uncle Mac's normally equable, avuncular manner. This was particularly the case if the record requested had even a hint of pop music about it.

"Now, children," Uncle Mac would grumble, "I'm going to have to put a record on the gramophone that I don't think is all that suitable for you. It's by a singer called Lonnie Donegan, and I want you to sit down quietly while you listen to it. If it was up to me I wouldn't be playing it, but [sighs] there we are, this is what happens when a persistent few keep asking for records like this. Perhaps those who requested this one should sit extra quietly, if you don't mind, and *just think about what you've done.*"

The other problem with music on the radio was that new, interesting stuff had been suppressed. The

261

paternalistic few in control of broadcasting had decided that just a few bars of "Rock Around the Clock" would unleash a storm of social change so terrible that it could easily destroy the whole fabric of British society.

The basic problem for them was that, in 1955, teenagers had been invented. Shortly afterwards a few had escaped from a secret laboratory somewhere in the Home Counties, and there was an ever-present danger that playing "popular tunes" could set up dangerous vibrations that would stimulate more to escape and spread around the country.

The 1950s solution to this danger was to use musical suppressants on a large scale. The Light Programme carried out this task, spraying out a fine mist of prophylactic "live" band and orchestral music to try to make sure that young people continued to have proper hairstyles and dance in predictable, geometric patterns.

It certainly was deadly stuff. The Light Programme was chock-a-block with little bands that seemed to be playing desperately quickly, as if they were trying to fit in one more number on the deck of the *Titanic* just before it tilted over. They had names like Frank Beige and his Sextet, Ian McGrunge and his Quintet and The Bryan Plonker Quartet. Then there was The Maple Leaf Four. They sang cheery Canadian folksy songs about waterfalls a' tumbling and logs a' rollin' and skies a' fallin' in.

But even worse, and surely winners of the Total Blandness Awards of the Twentieth Century, were the dreaded Adams Singers. They crooned seamlessly from one song to another through a half-hour programme

262

called *Sing Something Simple*. I experienced a sudden panic when writing those three chilling words. I have checked and looked nervously over my shoulder to make sure that the Adams Singers have gone off the air for good, and I think we're safe. But the reason to worry is that *Sing Something Simple* was the most terrifying of all the musical suppressants invented by the Ministry of Defence. Just two minutes' exposure to the insidious, creeping blandness of that programme could lead to paralysis of the limbs so that you couldn't talk, walk away or even lift a finger to switch off the radio. Fifteen helpless minutes later and you could undergo dental surgery without experiencing any pain. Twenty-five minutes and you'd be OK with any kind of surgery. Recovery was very gradual and might take all week. Even then you might be left with a residual nervous tic as you twitched to the endless, soporific tunes that the programme had implanted in your brain. But then, the programme would have succeeded — you'd be very wary of going anywhere near a music station ever again.

Those horrors apart, there were some compensations in listening to at least the introductions to a few light music programmes. For instance, there was the man with the vaguely sinister Mediterranean accent, Semprini, who used to play gushing, showy piano music against an orchestral background in his programme *Semprini Serenade*. His voice was aged, deep and sepulchral. I'm sure he was a part-time vampire. I always got a kick out of picturing Semprini (and his grand piano) covered in cobwebs as he

263

introduced himself. As he swept through a few bars of music, with a few bats squeaking past, he'd say in a gravelly voice from the crypt, "Old ones, new ones, loved ones, neglected ones . . ."

The beginning of Victor Silvester's ballroom dance music programme, *Music For Dancing*, was another laugh. It began with the violins of his light orchestra playing the swirling signature tune waltz, followed by a series of requests for dance tunes from couples living around the world. I say "around the world", but the weird thing was that Victor only seemed to deal with very suspect people living in the most reactionary, right-wing countries such as Rhodesia, South Africa, several South American republics where Nazis had covertly settled, and Eastbourne.

"And now," Victor would say, "a quick-step for Mr and Mrs Backlash of Bulawayo, Mrs Dawn Massacre of Cape Town, South Africa, Mr and Mrs Himmler of Bellevue Terrace, Eastbourne . . ." More tinkling introductory music. "And . . . a special hello to Mr and Mrs Smythe-Holocaust in their recently arrived submarine in Montevideo harbour. And a one, two . . . three!"

One of the best examples of inadvertent comedy I ever heard on radio happened on a light music programme, one New Year's Eve when I was 10, possibly 11. The radio was on in the background, and it was some nondescript band wearily playing numbers that were supposed to be lively and cheerful but just sounded tired.

I was just about to switch them off but something held me. It was a giggle. It came right in the middle of their mournful rendition of "Chattanooga Choo-Choo". Shortly after this I heard a drumstick fall on the floor and some suppressed guffaws. The band had obviously been doing a bit of preparatory New Year's Eve celebrating.

Suddenly, in mid-tune, the "Chattanooga Choo-Choo" came to a sudden halt. There was an awkward silence. I heard a muffled voice in the background say, "Oh, is that it?" There was a stumbling footstep and then some heavy breathing close to the microphone.

"Er, hello again, ladies and gentlemen," said a slurred voice. "We're here to see right up your. Start again. See you right up to midnight and New Year's Eve . . . And what better number to get us on the road, so to speak, than, er . . ." A pause, followed by urgent whisper away from the microphone: "What was it next?"

After several false starts and a few more suppressed giggles, the quartet launched into a ragged rendition of "I Left my Heart in San Francisco". But it wasn't going to work and after a few bars there was a complete collapse. You could hear at least two of the musicians weeping with laughter. A voice said, "It's flippin' live, ya stupid sods!" before bursting into giggles himself. Inexplicably, the fourth member of the quartet, hardly able to talk through his suppressed laughter, said "And now it's his tee-eeth!" Then there were unrestrained guffaws. There was a noise that sounded like someone falling over a drum kit and a long pause.

265

A calm BBC voice with an edge of steel said, "Well, we seem to be having some *technical* problems down in Studio Two with the Bryan Plonker Quartet, but I'm glad to say that we're now able to join Jimmy Shand and his Band for some Hogmanay fun . . ."

Towards the end of the 1950s, the BBC policy of indiscriminate musical suppression began to be revised. Very reluctantly, concessions were made to the idea of playing more "pop music" records, though this very much went against the grain of the Light Programme tradition of quartets and quintets playing medleys in a little studio somewhere.

And just as the Gestapo might have ordered the destruction of three whole villages in retaliation for a minor defeat, so the Light Programme insisted on inflicting endless pop "numbers", played by hitherto unknown little bands, on everyone in retaliation for the playing of a single record.

One example of this was *Parade of the Pops*, a programme that was described at the time as "a review of this week's popular music and predictions of hits to come". It featured painful and embarrassing renditions of current hits by live bands such as Bob Miller and the Millermen, The Raindrops, and Ken Jones and his Music.

When the Light Programme did play the music that millions wanted to hear, steps were taken to ensure that the one or two programmes with "disc jockeys" (an entirely new-fangled term) were buried late in the evening schedules. Pete Murray's show, *Pete's Party*, went out on Sunday evenings at 10.40p.m., and David

Jacobs presented *Pick of the Pops* at the same time on Saturday nights. They were also disguised by off-putting descriptions in the *Radio Times* — for instance *Pete's Party* was "a Sunday-night get-together round the gramophone to play his choice of records".

No wonder the cool people turned to Radio Luxembourg, though for me in the 1950s listening to Radio Luxembourg under the bedclothes was a pleasure yet to come. It wasn't going to happen until 1960, when Henry had joined the Merchant Navy. One day he came back from one of his three-month trips with a little red plastic box that had a dial and a shiny gold grille on the front. A marvel of the time, it was a transistor radio.

FROM BILL AND BEN TO WAGON TRAIN

As a young child, looking at the little TV screen with its fuzzy grey, black and white images was like peering at the rippling surface of a dark, peaty pond. Could you see anything magical in there?

The images you could make out were usually static — someone talking, or an object to look at for a while as interlude music played. During the younger children's television slot in the afternoons the BBC would show Andy Pandy or Rag, Tag and Bobtail moving slowly about. If it was Bill and Ben the Flowerpot Men, they'd be talking gibberish as well. They said things like "flobadob" and "flibadab" to each other. They prompted the thought, in my 4-year-old

267

mind, that they probably needed to get out more. They'd been in that garden too long.

Despite the limitations of children's TV in the early 1950s, though, I did begin to develop some primitive tastes and preferences. Viewing options were very limited because when I was 5 or 6 years old not many people had yet acquired a set. But Mrs Newport, a friend of my mother's, had one. Once or twice a week Mum would take me along to Mrs Newport's. While they had a cup of tea, a slice of sponge cake and a gossip, the television would be switched on for me.

I can't say I ever took to Andy Pandy, the puppet with the stripy dungarees and his two hangers-on, a certain "Teddy", and a crude stereotype of girlish incompetence, a ragdoll called Looby Loo. The main drawback in all three characters was that they all seemed to be recovering from an exhausting virus such as ME. They hardly seemed to have enough time to drag themselves on to the screen before they started yawning and crawling back into a large linen basket. Before you'd really got into it, a female voice would trill "Time to go home!" and that would signal the end of the programme. The basket lid would go down and that was it — most disappointing.

Bill and Ben the Flowerpot Men were much more interesting because at least there was some point to it all. In fact, every episode confronted the two main characters, Bill and Ben, with a major ethical dilemma: should they own up to whatever wrongdoing they had carried out? "Was it Bill . . . or was it Ben?" a slightly sinister female voice crooned every week, in the background.

You just knew that both Flowerpot Men were sweating, wrestling with their consciences, even though they couldn't express it very well because of their speech disorder.

Witnesses, such as their friend Slowcoach (a tortoise) and Weed (not marijuana, if that's what you're thinking, but a sunflower that always introduced herself in a piping voice as "Little Weeeeeeeed") tried to slide out of their responsibilities. They had to decide whether to inform on Bill or Ben.

In every episode things were resolved before the Gardener returned. Slowcoach would canter off-screen at a surprisingly fast pace, Little Weed retracted herself like a car aerial, and Bill and Ben got their arses back into the flowerpots very smartly indeed. It was much more impressive than Andy Pandy and the other ME sufferers. Also, my young mind thought that the underlying moral message, "If you're in trouble and in any doubt about what to do, hide under a flowerpot" was pretty sound, all things considered.

When I was 7, in 1955, the *Robin Hood* series was launched on children's television. This became a firm favourite to watch at Lloyd Passey's house. It was a British-made series, starring Richard Greene as Robin, and it started every week in a dramatic way with the twang of a bowstring and a whooshing arrow thwacking into an oak tree, followed by the title song:

Robin Hood, Robin Hood,
Riding through the glen.
Robin Hood, Robin Hood,
With his band of men!
[and a token woman called Marian . . .]
Feared by the bad, loved by the good,
Rob-in Hood! Rob-in Hood! Rob-in Hood!

Lloyd lived only a few hundred yards from what we grandly called "the woods". They were little more than a sizeable spinney with a stream on its boundary, so it was a very easy matter to watch an episode of *Robin Hood* and then gallop off to re-enact it with our own homemade bows and arrows.

Only one thing bothered me about *Robin Hood*, and that was a small detail of the sets they used. It's just that I couldn't get it out of my head that, however large Sherwood Forest was and wherever Robin and his band went in it, they were always leaning against or heartily laughing around the *same tree*.

But rather than seeing this as a limitation of the programme, I actually began to relate to this tree as an extra character. It could certainly get around, even though it was heavily built and looked a little overweight. I even began to wonder whether it couldn't be given a name and maybe a storyline of its own.

In addition to the mobile tree in Sherwood Forest there were quite a few other surreal things to watch on children's television. For instance there was *Billy Bean and His Funny Machine*, a weirdly prophetic programme in which Billy drew items on the screen of

270

his machine, just as you might with a touch-sensitive screen on a modern computer, and then waited for the machine to construct whatever he'd drawn. The machine itself looked like something you might find in Tate Modern. There were lots of dials, knobs and buttons, and, incongruously, a small birdhouse. A cuckoo with learning difficulties would emerge from this and do something inappropriate. At the moment when the machine was about to deliver a totally unexpected object, the cuckoo would lay an egg that rolled down a series of channels to the bottom.

I struggled with this. Like a contemporary art installation, it left you feeling somewhat disoriented. It was comforting, therefore, to take refuge in the more predictable fun of cartoons such as *Popeye*.

And if it was predictability you were after, it was there in bucketfuls in the many Westerns shown on both children's and evening TV in the 1950s. Looking back, it was astonishing how many there were. To name just a selection of the ones I was familiar with, there were *Champion the Wonder Horse*, *Davy Crockett*, *Hopalong Cassidy*, *The Lone Ranger*, *Rawhide*, *Roy Rogers and Trigger*, *Rin-Tin-Tin* and last but not least, *Wagon Train*.

Each one had a very formulaic storyline and format, but this added to their attraction rather than detracting from it.

Also, though the sedate plains of Cheshire were a world away from the USA and the plains of Montana or Arizona, there was a resonance there that people in an agricultural area like ours identified with. There

271

were some basic ingredients in Westerns that children like us, as well as men and women in the village, could readily see in our own environment — cattle, alert telepathic dogs, farmers, big skies, young women in farmhouses, sweaty men on horseback, double-crossing varmints from the big city. We were a bit light on deserts and cacti, rolling mountains, "First Nation" Americans, six-guns and community lynching, but that didn't seem to matter too much.

As with Robin Hood, watching a Western translated straight into the way we played together. After an episode of *The Lone Ranger* or *Rin-Tin-Tin* we'd run outside, our cap-guns cracking and smoking, excitedly arranging to ambush each other at carefully designated spots in the woods after tea. Even watching a Wild West movie today brings back that metallic, nose-crinkling gunpowder smell from the tinny toy revolvers we played with.

We were completely taken in by the characters and the situations in 1950s Westerns, and it's only in retrospect that their truly weird and surreal nature is apparent. For instance, it never occurred to us to question why Davy Crockett wore a dead cat with a long stripy tail on his head. Nor did it seem rather peculiar that the Lone Ranger always wore his mask. Surely it was pretty evident who he was by now, after the hundreds of daring exploits he'd carried out? You'd have recognised that slightly paunchy midriff anywhere, but even if you didn't, there would be that telltale habit of his shouting "Hi, Ho Silver!" instead of, "Cheerio, see you later."

The animals in Westerns were also rather strange. Nearly all of them had extraordinary powers of telepathy and communication, not least Champion the Wonder Horse, who could also move

Like a streak o' lightnin' flashin' 'cross the sky,
Like the swiftest arrow whizzin' from a bow . . .
Like a might-y cannon-ball he seems to fly!
You'll hear about him everywhere you go,
There'll be a time when everyone will know
The . . . name . . . of . . .
CHAMPION, THE WONDER HORSE!
CHAMPION, THE WON-DER HORSE!
CHAMPION . . . THE WON . . . DER . . .
     HOOOOOORSE!

Performer bunjees into the Grand Canyon on the last two syllables.

There was one Western, *Wagon Train*, which glued the village to its TV sets more than any other. It had forged a new kind of community bond — that of discussing a TV serial. It was so gripping that children and adults alike kept stopping to talk to each other in the village about what would happen next. And it had such a hold on the country at large that Hugh Gaitskell, the Labour Leader of the Opposition, requested that the date chosen for the General Election of 1959 should not coincide with an episode of *Wagon Train* so that voters wouldn't be distracted by it.

Each episode started with the rolling prairie, Big Country-style theme music and then showed the line of covered wagons trekking from St Joseph to Sacramento in the 1860s. It always focused on the gallant, tight-lipped efforts of Major Seth Adams in protecting the wagon train and the mainly foolish, naive travellers in it. He behaved rather like a harassed travel courier dealing with package holiday tourists in Spain.

The same basic elements in each story were permed in any combination each week. They were:

1. Hostile injuns (though there were always a few elderly wise ones left at the end, to negotiate with).
2. Wheel/ancient grandmother falling off wagon, *sometimes* simultaneously.
3. Little boy/girl wandering off and getting left behind.
4. Trusty dog (often named "Trusty") risking life to save said child.
5. Childbirth.
6. Broken crockery set.
7. The finger of God (useful for wrapping up any loose ends in the plot).

One summer (it might have been 1959), all these elements were to come together in a final episode that promised to be beyond all expectations in terms of its drama and human interest. So many threads were left dangling, and so many vital concerns aroused about key characters on the Wagon Train, that every inhabitant of Bunbury except Dad was on a knife-edge of excitement and anxiety in the days leading up to that final episode.

I felt left out of all the excitement, though, because we still didn't have a television set. I knew the gist of the story, but I hadn't been able to see the penultimate episode that was leading up to the grand finale. In the playground I tried to get away with knowing the various twists in the plot but, when it became all too clear that I didn't really know I looked pathetic.

Wagon Train was serialised on TV in the evenings, which meant that I couldn't easily ask to watch it at Lloyd's or Clive's. It was OK to play outdoors on summer evenings, but I felt it would have been frowned on if I'd asked to watch television in a friend's house after tea. I could sometimes watch TV at the Shores, next door, but for a reason I've now forgotten I wasn't going to be able to on that fateful night.

In the village the decks had been cleared. All social engagements for the evening were cancelled and all possible distractions eliminated. I felt utterly fed up. I'd happened to mention to Dad, for the very first time, that it wouldn't be a bad idea if *we* could have a television, and he'd just snorted and rustled the *Telegraph*. "Bally *Wagon Train!*" he said, sucking on his pipe as he settled into his armchair for the evening.

As Mum was ironing philosophically in the kitchen, I trudged around the village with the dog, kicking pebbles at fence-posts. There was half an hour to go. An unearthly hush had descended on the village. Everyone was indoors, waiting for *Wagon Train* to roll. But then I noticed that the silence had an extra depth to it. There was no sound from cars, bikes or people walking about, but the birds had also fallen silent. A peculiar

275

green-and-purple light was filling the evening sky. Looking up, I noticed for the first time that huge columns of inky cloud had gathered to the south. And they were heading towards Bunbury.

Then came the first deep rumble of thunder. Kim raised his wet nose and looked at me, flicking an ear to let me know he wanted to go home. Then the first, heavy splots of rain dotted the pavement, releasing a humid smell of greenhouse tomatoes into the close air.

Kim and I raced home, elated. As we ran up the garden path, the first sheet lightning came. The downpour soaked me even in those few steps. Laughing, I closed the front door and let the wet dog off his lead. As he arched and shook himself, showering me with raindrops, I heard Mum shouting down from the front bedroom, "Kenneth, come and look at the lightning!"

My mother and I shared a love of watching storms, and this one was the grandest ever. Not only was there a torrential downpour, so that we could see the garden path turning into a mini-Amazon, and the loudest thunder I'd ever heard, but also *purple* lightning. It came both in dramatic forks and in sheet lightning form, turning our excited and half-frightened faces into purple masks.

Dad walked into the little bedroom, smirking and holding his newspaper at his side. "O' course," he shouted through the deafening thunder, "nobody'll be watching *Wagon Train* tonight!" And he was right. Nobody in those days was ever brave or foolhardy enough to leave their television on in a thunderstorm.

276

Just one little prong of a fork of lightning down your aerial, it was thought, could turn your telly into a fireball.

There was one exception, of course, there always is. I've forgotten who it was exactly, except that he was an eccentric old geezer who lived on his own. He was determined to watch *Wagon Train* even if it was going to be his last episode as well as the serial's. Apparently he gained not only popularity for a week or so because he could fill people in on the ending, but also new-found respect for his bravery in indefatigably sitting there, watching the flickering screen as the heavens crashed down around him.

It was all very satisfying, for me, that evening. It had been the best storm ever, and *nobody* except one person in the entire village had been able to watch *Wagon Train* after all. The storm had put everyone else in the village on the same footing as me. Now *they* had to ask someone else what had happened in a crucial episode of a TV serial.

However, in the bright wet sunshine of the next morning, as we whooped and laughed about the storm in the school playground, that one exception made me realise that we in Sunnyside had become a bit odd. I was still getting nearly all my input from the outside world and all my media excitement through the Home Service and the Light Programme. I was still the radio kid. Everyone else my age had moved on to TV, and unless things changed soon I was going to be left behind for ever.

CHAPTER
NINE

Sixties Village

RESULTS

In July 1959 I reached the age of 11 and escaped the serfdom of the Steventons' village school. Their efforts to maintain the extensive gardens around their house by drafting us in as forced child labour, day after day, had been getting increasingly desperate. I can still remember the last July day at the school when, looking down at my blistered and soiled hands, I realised with huge relief that I was cleaning and oiling one of Mr Steventon's garden forks for the very last time. It was time to go in, collect our final school reports and listen to his valedictory talk about The Future. We were going to behave ourselves, not even think about hanging around telephone boxes and carefully consider voting Conservative when we grew up.

Just before then, that little brown envelope containing the result of my eleven-plus exam had dropped through our letterbox. I'd passed. It was bewildering. There had been no build-up in Sunnyside, and I'd forgotten all about it.

That morning in early summer I'd come downstairs to get some breakfast and found Mum waiting for me in the hall, smiling. And then something totally unexpected happened. With a whoop of joy she held me round the middle and danced around the hall with me.

It was one of those moments that stay with you for ever. The fresh green summer morning, sunlight dappling through the windows, the threadbare carpet on the stairs, the press of my mother's apron against my face, the giddy feeling as she swept me off my feet. And all this from a mother who'd rarely put her arm around me. For those few seconds I'd been grabbed and returned to early childhood.

When she stopped I smiled, embarrassed. It felt good, though the evident relief and joy in her face led me to wonder whether my parents had really expected me to fail. From Dad I just got a cheery smile and a "well done" as he sat at the breakfast table neatly polishing off his bacon and tomato.

When I got to school that morning John Cheers and Lloyd Passey told me that they'd passed, too. We looked at each other, wondering about a new kind of future together. John told me that only one girl, Pat Merrill, had passed from the Girls' School.

Clive Bevan, along with the handful of other boys in our class, had failed. He was sullen, red-faced with anger and disappointment, and couldn't bring himself to talk to us. All the worries he'd had about the impact on his eleven-plus chances of endless forced labour in the school garden had come true. It was sad because he'd been the one, I guessed, who had really wanted to pass. Much later, in September and after I'd started at the grammar school, I decided to go round to see him at his home, a little bungalow at the bottom of a big grassy hill in Beeston. It was an attempt to ask whether we could still be friends. We couldn't. He couldn't wait for me to leave.

School in the sixties

The sixties are sometimes referred to as the decade in which social attitudes loosened up and the way people dealt with each other became more informal than in the buttoned-up, respectable fifties. Those of a conservative bent often blame those years for the advent of "trendy liberal" teaching methods in schools and for the beginning of the decline that led, in the end, to a collective forgetting of what apostrophes are.

All that might have been true in some parts of the country or in some schools, at least in the late sixties if not the earlier years of the decade. But there was scant sign of any such social revolution in rural south Cheshire. While the Boys' School in Bunbury had clung on to an almost pre-industrial approach to schooling, Nantwich and Acton Grammar — the school to which I'd been assigned as a result of passing the eleven-plus — was continuing its long love affair with the 1930s.

For a village boy like me, though, it wasn't at all bad to be able to throw off the yoke of the nineteenth century and be able to move *up* to the 1930s. Not bad going, actually: only twenty-five years behind the present now!

280

Nantwich and Acton had an orderly, disciplined atmosphere, with its boys and girls dressed in a strict navy-blue uniform and its teachers flapping around in black gowns, but it was at heart a fairly laid-back place. It certainly didn't seem nearly as oppressive as the Steventons' regime at the village school. I eventually discovered from a teaching assistant at the grammar school, in my late teens, that the teachers in the staff room often laughed out loud when they talked about the Boys' School at Bunbury. Apparently Mr Steventon's approach to discipline, the cane and slave labour in the garden had given the place quite a reputation.

Unfortunately, the impact of the village schooling I'd received from the Steventons continued to have an influence on me at the grammar school. This showed itself particularly in the subject of maths. In Bunbury I'd often come out at the top of the very small class in feats of mental arithmetic. Sometimes these had required the rapid mental juggling of small, wholesome numbers like 8 and 5, as well as medieval units of measurement such as chains, rods, poles and perches. But, like priests and thinkers in the Middle Ages who would have nothing to do with the concept of nought, fearing it to be the work of the devil, so had Mr Steventon steered clear of zero, x and y. He hadn't prepared us for the grammar school at all, even by giving us just a simple warning to expect something called algebra and something else called geometry. Just mentioning the words would have helped.

In my first year of grammar school maths seemed to have become detached from its moorings and was floating about in a mist of abstract principles. I found it difficult to translate all the strange squiggles, numbers and diagrams on the blackboard into the clanking medieval machinery of rods and chains, although I tried valiantly.

Most of the other subjects were fairly easy, especially the geography lessons, in which the teacher put his feet up on a desk at the front and opened the *Daily Mirror* (usually on the racing page). Wagging his finger menacingly, he told us to be quiet and to do absolutely nothing at all for forty minutes.

But what neither my parents nor my teachers had prepared me for was the fact that the grammar school was actually two schools. At the end of the first year we sat a test that divided us into five sets. If you were selected for sets One and Two you were seen as potential middle-class material, likely to be in a non-manual occupation when you left school, to play tennis, be capable of learning Latin and stay on in the sixth form. If you were selected for a lower set then the logic was that you were more likely to leave school at 15 or 16, to pick up a skilled or semi-skilled manual job, to like football (boys), or prefer wearing make-up and going dancing (girls — well, mostly the girls, anyway). In the case of girls it would be better to be learning typing and secretarial skills; for boys, woodwork and metalwork.

I went into the end-of-year test like a novice sailor into a hurricane. No one had warned me of the hazards ahead. I'd looked with amused disbelief at the gaggles of girls around the playing field, their noses in their books as they revised for every minute of the lunch hour. It was only when I was faced with test paper after test paper demanding knowledge that I just didn't have, and with not a single reference to rods or perches, that I realised that something had gone badly wrong. I was put into one of the lower sets.

When I started the second year of grammar school I discovered a flaw in the "two nations" system they'd developed. The logic was that if you weren't good at Latin or other subjects reserved for the top sets, Nature had determined that you would be excellent at woodwork. But what if, as in my case, this logic didn't apply and that not being suitable for Latin or German *didn't* mean you were genetically designed to make a dovetail joint? This basic gap in the logic of the system didn't seem to have been recognised at all.

At least I wasn't alone, though. There were a handful of deviants such as myself who were, sometimes literally, square pegs in round holes. We did try. One of my fellow deviants who became a firm friend, Pete Walley (Wol), sawed at a piece of wood for over an hour, sweating profusely. It was only when there was a sudden crash that we discovered that he had sawn off the corner of the rock-hard woodwork bench that he'd been resting his plank on.

The rest of us were trying to fashion lumps of wood or metal into useful objects like a rack for a yard brush or a mystery box with a sliding lid. So challenging were the results that we thought it kinder to destroy them without trace than inflict such ugly sights on the rest of humanity. The best way to do this was to smuggle them out of school in the lunch hour and throw them into the neighbouring canal. There was at least an underlying convenience in the fact that we could weigh down the woodwork items with the avant-garde but ultimately disturbing pieces of metalwork we had created.

There was a positive outcome despite my failure, and Wol's, to fit into either of the two nations. He eventually did better at maths and science, left school at the age of 17 and successfully trained as an officer in the Merchant Navy. We scanned the newspapers for a few years afterwards for headlines about disastrous collisions at sea but all seemed to go well for him.

I did unexpectedly well in woodwork, scoring 90 per cent in the end of year assessment. It was the result of a bookkeeping error by Mr Orme, our absent-minded woodwork teacher. This must have meant that some other boy, possibly a potential master craftsman or cabinetmaker, had his confidence and faith in his own superb woodworking genius ruined by receiving my lowly mark. I never found out who that unfortunate person was. However, this and a few other better marks, together with the help of a sympathetic English teacher, Mr Simpson, helped me get promoted to one of the set Two classes (in English). I had to linger in the lower sets, where the kids failed all or most of their "O" levels, for all my other subjects.

GIRLS — PAT MERRILL, ESPECIALLY

There was an important redeeming feature about the grammar school — it was co-educational. Not that I was able to appreciate all the charms of girls straight away, because, having a July birthday, I was on the young side of my year and my hormones didn't kick in until I was 13. Nevertheless, to be in an environment with both a male and a female side was a great relief: it just seemed more human, interesting and relaxed. It's a shame, though, that I didn't manage to reciprocate the attentions of Pat Merrill.

She was the girl, also from Bunbury, who had passed the eleven-plus the same year as me. She lived in one of the council houses near to John Cheers's place. We were put in the same form and, more or less by chance, she sat at a desk just behind me. I'd been vaguely aware of her before in the village. One time a group of village kids, including Pat, had been entered for a short essay competition. We were only 9 or so then, and I'd been conscious of a colt-like girl with freckles and arched eyebrows wanting to get to know me, wanting to talk to me. I was still at the William Brown stage, though. I responded guardedly, politely and somewhat fearfully. What if Lloyd Passey had seen me talking to a *girl*?

In the first year of grammar school it was pretty much the same for me, but Pat was definitely getting interested. She would often giggle, blush and push me when she was talking to me. Sometimes she'd surprise me by hitting me over the head with a heavy book. I

285

liked her, despite the headaches, but couldn't quite see what was going on.

When I did twig it was too late, and I botched the whole thing. Perhaps it's inevitable, the first time. But instead of just chatting to her, being friendly and getting to know her, one day I thrust a secret note into Pat's hand. We must have been about 13 or 14 at the time.

The note asked her to meet me at the bottom of a quiet lane, near the village. It was a chilly autumn evening and almost dark when I waited at the chosen spot. My heart was thumping because I wasn't at all sure what to expect. When she came racing up on her bike, the heart inside my chest turned into a faulty foodmixer. I hadn't actually believed she would come. What on earth did I do now?

As Pat drew up, not dismounting from her bike, she was blushing. She told me angrily that it wasn't easy for her to make an excuse to come out on her bike at nightfall. "What do you *want*?" she asked, blushing again. My throat was constricted and full of cement.

"Er, I'm not sure, really," I said, eventually.

And that was that. I could only dream about holding her hand, getting close to those green-blue eyes, pushing her snub nose against mine. Of course, we did see each other and talk to each other again — school and shared lessons saw to that — but we never referred to the awkward assignation.

A few years later, when I was 17 or so, I saw Pat with a boyfriend in a pub in Nantwich. She came up to me, smiling, wearing a dark, tight dress that looked impossibly grown-up and sophisticated. Her boyfriend was smiling, friendly and looked as if he were about 25. I felt — and probably looked — as if I was 13 again.

By that time I was dating a girl called Margaret. Like me, she was in the sixth form — we'd both stayed on at school. And for a while life assumed a kind of order and predictability that I hadn't experienced for years. I'd cycle over to Nantwich to see Margaret; we'd go out on Saturday nights and I got to know her family. They were genuine, warm and really likeable people.

I was intrigued, though, as well as charmed, by the number of things in Margaret's house that had slots you needed to put coins in. I think that one side of the family must have had a frightening brush with debt once. As a result they had to be absolutely sure to pay their way, day by day. So you'd be sitting watching television in the living room and the lights would suddenly go out. There'd be a hunt in the dark for the jar with shillings in it. Or Margaret's dad would be heating a pan of milk on the stove and the gas would cut out. After feeding the gas meter back he'd go to the television with a hot drink, turn it on, favourite programme, and then *plonk!* — the screen would go black, the little white dot shrinking in the middle. There would be a collective groan and a searching in pockets or handbags. It meant that the television set needed a sixpence because its rent was paid for that way.

The most incredible example of the coin-in-the-slot life, though, was the day Margaret's mother came home from the coin-operated laundry in Nantwich, looked across at the clock on the mantelpiece and said, "Blow it, the clock's stopped!" I suggested that all they needed to do was rewind it. What I hadn't realised was that the clock needed a half-crown before it went any further that day. I looked across anxiously at Margaret. Where would a coin be needed next?

Despite the apparent solidity and permanence of those sixth form years, my relationship with Margaret didn't last beyond leaving school and home. A life putting coins into meters was not to be for me. A few years later, when I was home from university, Mum showed me a wedding photograph in the *Chronicle*. The bride was Margaret. She looked beautiful, almost matronly. The man standing next to her was tall, dark and handsome. I was impressed. In the grey newspaper photo he stood in a relaxed way, one hand resting in a trouser pocket. Was he thinking ahead, fishing for a sixpence?

And soon after that there was another wedding photo in the *Chronicle*. There was no mistaking the bride with the arched eyebrows and the snub nose. My heart wanted to turn back into a food mixer again. It was Pat.

"Looks nice, doesn't she?" Mum said. "Shame in a way. I used to meet her mother at the shops and we often wondered if you and she would get together one day."

THE GENTLY ROCKING SIXTIES

While life in a county grammar school in the sixties was pretty much insulated from the surges of social and cultural change that were beginning to wash through Britain, lives in the village — and in Sunnyside, too — did begin to float gradually away from their fifties moorings. But the effects of the sixties were more like those of gentle waves rocking a heavy, securely moored barge than of a big storm hitting a small boat.

In 1963, a few years after I left the Boys' School, the Steventons retired and, along with their teaching careers, the long dragged-out era of Victorian-style elementary education in Bunbury finally drew to a close.

The Girls' School, with its cheerful checked pattern of brickwork on the front, was closed and, for the first time, all the boys and girls were taught together in the same village school. Dougie Wright was now the head teacher. Dougie, who'd been a PE teacher at Nantwich grammar school, was a wiry, muscular man with a fierce expression, a bristling moustache and a humorous twinkle in his eye. Bunbury at last had a modern primary school.

And it was in the sixties that the first batches of new houses started to appear. To begin with they were inserted, artificial crowns in the gaps of an old jaw, just here and there. They were soulless sixties boxes, made of bricks that looked as if they had been washed in Daz or Omo before being stacked neatly for the builders to assemble. Their number has increased in more recent decades, creating a sizeable estate in one place. But their overall effect isn't a dominant one, and in a way they stood out more in the sixties, when they seemed to be the first, threatening sign of fundamental change, than they do now.

With the new houses came the commuters that were gradually going to change the social makeup of the village. As I was doing a newspaper round I could see the new arrivals setting off for work every morning. Many of them worked in what then seemed to us crazily distant places — Manchester, Liverpool, Warrington, Stoke-on-Trent. But the business executives, insurance salesmen and production engineers seemed happy enough to live in their cereal box houses, wave to their sixties wives with beehive hairdos, hop into their Minis and drive on the empty roads out of Bunbury.

What the newcomers weren't particularly interested in was catching the train. Even before new houses had started to appear in the village, though, it had been decided that the local railway station at Beeston Castle would have to close. It was a tiny part of the large-scale rail closure programme initiated by the Beeching Report in 1962.

So it was from the mid-sixties on that Beeston Castle station, an impressively large building that had always looked too big for its role as a local stop, stood empty and quiet as trains continued to rumble past its deserted platforms.

The *Chester Chronicle* reminisced about its past glories, when "county nobility took direct trains to Euston from there . . . and the forecourt used to be one of the most important centres of the social life of the county . . . with waiting drivers and outriders in full

290

livery." Most of the directors of the London and North Western Railway Company used to live within a 10-mile radius of the station, according to the *Chronicle*, as well as a duke, a marquis, two earls, three barons and a sprinkling of knights.

After the sixties the station itself completely vanished. Not only the building, but also the platforms and any signs that there was once a station there have been erased. It's a very odd feeling to walk past the place where you could once watch for the curl of white smoke in the distance that heralded the train to Chester, and to see nothing but an anonymous railway embankment. The gravelled forecourt where Dad would sometimes wait for us in the old Austin, the maroon-painted front doors that led to the ticket office, and the damp, echoing, white-tiled subway that led under the platform to the other side — they've all gone, a memory deleted.

In the sixties, though, that kind of complete change was yet to come. Mum and Dad were still alive, living at home, and though it was sad that Auntie Lu and my favourite uncles, Kenneth and Harold, had died, a mild kind of contentment began to waft under the front door of Sunnyside. After the mid-sixties I got the feeling that Mum was beginning to experience less of the frustration with life that she'd felt earlier on. And, as my parents were about as old as the twentieth century, they became pensioners in that decade. They were never well off, but at least pensions brought in some regular income. Every other year they seemed to set off to Canada to visit Jay, who was now married and had two children. The house was quieter without the twins in it or, after 1966, me. Mum and Dad seemed to enjoy life again, just a little.

But just as the sixties didn't really end until 1973, so they didn't start — in Bunbury, at least — until about 1965. For me, the sense of an end of an era came not with the death of President Kennedy but the funeral of Winston Churchill. It wasn't that I particularly hero-worshipped or admired Winston Churchill — he was just a distant, historical figure to me, an old Edwardian gentleman with a cigar. But the day of the funeral was a solemn state occasion when lots of people tuned in to the Home Service or watched television to follow it. That day felt like a throwback to the previous decade.

Someone decided that the church bells should be rung. I was involved because I'd started bell-ringing two years before, along with other kids in the village. The bells were half-muffled, which meant that each loud peal was followed by a ghostly whisper. When I heard the muted rounds, letting go the tenor bell, I had a sudden realisation that I was a teenager helping to enact a historical event. Nothing like it would ever happen again. We were helping the older people in the village to say goodbye not just to Churchill, but also to black-and-white newsreels of wartime disasters and feats of bravery, memories of rationing, and to the fifties, the decade that grew up under the shadows of the war.

CHAPTER
TEN

Then and Now

A SEPTEMBER MORNING

Why is it always a sunny morning when it's time to go back to school after the long summer holiday? It might be overcast in the last week of August but the first, second or third days of September are almost guaranteed to be china-blue perfect. The early September weather knows this. It taunts us. If we're trapped in school or in work, we can think of nothing better than being out in that sunshine, being free. The summer isn't over, surely? Can't we have just one more day?

It was just like that in 1959, when I started at the grammar school in Nantwich. And it was exactly the same when I went back to Bunbury to walk the fields and lanes of the village again, at the start of the twenty-first century.

I was alone, free of responsibilities for a day or two. There was a tinge of guilt — I was lucky to be outside on a September day, and such a beautiful one as this, while everyone else was inside, starting back at work or school.

I'd walked through the lower part of the village towards the higher part, where the large sandstone parish church dominates the skyline, then back towards the brook at the bottom of the hill. From there I could follow the brook through fields for a while and then cross towards Bunbury Heath and Sunnyside.

In early September the sun's rays are still hot but their lower angle in the sky begins to be noticeable. The shadows from trees and hedges are a little longer and a deeper purple-black, while the translucent September light brings out the sharpness and intensity of colours: the first few yellowing leaves, red berries on mountain ash, the lush greenness of wet pasture. It had rained heavily the day before. The air was clean and smelled of ferns and earth. Every path had large silver cobwebs spread across it, a spectrum of twinkling diamonds in each web.

I could feel tears coming. I hadn't walked this path since I was 18. I was a middle-aged man revisiting his boyhood haunts. I'd once known every little twist in the path, every hole in a hedge or fence, the way the sand collected in the bed of the brook, the places where I'd built dams with Lloyd Passey, Clive Bevan and John Cheers.

I was elated and surprised. At first sight everything looked much the same. I asked myself a question: if I were to jump over that stile ahead and meet my 11-year-old self coming towards me, across the next field, what would I say to him? Would I excitedly rush up to him, wanting to point out all the changes and differences, or, with some surprise in my voice, stress

294

how similar it all seemed? Would I actually remember how it all was in 1959 or have to ask him to remind me?

TELESCOPING TIME

The similarities struck me first. They just leapt out at me, and I didn't have to use my memory at all — it's as if all those familiar trees, hedges and paths physically *were* the memory.

As a physical environment the countryside around the village looks very much as it did in 1959. Perhaps this wouldn't be true in other parts of England, especially in the east where "prairification" has taken place on a large scale. But in this corner of Cheshire the same basic field pattern is just as it was. The footpaths are still there, most of the old familiar trees still rustle in the breeze, and black and white cows graze the meadows. In the distance you can still see the up-and-down outline of Peckforton Castle, looking like a child's drawing of a castle, and to its right the huge crag and the ruin of medieval Beeston Castle. In the distance, and in the September sun, the hills on which the castles stood had taken on a violet-blue colour.

There had been some minor physical changes but they seemed to be intriguing or exotic rather than negative or destructive. A tall, dense field of maize — a crop I wouldn't have recognised as a boy — blocked my path in one field. And when I came to explore a large sandy bank near the stream, a series of steep slopes where as kids we used to slide down at great speed, there was a shock. A stand of spruce and other coniferous trees, some as high as 30 feet, stood on the slope where we used to whoop and jump and slide down. The trees were varied and beautiful and seemed to have added something positive to the landscape.

It was a sobering thought, however, to realise that their considerable height was an indicator of how much of my life had been used up. When I'd left the village there had been no trees there at all. Now, after four decades, here was an imposing group that looked as if they had been standing for centuries.

Further on, I crossed another small field that had been set aside for trees and saw something magical — not just one or two, but whole groups of rabbits. Some stood on their haunches, noses up, while others nibbled the grass. This was something I'd never have seen as a boy when, as a result of the myxomatosis virus, a lone rabbit was a rare sight.

But it was still the similarities that stood out, at first. There was one sight in particular that caused me to gasp in amazement. It stood at the bottom of a hill — a small, rusting corrugated iron cowshed. One side was completely exposed to the elements and the corroded roof was paper-thin in places, with large rusted holes to let the sky through. The ground inside and around the hut had been churned with mud and sloppy cow dung into a foot-sticking mess. If anything was going to be demolished and tidied away long ago, surely it should have been this?

What astonished me, however, was that this mundane structure *had looked like this in my childhood*. While the new stand of trees by the brook had seemed to emphasise how much could change in a few decades, this little hut did the opposite. In fact, it led me to say to myself, "If it's here now, more than forty years later, how long was it sitting there, rusting away quietly, *before* the 1950s?"

Suddenly the decades telescoped into themselves. I could imagine not just my 11-year-old self excitedly running up to me, in that September field by the cowshed, but also dozens of other shrieking and laughing children from the 1940s and 1930s and from even earlier decades. Perhaps we would all recognise that shed, this field and the surrounding countryside.

As we get older, I reflected, the past gets nearer rather than further away. When I was 9, sitting in the village hall watching the German bombers in *Reach for the Sky*, the Second World War belonged to a different epoch, a strange fascinating time but one that had no connection to me. Now I can see that I was born just a few years after a war that included, among a myriad acts of destruction, the random dropping of a land mine on Bunbury village that destroyed several old black and white houses and severely damaged the church roof. The years 1939–45 suddenly shuffled much closer. Similarly, if a middle-aged man had talked to me in my teens about the 1920s I would have thought he was describing an age as distant as the eighteenth century. But if I talk to a teenager now about the 1960s, the time gap is the same. For me, though, the sixties are close enough to touch.

CHANGES

Although it was the similarities and the continuity that hit me first, as I walked around Bunbury, bit by bit, the changes and differences became more evident. In what we'd always called "the village" — the cluster of shops, garage and pub in Lower Bunbury — only one grocery store was still functioning, with a post office counter inside. The three thriving village stores that I'd known as a child had all closed down. One had already been converted into a house, while another lay empty and had a "For Sale" notice outside. Peering through the dusty shop window of what had been the newsagent's, I could see only a few crates and cobwebs where a counter crammed with sweets and newspapers had once stood. This was where, as a 12-year-old, I'd gone with Mum's old bike to start my paper round (and since my first revisiting of the village, this shop has also been turned into a house).

There was still a butcher's shop being run by the same Burrows family, and the Nag's Head, but the garage has just been knocked down to make way for more houses. The separate little Post Office building has also been demolished, and the few other little shops that had existed in the 1950s and 1960s, including a part-time Midland Bank (Fridays 10.00a.m. to noon) and a draper's shop, had apparently long gone.

298

The vicarage — a large house that had appeared gloomy and neglected in the 1950s, with its grey render and its solemn yew trees — had been sold off and turned back into an elegant Victorian mansion with immaculate, sweeping lawns. Next to the old vicarage there's a new detached house for the current vicar and his family to live in. It's neat suburban redbrick. A sign outside informed passers-by that "Rick and Lin" lived there.

Above all, it was the quietness that struck me as the biggest change. I'm sure that a dispersed rural settlement like Bunbury has always been pretty quiet, but in the 1950s there would have been more passers-by, more cyclists and pedestrians greeting each other than on that silent twenty-first-century September morning. Cars pass by, but they glide along country roads powered by engines that sound hushed and discreet compared to the throaty rattle of many 1950s vehicles.

As I retraced my steps from the village back up the hill towards my old home, it began to seem as though the whole place had been depopulated by a radiation attack that had left buildings intact but destroyed all human life.

The serene atmosphere of that sunny September morning suddenly took on an eerie quality. I began to experience a disembodied feeling. I was only a ghost visiting my old haunts and, as such, I couldn't connect with anyone. And it wasn't likely that a passer-by would accost me, say hello or narrow their eyes curiously at me, because there were no passers-by.

299

It suddenly occurred to me that I would visit the village, stand to look at Sunnyside for a few minutes and leave in an hour or so without anyone knowing that I'd been back. I was tempted to knock the front door at the next house up from Sunnyside to say hello to our old neighbours since the 1960s, Blanche and George Wilgose, and let myself in for surprised and excited greetings, perhaps a lengthy conversation. But something stopped me. I should have contacted them first. And what would it have meant if I did see them? I might have become "real" again, for an hour or so, but what difference would it make in the long run? What would my future connection with the village be?

I decided to remain transparent, de-materialised, not leaving a mark: not a purchase in a shop; not a greeting; not even a half in the Nag's Head or in the Dysart Arms next to the church.

I believed — hoped — that Blanche and George were still living next door to Sunnyside, but would I know where anyone else was, after such a long absence? Where were Clive Bevan, Lloyd Passey and John Cheers now? Where was Susan Walker, the girl who lived in the wooden bungalow, or Pat Merrill, the girl I had a crush on when I was 14?

Perhaps they're all living somewhere nearby, but that eerie quietness of the village that day was a sign of the biggest change of all since the 1950s. The village at the start of the twenty-first century might look more or less as it did in 1959, with the same hedges and fields and some extra houses, but that appearance is very deceptive.

300

Look more carefully at the older houses. They're so much neater than they were in 1959: they're better painted and maintained, their windows are bigger and double glazed, they exude an air of affluence. Even their surrounding shrubs look healthy, dark green and suburban.

Walking along the road that passes Sunnyside I noticed how several small dwellings — what used to be two or three small cottages in the 1950s and 1960s — had been knocked into single detached houses. One in particular caught my eye. It was a twee country cottage with a carriage lamp on the side wall and ivy growing around it.

When it was two houses, I remembered, Miss Groucott had lived in one of them. She was a genteel, lonely old spinster, a retired seamstress from Birmingham who wore bent wire spectacles and a rather bewildered expression. She was very poor and her tiny cottage was shabby and down-at-heel.

Miss Groucott had never been able to afford to pay for a WC to be installed. She must have been about the last person in the village to be dependent on the local council's sewerage truck for weekly calls to empty her earth closet. This vehicle — which we kids used to call "the cack cart", grinning and holding our noses while we said it — carried with it not only a disgusting stench of excrement but also the smell of social stigma. The rat-like men who operated the truck wore funny smiles, furtive but defiant.

"I hate that council lorry coming, I'm so sorry it has to come up our road because of me," Miss Groucott once said to me. I was a small boy looking wonderingly at the single tear in the corner of her eye, as she dabbed it with a neatly folded embroidered handkerchief.

I blinked and was back in the twenty-first century. The memory of the truck laden with excrement calling at Miss Groucott's house belonged to a different world. Now, Bunbury, like almost every village in England and in many other parts of the UK, has been safely modernised, suburbanised and sanitised.

The silence I'd noticed was the daytime silence of a dormitory. And in Bunbury's case it's a very expensively purchased silence that only a certain income range can afford. Consequently the variety of social or class backgrounds of the people in the village in the 1950s and 1960s has gradually given way to a more exclusive and affluent band.

Their desire to recreate an authentic country atmosphere is very selective. It extends only as far as carriage lamps, those leaded windows with little diamond-shaped panes and a 4×4 on the drive. For them, evoking the past is a necessary part of creating their vision of rural life, but that vision doesn't want to be encumbered with too many of the realities of the past. I certainly couldn't imagine a rustic wooden sign swinging in the breeze outside Miss Groucott's old house that read "Cack Cart Cottage".

I stared at Sunnyside for a few moments, taking in the changes. The stumpy red chestnut tree by the front gate had gone and there was now a space to park a car in front of the house. Apart from that, and smarter paint-work on the front door and windows, the front of

302

my childhood semi-detached home looked just the same, except that it had become much, much smaller than when I was a child.

With memories of Dad in stained oily overalls, breezing up the front garden path, his *Telegraph* rolled under his arm, and of Mum smiling tiredly as she wheeled her bike through the gate, I walked across the village once more to find my car next to the churchyard.

Before I left, I made a half-hearted attempt to tidy away the weeds and long grass around the grave. None of us live anywhere near Cheshire now, so it's rather neglected. The bulky church tower of pink-red sandstone stood silently against the deep-blue September sky.

As I walked away I looked back to the stained white headstone, which says:

WILFRID BLAKEMORE 1897–1972

BERYL BLAKEMORE 1901–1981

"All that survives of us is love"

THE MAGICIAN WITH A SUITCASE

That evening I ate alone in an "Indian" restaurant called Hannah, in Nantwich. It was the most homely, tasty Punjabi food I'd ever eaten. This was surely a positive and cheerful change from the 1950s when you'd have been lucky to find a fish and chip shop open.

I drained a glass of Cobra and reflected on social changes in Bunbury and other English villages since the fifties. If I had to select some themes to summarise the contrasts in life between now and then, what would they be?

As a start, I thought that one thing would be very important. I wouldn't try to glorify village life in the 1950s, which is easy to do if you're looking back at the decade through a child's eye. As a child I didn't have adult responsibilities or worries. But when things did go seriously wrong or if there were family tragedies the 1950s might have been a terrible period. For instance, people in institutions or in long-term hospital care were often dehumanised and subjected to terribly humiliating experiences. These were the forgotten people with mental illnesses, disabled people, or older people like Aunt Annie (who did end her days in the geriatric care ward of a large, Poor-Law-like hospital).

The 1950s have also been pictured as the decade of conformity and the re-imposition of "family values". After the dramas, crises and relative loosening-up of society in the war years of the 1940s, stability and homeliness were valued above everything else.

But those cosy, paternalistic attitudes carried a cost, for example, in the form of prudish attitudes towards sex education and contraception, which fostered the conditions that led to rising numbers of back street abortions. In the 1950s it was a criminal offence to engage in homosexual relations. And it was the decade in which thousands of black people came to work in Britain, chiefly from the Caribbean and West Africa but also from other places. Yet apart from some news coverage and film documentaries there were few black voices on the radio and scant sign of any black people on early television programmes. And it was quite legal for landlords to put up notices that specified that their accommodation could not be used by "coloureds", dogs or other pets.

I believe I saw only one person with a brown skin during my whole village childhood, except for the glamorous Indian family we'd seen getting off a plane at Heathrow who we saw on our school trip. He was a Sikh door-to-door salesman and he carried a large, battered suitcase. He wore a crumpled grey suit and a turban, and he tiredly walked up the garden path at John Vickers's house in Queen Street while we were playing outside. I was about 8 years old then. I caught the man's eye as he smiled at me and asked politely if anyone was at home. He then opened the suitcase lid to show us roll upon roll of brightly coloured samples of cloth. All were vivid, and some seemed to gleam with gold tracery.

John and I went inside to tell his grandmother that a magician with a funny hat had come. John's elderly grandmother was the only adult at home, and she came wheezing into the front room to peek through the lace curtains, inspecting the visitor suspiciously before deciding whether to open the front door.

When she saw the Sikh man John's grandma gave a shriek of terror and hid behind the sofa. John and I looked at each other. He shrugged his shoulders. Grandma was gibbering something to us, wanting us to hide as well. But we decided we ought to go outside to tell the visiting magician that nobody was at home after all.

I wonder if that man, as he trudged back along the dusty unmade road from John's house, would ever have believed that an Indian restaurant would be flourishing near this bush place, fifty years on? I'd have thought he would have been sceptical.

WE NEVER HAD IT SO GOOD?

And yet, I reflected as I paid the bill (with a hefty tip as an indirect thank you for the memory of the Sikh salesman), there are two stories to tell about the fifties. The first is the one I've just summarised. It was not a very open-minded or progressive decade. It was a period in which people were complacent, not only about their own values and their own lives, but also about the unquestioned superiority of Britain.

British machinery was assumed to be the best, British bikes were the best and — despite plenty of evidence to the contrary, especially in Dad's little garage — British motor cars were the most reliable in the world. And though Great Britain was busily untying the knots that held the strings to the colonial territories in Africa, Asia and elsewhere, the colonial mentality was still very much alive and kicking.

For instance, one day at school the vicar came into the classroom to introduce a missionary to us. Bunbury

School was a Church of England school, and it was thought to be educational for us to listen to the vicar having a conversation with the young missionary, after which we could put up our hands to ask a question.

The missionary was a sallow-skinned man with a coif of curly blond hair who lounged back in his chair, cradling the back of his head with crossed arms. He stuck his legs out, sighed and talked lazily, mentioning how the great heat of Africa made it virtually impossible to do anything much.

"And can you tell us about how well your African students learn?" asked the vicar. "Do you think that it is wise to teach them much western civilisation?"

"Well, put it this way," drawled the missionary. "One of the young men in my theology class came on in leaps and bounds. I found," and the missionary said each word slowly from now on, for maximum effect, "that he could actually listen to Beethoven within about three months."

British complacency reached its zenith in 1959 when, during a glorious summer, the Conservatives celebrated another General Election victory that they had won under the leadership of Harold Macmillan on the slogan "You've Never Had it So Good".

But I think it would be wrong to conclude that the 1950s were completely stuffy, complacent and narrow-minded. There is a second story to tell, at least as far as my village was concerned.

TEENAGERS WITH GUNS

The story starts with the example of trust. I believe that one of the positive aspects of life in my village in the 1950s was that people were generally more trusting — perhaps rather naively so, in some cases — than they are now. And perhaps young people, who today are not always trusted, were more likely to be given the benefit of the doubt.

What's the evidence for that? Well, for starters, how about the example of young teenagers being allowed to play with army rifles that they'd found in a large chest in the village hall? Henry and other young lads in the local Scout troop did this for months at some point in the early 1950s.

Quite what the guns were doing there, in an unlocked chest in a village hall, no one was quite sure, but they had probably been used by the Home Guard. They were all Lee Enfields, except for one Martini-Henry of the type that had been used at Rorke's Drift during the Boer War. Fortunately there was no ammunition, though Henry knew that there was a single 303 round in Mr Ewing's shed, and for a moment it had crossed his mind that he could shoot Mr Steventon with it.

Admiring the heavy, oiled rifles, Henry and pals played with them to re-enact the war films or Westerns that they had just watched in the village hall, and they responsibly decided that they could not take them beyond the environs of the hall itself. In a failed attempt to gain more permanent ownership of the rifles, they politely asked two retired army officers in the village for permission to borrow them for a longer period. And this is the most astonishing thing about this story, from today's perspective: they didn't run off with them, giggling, to hide them in the woods or in garden sheds, or scare motorists witless by waving the rifles menacingly at passing cars.

Trust blends into carelessness, though, when someone leaves a revolver in an unlocked drawer. This is what Dad had done. It lay in the third drawer of the highly polished bureau in the kitchen, a gun that had come from Grandpa Blakemore's veterinary surgery in Hyde and had been discovered when Uncle Kenneth's possessions were being sorted out, after his death. This gun, a five-shot .38 revolver, was an old grey-black Edwardian-looking piece. The gun just seemed far too exotic or melodramatic an object to have in our family. You could never imagine Mum or Dad running around the kitchen shouting "Caramba!" and shooting holes in the ceiling.

However, one day Henry decided that it ought to be tested. Maybe he assumed a little readily that he would be trusted to do this carefully. But be that as it may, he did take a lot of precautions. I was allowed to watch. It was a late afternoon in summer. Henry and Peter Frodsham carried out the experiment by lashing the revolver securely to a tree in the field at the back of Sunnyside. They had found what they hoped were suitable bullets, in a barn in Beeston. The gun was pointing at the majestic beech tree in Mr Ewing's field.

Henry and friend crouched down some 30 feet behind the gun, a length of string trailing from the trigger to Henry's forefinger. They'd decided that holding the gun was too dangerous. It was a very old firearm and, for all they knew, it might blow into fragments in the explosion. I hid behind a neighbouring apple tree, focusing on the gun. I had been told that it was very unlikely that such an old thing would actually fire.

Henry tugged the string. There was an extremely loud bang and an impressively long tongue of red flame shot out the barrel. The force of the blast was so great that the gun, so securely lashed to the tree as we thought it had been, had nevertheless twisted itself to one side in the explosion like a desperate prisoner struggling to be unbound.

As the smoke cleared and crows squawked loudly overhead, we walked up to the tree. Henry checked the angle of barrel, which was now pointing vaguely in the direction of a nearby cottage. "Mmm," he said anxiously, "I *think* it missed."

Perhaps there are easier ways of demonstrating how young people enjoyed trust in the 1950s than by relying on stories about the way they responsibly handled the firearms they happened to stumble across.

One example of trust and honesty in those days, not only in relation to young people but also to the community as a whole, was the way you could leave your bike unlocked or unchained at the bus stop or the railway station. Whether your bike was a fancy racing model like Henry's or a rusty old machine like Mum's, it was going to be there when you came back.

Another classic example of trust and security in any community is the feeling that it's safe to leave doors unlocked. This was at least half true at Sunnyside. For some reason Mum insisted on locking the back door while we were out even though the front would usually be left unlocked. I think she carried an image of Mexican bandits leaping over the hedge in the back garden and furtively letting themselves in to plunder the treasures within.

But a moment's thought would have led us to realise that a burglary was most unlikely because we didn't have anything of value to steal in our spartan household. True, it wouldn't have been dead easy to find the back door key, which was always placed right next to the tame toad under the mop in the wash house. However, it wouldn't have involved a quantum leap in daring and ingenuity for a burglar to try the front door handle and conclude, "Oh, I can open this." Actually, they could have done the same with the back door even when it was locked, simply by leaning gently against its rotting frame.

CHARACTERS

While trust and freedom from worry about theft were hallmarks of life in the village in the 1950s, another positive aspect of life then, I believe, was an acceptance of deviant characters as long as they were perceived as

311

harmless. I must be careful about this point, though, because I'm sure there were strict limits to acceptance. Conventionality and politeness were highly valued in the 1950s, and rules were rules.

However, within those limits, it was surprising how many odd people there were in the village. There were several with mental health problems, and it's interesting to reflect that they were living at home despite the tendency to lock people away in mental hospitals in the 1950s. For instance, there was the quiet, middle-aged couple living in the cottage at the very end of our road. They didn't go to work and rarely opened their door. The man had a sad expression and a squashed-down brown hat. The woman never spoke to anyone, though sometimes her face appeared at one of the front windows. Sometimes more than her face appeared because she liked to walk around without any clothes on. No one minded this, least of all the postman.

I began to realise that some adults had a screw loose when a woman who lived close by called me over to look at something. She could hardly contain her excitement. I was with Lloyd Passey at the time, and we dutifully walked over to her gate. With a flourish, she produced a large pink greeting card. We held it and looked at it, puzzled. "Go on then, open it!" she cried, giggling. I opened the card and yes, it did feel rather heavy. Spread-eagled across the inside, its wings stapled neatly to the card, was a dead bat. In rigor mortis, its toothy mouth had set itself into a leering smile.

As we walked away we agreed that the woman was nutty. I began to go over other examples of strange adult behaviour that I'd observed when I was very young. There was the old man with a red face, who sat on a horse that was led around by a strange, thin woman with long, unkempt grey hair and a weather-beaten face. She never talked or moved her head from looking straight ahead, just walked on, leading the horse in a determined way. The man would stop the horse at various points around the village and then, lifting a hunting horn to his lips, blow it loudly. It sounded like the long, plaintive call of a lonely sperm whale. What was that all about?

Other Bunbury people might not have been that eccentric but they did stand out somewhat against the conventional village background. For example, there was the tall woman who lived in the house at the bottom of the hill near the church. She wore men's clothes — long, masculine raincoats and wide, straight trousers with creases and turn-ups. She could be observed going for long striding walks most days, walking very fast but nevertheless pulled along by two large Airedales.

And then there were road men, Thunder and Lightning. They were a Laurel and Hardy pair. Lightning was a thin, undernourished man with a rather vacant expression and Thunder a very fat, red-faced man who sometimes wore a red kerchief around his gleaming, bald head. They were supposed to keep the kerbsides of Bunbury clean and tidy, but everyone accepted that they did very little. Their function was largely ornamental but, like the other odd characters in the village, they were accepted for what they were.

Time to go

It was time to stop being a wandering ghost in my own past. And it was also time to stop trying to draw up a balance sheet about whether life in the fifties was a more positive experience than it is now. I pushed back my chair and stood up stiffly, putting my notebook of memories in my coat pocket.

A lot more people were in the restaurant now. I'd come in early, about 6.30p.m., with shafts of evening sun slanting through the windows. Now six or seven tables were occupied and young children were scampering around, chattering excitedly. I waved to the Pakistani woman who had served me and said goodbye, but she was talking animatedly to other customers. I was invisible again, then.

I had to get back to my car. As I walked out of the restaurant on to the street, the low evening sun caught me full in the eyes. I walked on through the September light, feeling the first chill of early autumn.

This part of town had been turned into a pedestrian zone in the 1960s. I stopped at its edge, looking down a slight incline to the bridge over the River Weaver. Welsh Row, the main road out of Nantwich, curved beyond out of town. Round that bend, the road continues north-west from Nantwich, past the red brick comprehensive that was my old grammar school. Then

314

it goes on towards Tarporley and — if you're prepared to divert yourself some distance off the main road towards Bunbury — my childhood.

As the sun set over the roofs of the black-and-white half-timbered houses and Georgian buildings on either side of Welsh Row, I took one more look before turning away to make for the car park in the town centre.

But then something held my attention, made me freeze. A battered, dark green Range Rover had pulled up at the kerbside about thirty yards away. It was facing me and was parked on double yellows, the engine running. The driver, a slim middle-aged woman, was getting out on to the road, laughing and talking happily to a teenage girl dressed in horse-riding gear and holding a black riding helmet. As the girl got out so did some stalks of straw, falling on to the pavement.

For a moment I thought they'd stopped for me, but no, they hadn't. The woman was continuing to talk to the girl but was now retracing her steps to open the driver's door again. She was saying goodbye and the girl was turning to go, smiling and joking. I couldn't be sure that the middle-aged woman was who I thought it was . . . *could* it be?

It was the voice that had held me. It wasn't abrasive, but it had that familiar, husky, penetrating quality. I walked quickly forwards, wanting to check her face. Yes! There was the snub nose, the freckles, the same chin and cheekbones — all in a face that had changed with time, of course, but was still much the same.

She gave a final wave to the girl and slammed the car door. My heart was pounding. I stopped and stared, only ten yards away, at the woman looking down at her car keys, putting on her seatbelt, looking in her mirror and flicking a curl on her forehead. As she drove past me I fell into her eyes. The same green-blue, the same bold, friendly glance. She gave me a wave, uncertainly and enquiringly, her eyebrow arching in that familiar way.

For a moment, it was Pat Merrill driving past me there.

Also available in ISIS Large Print:

Living on Tick

Hazel Wheeler

"Part of our war effort at Central Stores must surely have been in helping to keep people's spirits up. Even in wartime there has to be humour or we'd all be dead. Not from bullets but from sheer monotony."

The corner shop in the 1920s and 1930s was much more than just a place to buy the groceries. It was a meeting place where familiar faces, on both sides of the counter, swapped stories and helped each other out. People bought groceries daily, so visits to the shop were a frequent occurrence and when times were hard it was common for a customer to ask for, and usually get, goods "on tick". Hazel Wheeler grew up in her father's shop in Deighton near Huddersfield and recalls her memories of those times. She remembers the people, the goods they sold in the shop and a way of life that has now vanished.

ISBN 0-7531-9362-0 (hb)
ISBN 0-7531-9363-9 (pb)

Country Boy

Colin Miller

"My childhood, especially during and soon after the war, was a delightful experience that I look back on with great affection and all of my family, not just my parents, made that possible."

Colin Miller was born in 1940 in Rollesby, a village near Great Yarmouth. In Rollesby, as in so many other rural communities at this time, drinking water was drawn from a well, the lavatory was a bucket in an outside privy, transport was a bicycle or a bus, and entertainment was provided by the radio, whist drives at the village hall or a rare visit to the cinema. As the 1940s and '50s progressed, this way of life changed dramatically — some would say disappeared. Colin Miller chronicles these developments through the eyes of a Norfolk schoolboy and teenager.

ISBN 0-7531-9358-2 (hb)
ISBN 0-7531-9359-0 (pb)